T0306179

THE FUTURE OF CHARITY MARKETING

Charities play an increasingly important role in our society. Whether caring for the vulnerable, campaigning for change or enabling access to the arts, they are organisations on a mission, underpinned by social purpose. However, charities now face unique challenges in a turbulent global economic climate due to structural changes in society post Covid and pressure on disposable incomes. Charities need to transform and, in some cases, modernise for sustained increasing demand from their service users. They need to engage with a wider range of stakeholders, meet higher public expectations on transparency and governance and compete for resources from existing as well as a continuous range of new competitors.

This book brings together leading scholars to think about what is needed to future proof the nonprofit sector in areas such as partnerships, collaborations, branding, communications, income generation and fundraising, stakeholder involvement and meeting the future needs of service users. This edited collection builds upon the research in the editors' first book *Charity Marketing: Contemporary Issues, Research and Practice* to challenge students, researchers and practitioners in understanding the challenges and opportunities ahead and think about how to future proof nonprofit marketing.

Drawing from a diverse group of academics and deep-thinking practitioners, *The Future of Charity Marketing* focuses on how charities can prepare for the future through sharing big ideas and examples of best practice. Presenting contrasting perspectives and the latest thinking on a range of challenges, this book gives topics for classroom debate, identifies areas for future research and offers practitioners useful insights.

Sarah-Louise Mitchell is Research Area Lead in Marketing at Oxford Brookes Business School and Co-Lead of the Children and Young People Research Network. She holds a PhD from Henley Business School and an MBA from London Business School. Her primary area of research focuses on providing academic insights for the nonprofit sector, particularly understanding the role of brand for nonprofit organisations through decoding nonprofit brand storytelling and repositioning volunteering for the next generation. She is a member of the Editorial Board of *Journal of Philanthropy and Marketing* and the BAM Peer Review College. She leads the national thesis awards for the Worshipful Company of Marketing and is a member of the National Education Committee for the Academy of Marketing as well as an elected member of the BAM Marketing and Retail SIG. Previously, she worked in marketing practice across consumer goods, food retail and nonprofit sectors.

Fran Hyde is Associate Professor in Marketing at the University of Suffolk having previously been a marketing practitioner before moving into marketing education. An experienced but always curious 'social value' focused marketing educator Fran's examination and interest in charity marketing began during a presentation to a group of students from the Marketing Director of a Hospice. Continuing to combine teaching with research Fran works to ensure that in the teaching of marketing students get to see first-hand how marketing can have a positive impact in society. Fran is a member of the National Education Committee for the Academy of Marketing as well as a member of Worshipful Company of Marketors and Chair of the Marketors Education and Knowledge Development Committee. Continuing to be active within the charity sector Fran is Deputy Chair and Chair of Corporate Governance and Risk Committee at St Helena Hospice, Colchester.

Routledge Studies in Marketing

This series welcomes proposals for original research projects that are either single or multi-authored or an edited collection from both established and emerging scholars working on any aspect of marketing theory and practice and provides an outlet for studies dealing with elements of marketing theory, thought, pedagogy and practice.

It aims to reflect the evolving role of marketing and bring together the most innovative work across all aspects of the marketing 'mix' – from product development, consumer behaviour, marketing analysis, branding, and customer relationships, to sustainability, ethics and the new opportunities and challenges presented by digital and online marketing.

For more information about this series, please visit: www.routledge.com/Routledge-Studies-in-Marketing/book-series/RMKT

THE FUTURE OF CHARITY MARKETING

Edited by Sarah-Louise Mitchell and Fran Hyde

Routledge
Taylor & Francis Group

LONDON AND NEW YORK

Designed cover image: Tyler E Nixon, Getty Images

First published 2025
by Routledge
4 Park Square, Milton Park, Abingdon, Oxon OX14 4RN

and by Routledge
605 Third Avenue, New York, NY 10158

Routledge is an imprint of the Taylor & Francis Group, an informa business

British Library Cataloguing-in-Publication Data
A catalogue record for this book is available from the British Library

ISBN: 9781032500713 (hbk)
ISBN: 9781032498478 (pbk)
ISBN: 9781003396802 (ebk)

DOI: 10.4324/9781003396802

Typeset in Sabon
by Newgen Publishing UK

CONTENTS

FIGURES

TABLES

CONTRIBUTORS

Ahmed Al-Abdin is Senior Lecturer in Marketing and Deputy Associate Dean (Internationalisation) at the University of Liverpool Management School. He specialises in branding, transformative services research, brand activism and health marketing. Over the past few years, he has completed projects investigating consumption practices in conflict/disaster zones and how consumers manage the 'new normal'. He has also researched widely into service experiences in end of life care and as part of a team, has worked with hospices/palliative care units across the country and internationally. His work has been published in a variety of publications including the *Journal of the Academy of Marketing Science*, *Journal of Service Research*, *Journal of Business Research*, *Tourism Management* and *Annals of Tourism Research*.

M. Bilal Akbar is Senior Lecturer in Marketing at Nottingham Business School, Nottingham Trent University. Bilal's research includes social marketing theoretical development and its applications in practice, behaviour change, consumer behaviour, customer experience, SDGs in marketing education and the Delphi research method. Bilal teaches various undergraduate and postgraduate marketing modules and regularly delivers social marketing lectures for MA Public Health students.

Shalini Bisani is Senior Lecturer in Marketing at De Montfort University. She has taught on a range of subjects in business, marketing and tourism management. She became interested in 'place branding' research during her MA in Design and Branding Strategy and published her dissertation on 'Fostering brand advocacy through city-citizen interactions'. Enabling the engagement and participation of marginalised communities in place-based decision-making has been a central theme in her research. Her PhD in 'Exploring Stakeholder Participation and Representations in Region Branding: The case of Northamptonshire, UK' serves as the inspiration for this chapter. In addition to stakeholder engagement in place branding, her research interests include media-induced tourism to lesser-known destination sites. She's a reviewer for the *Journal of Place Management and Development* and *Qualitative Market Research*.

Alison Body is Senior Lecturer in Philanthropic Studies and Social Policy at the University of Kent's Centre for Philanthropy. Beginning her career in children and youth charities in 2001, she focused on early intervention services and advocating for children's participation rights. She is an experienced practitioner, having held multiple leadership positions within the third sector, and as a commissioner of early intervention services. She was awarded her PhD from the University of Kent, investigating the relationship between children's charities and the State. Body's research critically explores charity, philanthropy and the third sector, particularly concerning children, young people and education. Her academic publications span youth participation, voluntary action in education, how children and young people learn philanthropic behaviours, and the co-production of public services. She has authored two books, *Children's Charities in Crisis: Early Intervention and the State* (2020) and *Children as Change-Makers: Unleashing Children's Real Philanthropic Power* (2024).

Julia Carins is a social marketing researcher at Social Marketing @ Griffith in the Department of Marketing in the Griffith Business School at Griffith University (Australia). Julia's research takes a consumer and systems approach to behaviour change. She has a strong track record in partnered research, currently leading a large-scale, collaborative research program designing, implementing and evaluating social marketing programs to improve nutritional behaviour. Her research seeks to understand and optimise the effectiveness of social marketing and to advance the impact it can have for society.

Edward Cartwright is Professor in Economics at De Montfort University. His main research interests include behavioural and public economics as well as the economics of cybersecurity. A theme throughout his research has been the application of behavioural economics to address societal challenges, such as how to incentivise giving to charities. One strand of his research looks at regional economic policy, and the role that community organisations and the voluntary sector play in local economies. Underlying this research has been an interest in community engagement to enable diverse audiences to feel they have voice in economic and social policy. Edward is the author of two textbooks: *Behavioral Economics* and *Microeconomics and Behavior.*

Irene Garnelo-Gomez is Lecturer in Marketing and Sustainability at Henley Business School, University of Reading, where she is the Programme Director for the BSc in Business and Management (Marketing). She is a member of the John Madejski Centre for Reputation, and her research interests include pro-social and sustainable behaviour, social marketing and corporate social responsibility, in particular looking at the psychological mechanisms influencing responsible practices (by consumers and organisations). Irene has presented her research at reputable conferences such as the Academy of Management Conference and the World Social Marketing Conference, and she was a keynote speaker at IAPNM's 19th International Congress. Her research has been published in top journals, including the *European Journal of Marketing*.

David J. Hart is Associate Professor in Marketing in the Department of Marketing, Operations and Systems at Northumbria University. His primary research interests include charitable marketing, sports marketing and customer loyalty. His most recent projects have investigated the role of donation destination in donor decision making, cause-related marketing campaigns and digital forms of giving. On a pedagogic level, he has won multiple student-nominated awards for his teaching in the areas of digital marketing, relationship marketing and consumer behaviour. He also has extensive experience in the design, validation, implementation and leadership of undergraduate and postgraduate marketing programmes spanning full-time, apprenticeship and distance learning delivery modes.

Sebastian Isbanner is Research Fellow at Social Marketing @ Griffith (Australia). His research focuses on the promotion of societal and planetary health, which includes research on healthy eating in schools (e.g., increase of fruit and vegetable intake in school-aged children) and sustainable food choice in workplace settings (e.g., increase of plant-based foods). Sebastian is particularly interested in how behaviour change interventions targeting one behaviour can spill over into other related health or sustainable behaviours, thereby maximising intervention efficiency and fostering broader lifestyle changes.

Rita Kottasz is Associate Professor of Marketing in the Department of Strategy, Marketing and Innovation at Kingston University, London and is Editor-in-Chief of the *Journal of Philanthropy and Marketing* (Wiley). Her current research interests are predominantly centred around understanding the 'what', 'how' and 'why' behind the disintermediation of the charity sector and is working her way through MacQuillin et al.'s (2023) disintermediation typology to uncover the motivations behind (i) donation-based crowdfunding initiatives and (ii) the *hijacking* of the charity fundraising function by new entities operating within the markets for philanthropy and social purpose. Rita also continues to develop the concept of post-series depression that has been linked to addictive behaviours within the arts, tourism and entertainment industries. Her recent works have been published in the *Journal of Marketing Management, Transportation Research Part A: Policy and Practice*, and the *European Management Review* and were featured in *The Conversation* and *Popular Science*.

Alison Lawson is Head of the Discipline of Marketing and Operations at Derby Business School at the University of Derby. Her research interests are in social marketing, sustainability and consumer behaviour. Her teaching specialisms are social marketing, marketing communications, services marketing and research methods. Before joining academia, Alison worked in the book publishing industry and a nonprofit contract research organisation specialising in education. Now an academic manager, she supervises PhD and DBA students on various topics and writes a blog called Musings on Methodology.

Ian MacQuillin (MCIoF[Dip]) is Director of the international fundraising think tank Rogare, which he founded in 2014, and holds a Visiting Fellow position at Kingston University Business School. He is recognised as a leading thinker on fundraising ethics, whose ideas have been published in the *Journal of Business Ethics* and the *Journal of Philanthropy and Marketing*, for which Ian is also an associate editor. His main contribution to the field is the development of a new normative lens of fundraising ethics called Rights Balancing Fundraising Ethics, which reintroduces beneficiaries as a key ethical stakeholder, redressing previous approaches to fundraising ethics that focus almost exclusively on the rights of donors. Rights Balancing Fundraising Ethics has gained considerable traction in the global fundraising profession, being incorporated into professional qualifications in the UK and Europe. Ian leads Rogare's research agenda, with major work streams on ethics, the philosophy of fundraising (within which Rogare's project on disintermediation sits), the professionalisation of fundraising, gender issues and the ethics of donor relationships.

Kerry Martin has over ten years of professional experience in marketing, having worked extensively within the in-house marketing teams of charities, public bodies, consumer brands and business-to-business (B2B) organisations. Kerry holds a Bachelor of Arts (Honours) degree in Media and Communications from Glasgow Caledonian University. Additionally, she has recently completed a Master of Science (MSc) degree in Digital Marketing at the University of the West of Scotland. Kerry's academic interests lie in the development of recruitment marketing and employer branding and how digital can shape both of these areas positively. Kerry's MSc research focused on how online discussions and the discourses that emerge within these forums influence marketing outcomes.

Trevor Meagher is a PhD candidate in the Department of Public Affairs at the University of Texas at Arlington (USA). His research explores the role of arts organisations in modern society, the nonprofit sector, the cultural economy, creative placemaking, urban identity, cross-sector collaboration, universities and organisational strategies for achieving local institutionalisation. Trevor regularly presents his research at the Association for Research on Nonprofit Organizations and Voluntary Action annual conference, and his work is published in the *Journal of Philanthropy and Marketing*. A Dallas-Fort Worth native, he holds an undergraduate degree in Music Performance with minors in Arts Management and Arts Administration. He holds a Master of Public Administration with a focus in Urban Nonprofit Management. At UTA, Trevor is fortunate to study with Drs Karabi Bezboruah, Jiwon Suh, Emily Nwakpuda and Alejandro Rodriguez. He is grateful for their mentorship, as well as that of Dr Kathleen Gallagher and Mr John Kitzman.

Simon Pickering is Founding Director of Dot to Dot Training & Consulting. Dot to Dot is a for-purpose driven organisation, specialising in supporting charities and social enterprises to increase their reach and impact potential. Dot to Dot offers a broad range of services including start-up and scale-up learning programmes that support charities and social enterprises to develop and scale more quickly. Dot to Dot has supported over 300 organisations. Simon co-presented a podcast series called 'This Much We Know' which provides detailed insight into the development of some of the UK's best-known social enterprises. Simon has a degree in Environmental Studies and prior to founding Dot to Dot, Simon had a career in Youth and Community work. Simon is a non-executive director for a number of social enterprises, including a green tourism social enterprise based in Cambridge employing individuals with lived experience of hardship (primarily homelessness). Simon also holds a number of trusteeships for charities.

Emma Reid is Lecturer in Marketing at the University of the West of Scotland and PGR Lead for the School of Business and Creative Industries. She holds a PhD from the University of Strathclyde. Emma teaches across the undergraduate and postgraduate marketing programme. Her research focuses on marketing innovations, charity marketing and digital marketing.

Prior to her academic role, Emma worked for small agencies specialising in social media monitoring and social listening.

Sarah Rogers is Lecturer in Marketing at Oxford Brookes University. Her consultancy work with churches and church charities started in 2015 exploring different operating models many churches and faith-based organisations (FBOs) are piloting or delivering. She has worked as a development consultant with a focus on arts, culture and social enterprise, with St Martin's in the Field's HeartEdge network of churches and under her own consultancy business Watermark. Projects mainly include Heritage Fund restoration projects aimed to scope and operationalise revised business models, scope routes to marketing commercial and cultural portfolios, evaluating social return on investment for community-led enterprises, including less tangible outcomes needed for financial stability.

Sharyn Rundle-Thiele applies marketing to improve people's health and well-being and to protect the planet. She founded Social Marketing @ Griffith (Australia) and co-founded the *Journal of Social Marketing*. She is currently serving as Vice President of the International Social Marketing Association (ISMA). Sharyn has co-created behaviour change programs with community and stakeholders. Her projects deliver outcomes and impact including removing leaves from waterways, improved social connections for adolescents, reduced koala deaths from dog attacks by 40%, reduced koala deaths from car strikes by 83% and more.

Joe Saxton is Chair of the Association of Chairs, the umbrella body for charity board leaders, and a trustee of the farmers' benevolent fund RABI. He runs his own website with insights for nonprofits – Heyheyjoe.info. Joe Saxton was founder and driver of ideas at nfpSynergy a research consultancy for charities, until he sold the business to two colleagues in November 2021. He has been the chair of six different charities and founded two. He was chair of the Institute of Fundraising for three years, and co-founder and chair of CharityComms for seven years. He was chair of Parentkind, the umbrella body for PTAs. He also sits on the board of two small grant-makers. In total, he has worked with over 200 charities.

Alan Shaw is Chair of the Retail Institute Special Interest Research Group. He is also Chair of Trustees at X-PERT Health, founder of Strategic Planet and member of the Social Media Research Foundation and the Association of Internet Researchers. Alan's main research interests are in generative AI, social marketing, social media marketing, social network analysis and social listening. Much of his research focuses on the health sector. Alan has over

25 years of experience working in the private sector, much of which was in health.

Claire van Teunenbroek is Assistant Professor at the University of Twente (the Netherlands), in the Department of High-tech Business and Entrepreneurship, Faculty of Behavioural, Management and Social Sciences. Specialising in entrepreneurship and marketing, her research is twofold: (1) examining donation-based crowdfunding as a mechanism to foster prosocial behaviour and (2) exploring reward-based crowdfunding in the context of (high-tech) product development. Currently, Claire's work is centred on studying the viability of crowdfunding as an alternative financial method for supporting organisations, institutions, and charities. She is particularly interested in understanding the extent to which experts and the general crowd align in their support for similar projects. Her approach to research is interdisciplinary, drawing on principles from organisational psychology, behavioural economics and business administration. Her contributions have significantly advanced academic understanding of crowdfunding dynamics and provided practical insights for practitioners in the field.

Barbara Tomasella is Senior Lecturer at Derby Business School, Fellow of the Higher Education Academy and Fellow of the Institute of Corporate Responsibility and Sustainability. She is the Programme Leader for the Postgraduate Marketing. She teaches and supervises at the undergraduate, master, MBA and postgraduate levels. Her research interests include corporate social responsibility, social entrepreneurship and responsible management/marketing/enterprise education. Before joining academia in 2014, she worked for 15 years as a professional in sustainability marketing. She mentors young CSR industry professionals, as well as consults businesses on their sustainable marketing and certification strategy.

Luan Wise is a Chartered Marketer and Fellow of the Chartered Institute of Marketing, with over 20 years' experience in agency, client-side and consultancy roles. Luan is a specialist in social media, training thousands of professionals across the world to understand and maximise the opportunities available from an ever-changing landscape. Luan is a LinkedIn Learning course instructor, an accredited lead trainer for Meta (Facebook and Instagram) and a coach for Google's Digital Garage initiative. Luan is the author of *Relax! It's Only Social Media, Planning for Success: A Practical Guide to Setting and Achieving Social Media Marketing Goals* and *Using Social Media for Work: How to Maintain Professional Etiquette Online*. Luan regularly shares social media news and updates via her resource website, www.thelighthouse.social.

Walter Wymer is Professor of Marketing at the University of Lethbridge (Canada). His primary areas of research include nonprofit/charity marketing, social marketing, brand strength/loyalty, higher education marketing and scale development. His early work focused on volunteer psychology, segmenting volunteer subgroups and gender differences in volunteering. Another interest concerns formulating effective social marketing and public health communication strategies. His current research endeavours involve charity brand topics and crowdfunding on social networking sites.

FOREWORD

Introducing *The Future of Charity Marketing*

Sarah-Louise Mitchell and Fran Hyde

> The pandemic and the impact of the cost-of-living crisis have brought about two major realisations. How dependent society is on the contribution of civil society and civic spirit, and the extent to which the external environment can have a long-term impact on the charity sector.
>
> (Charities Aid Foundation, 2023)

Building on the success of our first book *Charity Marketing: Contemporary Issues, Research and Practice*, we were encouraged to project forward. Day in, day out, charity professionals are facing a volatile world and unprecedented challenge. However, this also presents opportunities. By harnessing insights from academics who believe in understanding the nonprofit context, the opportunities and potential navigational pathways become clearer. The balance between the demand for charities to support the most vulnerable, both people and planet and the resources they need to deliver are currently out of balance. How to resolve that imbalance is a debate we feel is worth having.

This book starts with an overview of the structural changes facing our sector by **Joe Saxton**. The first collection of chapters then considers the next generation and how we can directly engage them in charitable organisations. **Alison Body** argues that for structural change in civic participation we need to start young, embedding good practice through primary school. **Rita Kottasz, Ian MacQuillin** and **Claire van Teunenbroek** then observe the phenomenon of people, especially younger supporters of causes, bypassing charities to donate and advocate directly. **Sarah-Louise Mitchell** and **Irene Garnelo-Gomez** address how charities can attract the next generation as volunteers, a vital resource for service delivery. **Walter Wymer** extends this for the next generation of donors, particularly considering the Canadian context.

The book then considers the implications of rapid digital change. **Luan Wise** identifies some of the missed opportunities for harnessing social media. **Alan Shaw** focuses on the tools for strengthening search engine optimisation and keyword analysis and **David J. Hart** explores the digital implications of online giving. Next the book considers some of the structural issues facing charities as Emma Reid and Kerry Martin explore attracting the right individuals in their discussion of charity recruitment. Also paramount is the need to explain the social impact delivered in order to attract new funds and partners, with **Julia Carins, Sebastian Isbanner** and **Sharyn Rundle-Thiele** leading the thinking on this, particularly in the Australian context. **Fran Hyde** and **Simon Pickering** question whether the underlying business case for charities needs to be reconsidered through a move to a social enterprise model.

The last section of the book considers specific cause contexts and implications for charity marketing. **Trevor Meagher** shares the experience of American arts-based organisation and the connection to place branding. **Sarah Rogers** opens up the opportunity for faith-based spaces and the importance of brand heritage. **Shalini Bisani** and **Edward Cartwright** extend the thinking on place and the link to brand identity. **M. Bilal Akbar, Alison Lawson** and **Barbara Tomasella** highlight the importance of co-creation and collaboration to solve some of the world's wicked problems, such as reducing food waste. Likewise, to make progress on the major issues facing our society, **Ahmed Al-Abdin** argues for using a peace marketing approach to build cohesive communities.

When viewed as a whole, this book draws from a diverse group of academics and deep-thinking practitioners and presents contrasting perspectives and the latest thinking on the challenges with the aim of stimulating classroom debate and future research. The approach of this book, as with our first book, is to contribute to the growing phenomenon of Theory + Practice in Marketing (TPM). Despite the recent theoretical development of the 'strategy-as-practice' construct and special journal editions focusing on TPM, the charity sector has been largely absent from the debate. This is an oversight given the importance of the sector to the jobs, economy and social fabric of many countries. The book provides a bridge between the practice of contemporary nonprofit organisations, charity marketing and recent academic insights into the challenges, culture and communication and exemplary case studies of nonprofit and charity brands.

Audience

This book is for students, charity marketeers and fellow academics. There are an increasing number of postgraduate and undergraduate courses at universities that focus on nonprofit and charity marketing and management, as well as students studying for professional marketing and management qualifications, such as with the Chartered Institute of Marketing and Chartered Institute of Management, who are required to extend reading beyond core texts for certain modules and their final projects. Charity and nonprofit practitioners will also find this book helpful in seeking to find new ways of thinking to improve the effectiveness of their organisation's marketing. Finally, for academics researching the nonprofit sector, we hope this book will be a useful update on the latest thinking in the sector and one that builds upon the foundations laid by our first book *Charity Marketing: Contemporary Issues, Research and Practice*.

Reference

Charities Aid Foundation (2023). Key challenges and opportunities facing the charity sector. www.cafonline.org/about-us/blog-home/charities-blog/challenges-and-opportunties-facing-charity-sector

ACKNOWLEDGEMENTS

The editors would like to thank the Academy of Marketing for its support for our work, including hosting the nonprofit workshop at their conferences in 2023 at which many of our co-authors presented and the idea for this second book was developed.

THE THREATS TO THE EXISTENCE AND EFFECTIVENESS OF THE CHARITY SECTOR

Joe Saxton

Introduction

In this chapter, I argue that there are a range of different threats to the charity sector, and these threats do not come from a single source but a variety of different factors. Overall, these different factors are likely to diminish the impact and efficacy of the charity sector over the next few decades. These threats are divided into three main areas: the first is the impact of changing demography and lifestyles, compounded by the lingering impact of COVID. The second area is how the nature of 'doing good' is changing, and the third is political perception of the importance of charities.

Area 1: Threats Because the World Is Changing

A declining youth workforce

There are fewer young people in the population than a generation ago. ONS analysis sets out the challenge[1]: "there were 605,479 live births in England and Wales in 2022, a 3.1% decrease from 624,828 in 2021 and the lowest number since 2002". The total fertility rate (TFR) is now around 1.5 children per woman. Back in the 1960s, the TFR was nearly 3 per woman. A TFR of around 2.1 means the population is stable assuming no immigration or emigration.

This kind of population structure with less young people (and more older people as we will see below) means the demands on young people in terms of jobs that society needs from them is ever more intense. Younger people will be wanted to be doctors, nurses, lawyers, engineers, teachers and the like. As immigration is restricted and the private sector, and government pays more to get the workforce it needs, who will want to work in the charity sector?

Post-COVID and cost of living crisis has impacted the workforce and charities

Life after COVID-19 has had a profound impact on society. In particular, there has been an increase in the number of people who are not economically active, or who are determined to make the most of life rather than just work. This could impact on those who are prepared to volunteer for charities – especially in areas like fundraising or retail. Indeed, COVID-19 seems to have increased the number of economically inactive people – there are now 2.8 million people aged 16–64 years who are not in the workforce due to ill health, and this has increased by nearly 70,000 since the pandemic.[2] This combination of a declining fertility rate, increasing rates of economic inactivity (both impacted on by the pandemic) is then compounded by the next factor.

The static workforce and the ageing population over 70

The number of people in the world of work is fairly static. An analysis of ONS data shows that between 2020 and 2030, the number of people aged 25–55 is pretty static (an increase of around just 100,000 out of 22 million).

However, an analysis of ONS[3] data shows that there will be 1.6 million more people over the age of 70 between 2020 and 2030.

This means the tax base of working people is not increasing, but the people who are more likely to depend on the state – for pensions, for social care, for the NHS, is increasing. As society ages, people need to wait longer for their pension. This reduces the number of people able to volunteer. Equally important as people live longer the demands for support and social care will only increase the demand on social welfare charities – possibly at the expense of other types of cause. So, charities will face increased demand for their services, but a decrease in volunteers and those likely to donate.

Digital is supreme, just not in charities

For most people, digital is now the default, not the exception. In 2015, around 12% of sales were online and by 2022, they had hit over 25% with a peak in the second lockdown of over 35%.[4] The age differences in this rise are predictable – young people use digital more than older – though not by as much as might be expected. In 2023, 82 % of the individuals in the EU aged 16–24 years bought or ordered goods or services online, while the individuals aged 45–54 years were at 75 % in 2023.[5] Even the over 65s were at 60%.

However, in charities, there are very few digital insurgents – no charity equivalents of Google, Amazon, Facebook, Microsoft or Apple – who have grown big using digital technology and usurped the market incumbents.

Equally, I would argue that there is little evidence that digital fundraising is as successful as real-world fundraising. Digital is good for emergencies and fundraising events, but it has not been transformative in the way it has in the commercial sector. How will charities cope as society is increasingly made up of digital natives. Fundraising is a people-to-people business. The growth of AI will only compound this trend, as the commercial world exploits AI to the full, while the charity world struggles to make full use of it.

Area 2: Threats Because 'Doing Good' Is Changing

Doing good is not a charity monopoly

If nothing else, charities tend to think they have a monopoly on 'doing good'. However, increasingly people and companies can do good without going anywhere near a charity. Individuals can go Vegan and use renewables. Companies can create meat-free technology, put up windfarms or reduce their carbon footprint. Charities are in risk of being disintermediated from the very area they think is their raison d'etre.

Government bodies becoming charities

There are a growing body of charities that have been created out of the assets of the state. Two of the best known are English Heritage and the Canal & River Trust. Both used to be non-departmental public bodies, but now they are charities. Alongside these high-profile examples are leisure centres, schools and sports bodies and more that have become charities. There is no inherent problem with an individual body becoming a charity, but collectively, it blurs the lines between the state and charities, not least because many of these charities keep behaving like they are part of the state. 'Brand charity' is thus weakened.

Companies and government have the scale that charities do not

Charities are caught in a cleft stick. Their campaigning work to influence policy is disliked by elements of the political right, but they do not have the scale to really make a difference in terms of income or people. In contrast, one venture capitalist recently boasted in Harvard Business Review that they could put 50,000 people onto any problem they choose to tackle. Will charities still be relevant in the face of serious effort by the state or corporate world to tackle some of the major issues that the world faces – such as climate change or poverty.

The biggest problems are very complex

While some problems are straightforward to tackle such as an infectious disease, others are hugely complicated such as climate change, poverty or racism. Equally challenging is that solutions to these problems do not stay sorted – progress in climate change can be reversed in a political whim. More important for charities, the solutions are beyond the power of charities to tackle alone. Climate solutions require the State, individuals and the companies all to play their part. What is the role of charities in tackling these problems then?

Increased regulation has suppressed some sources of income

Over the last decade, regulation has made a number of forms of fundraising diminish markedly. The most powerful of these regulations is GDPR. The need to get informed and clear consent to receive specific fundraising requests has been devastating for outbound telephone fundraising, and impact on postal appeals. The former because so few say they want to get telephone calls, and the latter because getting a fundraising email may feel like equivalence to a postal appeal, but the results say otherwise. On top of these, the work of the Fundraising Regulator has made certain types of fundraising, along with lifestyle changes, more highly constrained. Fundraising events are a case in point.

Area 3: Threats Because of How Charities Are Seen

Charities are disliked by much of the British right

There has been an ongoing campaign in recent years by elements of the political right to condemn some of the actions of charities. For instance, the Royal National Lifeboat Institution (RNLI) rescuing migrants in the Channel, the National Trust talking about its history of slavery in its properties and overseas development charities talking about anti-racism. This has created a climate in which the value of charities is easier to dismiss or diminish. So, the Lobbying Act and the restrictions on government contracts in terms of lobbying are the by-products of this political hostility. They all contribute to reduce the status and role of charities.

Charities are invisible in many political problems

In many of society's problems, the role of charities in solving them has been all but invisible under the current government. In other words, there are many areas in which those in charity sector would say that charities have a significant role in tackling, but government policy appears to be indifferent to the role of charities. Politicians do not involve charities, rarely talk about them as part of the policy, or sometimes appear to be actively hostile. To paraphrase George Bernard Shaw, "The worst sin toward charities is not to hate them, but to be indifferent to them: that's the essence of inhumanity".

Three solutions to these existential threats

How does the charity sector respond to these threats? It is not easy but here are three ways to start the process.

1 **Have a plan.** The landscape is challenging in a variety of ways on top of the issues I address here. Charities individually and collectively need a plan. The importance of a plan for an individual charity is obvious. Equally important is the need for a collective plan: to tackle those issues that a single charity alone cannot do.
2 **Plagiarise.** I know its anathema to every academic but borrowing other people's ideas and using them to the full is critical for adapting to a changing world. How is the private sector and government responding to the common problems they face (like ageing population and static workforce)? It can make no sense to try and tackle problems without having some idea of how others are tackling the same problems.
3 **Know your business.** Every MBA student is told about how the US railroads declined in the early 20th century because they thought they were in the rail business not the transport business. Charities suffer the same marketing myopia. They think they are in the 'doing' business, when they should consider themselves to be in the 'ideas' business. What charities are really good at is pioneering, influencing and changing hearts: that is how they will change the landscape in this challenging turbulent world.

Notes

1 www.ons.gov.uk/peoplepopulationandcommunity/birthsdeathsandmarriages/livebirths/bulletins/birthsummarytablesenglandandwales/2022refreshedpopulations
2 www.health.org.uk/news-and-comment/news/health-foundation-responds-to-ons-update-on-economic-inactivity-due-to-long-term-sickness
3 This is my own analysis of the ONS data for each year group in 2020 and a project in 2030.
4 www.ons.gov.uk/businessindustryandtrade/retailindustry/articles/howourspendinghaschangedsincetheendofcoronaviruscovid19restrictions/2022-07-11
5 https://ec.europa.eu/eurostat/statistics-explained/index.php?title=E-commerce_statistics_for_individuals

1

EDUCATING FOR PUBLIC GOOD

Concepts, Problems and Possibilities for Cultivating Philanthropic Citizenship in Primary Education

Alison Body

Introduction

The concept of raising charitable children receives little challenge within primary education. And, why would it? The idea of raising kind, compassionate, empathetic and prosocial children is at the heart of education and central to a fair, democratic society and firmly embedded as a cultural norm within Britain. Thus, from the young age our children are commonly engaged in charitable and philanthropic behaviours, in hope that in a cumulative fashion, these attributes increasingly become more sophisticated as our children grow up. Indeed, from fundraising through telethon appeals, donating to foodbanks, participating in litter picks or helping the homeless, children regularly display a multitude of formal and informal philanthropic behaviours. As well as providing vital support for many worthy causes, the hope is that engaging children in active civic behaviours through philanthropic acts helps develop 'habits' of giving that stay with them throughout their lives. I refer to this as philanthropic citizenship, defined as a "form of civic engagement and citizenship behaviour, associated with intentions and actions that intend to produce social and/or environmental benefits for example helping others, volunteering, social action, charitable giving, advocacy and activism" (Body, 2024, p. 2).

In this chapter, I first briefly conceptualise the idea of philanthropic citizenship and discuss why this should be a priority for children's moral and social development. Second, drawing on research from data from our Economic and Social Research Council funded project, 'Educating for Public Good' (see Body et al., 2023b) and other studies in this field, I problematise the way in which philanthropic citizenship is currently encouraged among

DOI: 10.4324/9781003396802-1

younger children, particularly in the context of primary education in England, arguing that too often in our pre-occupation to create philanthropic 'habits' framed around the donating of money, too little attention has been given to *how* these ideas are cultivated, risking promoting charity as a transactional act, missing opportunities for critical engagement around ideas of social justice and potentially exacerbating inequalities. I conclude by considering the implications for practice in cultivating children's philanthropic citizenship.

Conceptualising Philanthropic Citizenship

Theoretical and empirical studies across the fields of education, social and developmental psychology consistently underscore the significance of middle childhood and the primary school years (ages 4–11 years) in shaping and normalising civic behaviours (e.g., Arthur et al., 2017; Taylor-Collins et al., 2019; van Deth et al., 2011). Furthermore, research indicates a positive inclination among children to willingly participate in philanthropic behaviours (Body et al., 2020; Lau & Body, 2021; Power & Smith, 2016), coupled with their high expectations regarding the role of charitable organisations in addressing societal challenges (CAF, 2013; Power & Taylor, 2018). The research further reveals that concepts of charity and altruism are deeply ingrained in the mindset of primary school-aged children (Wörle & Paulus, 2018), and these tendencies are likely to intensify during the primary school years with appropriate encouragement (Body at el., 2020; Paulus & Moore, 2012). Consequently, outside of the family, primary school frequently serves as one of the initial arenas where children encounter and engage with concepts of charity, benevolence and voluntary contributions for the social good (Body et al., 2020; Power & Taylor, 2018; Simpson, 2017).

My own research with colleagues highlights that encouraging philanthropic acts, such as giving to charity, volunteering and social action, has become increasingly mainstream in education and more broadly in society (Body et al., 2024; Power & Taylor, 2018). Of course, this should be celebrated. Nonetheless, it also raises questions about 'how' this activity is happening in schools. For example, in a previous study working with 150 children aged 4–8 years old, we found that while almost all children engage in some form of giving in schools, less than 20% were aware of the cause they are supporting, and only around 8% were afforded any meaningful engagement in decisions about which charities they support (Body et al., 2020). However, more encouragingly, research finds that when children were pro-actively engaged in giving decisions, they were significantly more likely to continue these behaviours (Arthur et al., 2017). Indeed, we found, when children were facilitated to research and lead on charitable giving decisions and were asked about their views and perceptions of charity, they focused on acts of everyday kindness, viewing charity as much more than monetary donations. For them, the idea of charity is an embodiment of a set of behaviours, actions and values that are rooted in ideas of fairness and empathy, the very building blocks of social justice and democracy (Body et al., 2020). We argued that this calls for greater emphasis, not just on teaching children to be charitable but on how schools and communities engage children in conversations concerning charity as active citizens (Body et al., 2021; Simpson, 2017; Westheimer, 2015).

Joel Westheimer, an US professor of democracy and education, and colleagues have conducted extensive research into the type of citizenship programmes operating in schools and the types of citizenship promoted through these programmes (see Westheimer, 2015; Westheimer & Kahne, 2004). Westheimer identifies three versions of citizenship promoted by educational programmes, the personally responsible, the participatory and the justice-orientated, each with a specific suite of characteristics as shown in Table 1.1. The personally responsible programme of activity focuses upon improving individual's actions, without engaging in wider cause areas, for example, this person would donate to the food bank but not necessarily question the underlying causes/inequalities that results in the need for the food bank. The participatory programme, characterised by Westheimer (2015) as the type of citizenship promoted through service-learning education, is when individuals are encouraged to play an active role in the community, for example, they would organise a collection for the food bank, engage in active service but within the current status quo. Finally, the justice-oriented citizenship programme, focuses on providing individuals with the knowledge and capabilities to address the root causes of problems, seeking to encourage citizens who critically assess social problems and seek for structural change to find solutions to societal issues like food poverty.

TABLE 1.1 Three versions of citizenship

The Individualised Citizen (Contributory)	The Participatory Citizen (Participatory)	The Justice-Oriented Citizen (Justice-orientated)
Acts responsibly in his/her community. Obeys rules and follows laws. Recycles, gives to charity, gives blood, etc. Volunteers to 'lend a hand' in crisis. Gives to a food bank.	Active member of community organisations and/or improvement efforts. Organises community efforts to care for those in need. Engages in collective tasks. Organises a food drive.	Critically assess social, political and economic structures to see beyond surface causes. Seeks out and addresses areas of injustice. Knows about democratic social movements and how to effect systemic change, for example challenge food poverty.

Source: Adapted from Westheimer (2015).

Crucially, Westheimer (2015) argues that educational programmes which hope to develop the personally responsible citizen, who contributes to society, are commonly framed within an individualised framework, focusing on individual characteristics and developing virtues but often fail in increasing children's participation in local and national civic life. Equally, Westheimer's research shows that educational programmes that emphasise participatory citizenship, do not necessarily develop children's skills to critique root causes of social problems. Nonetheless, educational programmes which focus on critiquing the root causes of social problems, without participatory involvement, are also shown to be unlikely to increase children's future citizenship engagement. Indeed, Westheimer argues that to increase active and critical citizenship engagement, educational programmes must include both participatory actions, *combined with* critiquing root causes of social problems (Westheimer, 2015). Thus, now that we have established the core components of critical citizenship education, we must question what does philanthropy education look like through this lens?

What Do We Mean by Children's Philanthropic Citizenship?

Philanthropy is a contested concept (Daly, 2012), often regarded as inherently problematic, with critics highlighting its potential contradictions to social justice (see Giridharadas, 2018; Reich, 2018; Vallely, 2020). However, these critics often associate philanthropy primarily with the super-wealthy, potentially overlooking everyday philanthropic contributions. This is not to dismiss the ongoing debates surrounding 'big' philanthropy but rather to shift focus towards reframing philanthropy within a broader global citizenship perspective for the common good. Viewing philanthropy from a global citizen perspective entails encouraging active roles, both locally and globally, in fostering peaceful, sustainable, equal, tolerant and inclusive societies taking into account the diverse circumstances in which all citizens live and striving for a common good (Nussbaum, 1998). Thus, under this definition of philanthropy, we embrace a positive, progressive idea reflecting Schervish's (2014) call for recognising the 'moral content' of philanthropy and its relational aspects, where we attend directly to people in their needs (Schervish, 2014).

Philanthropic actions are often perceived as acts or activities grounded in widely recognised virtues, including generosity, compassion, courage, fairness and integrity (Martin, 1994). Virtues are considered traits of character, offering individuals morally desirable ways to relate to people, practices and communities (Martin, 1994, p. 5). Virtuous philanthropy aims to nurture caring relationships and draws upon these behaviours. Martin (1994) identifies a total of 30 philanthropic virtues, categorising them into participation virtues and enabling virtues. Participation virtues, such as benevolence, justice, reciprocity, enlightened cherishing and self-affirmation, focus on motivating giving, while enabling virtues provide the moral resources for effectively pursuing philanthropic actions, such as respect for others, self-direction and moral leadership.

In contrast, critics of character virtue learning argue that focusing on personal ethics may address broader social, political and environmental issues only at an individual level, rather than at a community, local or global level (Jerome & Kisby, 2019; Kisby, 2017). Suissa (2015) asserts that without a more radical understanding of 'the political' and engaging children in debates about how political aims, ideas and values intersect with, yet are distinct from, moral values, it's impossible to involve them in creating a more socially just and less oppressive society. Acknowledging these challenges, we reject the binary view of character virtues and citizenship, recognising them as interconnected (Peterson, 2019). Martin (1994) emphasises that it's the combination of these virtues in philanthropic action that provides a platform for moral creativity, puts our vision of a good society into practice and fosters caring relationships that enrich individuals and communities alike.

Expanding on this, a citizenship approach to philanthropic giving seeks to integrate social justice, encouraging children to develop virtues to respond to social needs while critically exploring the underlying issues behind charitable notions (Body et al., 2020; Simpson, 2017). Peterson (2019) suggests that engagement in communities and deliberation with others are central to developing individual character virtues, alongside recognising and challenging structural injustices. Many education scholars argue that citizenship education is essential to help children and young people become critically literate (e.g., de Andreotti, 2014; Weinberg & Flinders, 2018). Simultaneously, many critics of philanthropy argue that it ignores critical inquiry into the root causes of injustice, thus reinforcing social inequalities (Giridharadas, 2018; Reich, 2019; Vallely, 2020). In a global citizenship education context, Jefferess particularly cautions against what he terms a "politics of benevolence", where privileged global citizens give to the needy "other", perpetuating unequal power relations (2008, p. 27). Instead, by viewing philanthropy through a citizenship lens within an education context, we aim to consider how philanthropic acts can be linked to broader social and political frameworks, striving to create a better world 'with' rather than 'for' others (Jefferess, 2008).

In breaking down the definition of philanthropic citizenship, several core components are identified. Firstly, it involves an act of giving, typically entailing the donation of one's resources without expecting comparable economic compensation (Martin, 1994). Philanthropic citizenship includes an intention, rooted in the virtues discussed earlier (Martin, 1994), to engage in acts such as volunteering, social action, charitable giving and activism. Secondly, it implies an active participative role, which, from a children's rights perspective, necessitates their involvement in decision-making processes (Nolas, 2015). Moreover, the discourse on children's rights goes beyond merely recognising children's competence to considering how children's rights education can promote the democratisation of human rights (Jerome, 2016). This leads us to identify a third crucial element of philanthropic citizenship: empowerment, another vital aspect of developing children's moral capabilities (Covell & Howe, 2001). Another crucial element is the intention 'to produce social and/or environmental benefit'. Here, two key aspects are identified: firstly, the critical thinking required to identify the problem the act aims to address, its root causes and the best ethical approach to addressing it (Jerome & Kisby, 2019; Kisby, 2017; Suissa, 2015). Secondly, the intention to produce some form of environmental or social good, broadly concerning the protection of human and/or environmental rights (Martin, 1994). Thus, advocates of philanthropic citizenship within education advocate for critical thinking within a justice-oriented framework (Body et al., 2020; Nussbaum, 1998; Simpson, 2017; Westheimer, 2015). As Simpson (2017, p. 90) states, "a social justice mentality or mindset could be considered a commitment to equality, developed critical or independent thinking which results in ethical action". In the next section, drawing on survey data from over 2000 primary school teachers and leaders, I now problematise some of the prevalent approaches to encouraging children's philanthropic citizenship within primary education, and then seek to explore the possibilities for doing things differently.

Problematising Current Approaches to Cultivating Children's Philanthropic Citizenship

Problem 1 – Charity is viewed as important but often framed as a transactional act

We surveyed over 2000 primary school teachers across England. We found primary school educators are committed to promoting ideas of charity within their school. 76% of all primary school teachers agreed or strongly agreed that teaching children to be charitable should be embedded within the primary school curriculum (Body et al., 2023b). This figure is relatively consistent across all schools, regardless of OFSTED rating (England regulatory body for assessing schools), Free School Meal data (which provides a proxy indicator for levels of deprivation within a school community), school governance type or teachers own personal characteristics, such as age, gender and years teaching. Even within the remaining 24%, only 2% actually disagreed that these activities should be embedded within the school curriculum, with 22% saying they were unsure. Reasons given for those teachers who were unsure, tended to be focused on concerns about lack of confidence about discussion issues relating to charity, how full the school curriculum already is, lack of support to deliver these opportunities, time constraints and children's capabilities.

Positively, this research also revealed that almost all schools facilitate some form of charitable engagement, with most of this activity centred around fundraising and the giving of money. Indeed, teachers reported that 92% of primary school children regularly engaging in fundraising activities, most often centred around gifting of money to national campaigns, school fundraising projects and local charities, with less than half of schools engaging in any form of social action. This potentially reduces children's experiences of charity to a financial exchange, and overlook wider contributions children can make, such as volunteering, social action, advocacy and campaigning. Furthermore, previous research highlights that while most primary school children give to charity in schools, most associated their giving with a reward, for example, dress up in funny clothes, or for a token reward such as a red nose (Body et al., 2020). This poses a risk that charity and philanthropy is promoted as a simple economic 'transactional process', where the child exchanges a gift for reward. Research shows such extrinsic rewards can override intrinsic philanthropic behaviours, actions and values (Worle & Paulus, 2018). As well as shifting ideas of philanthropy and charitable giving away from a sense of 'fellow feeling', this economic focus potentially reduces children's learning about supporting others to being simply about money and funding, rather than the wider, holistic social change and justice (Power & Taylor, 2018; Simpson, 2017). This is counterintuitive to cultivating active, long-term philanthropic citizens who are intrinsically motivated to help others, and understand the whole philanthropic ecosystem, beyond that of donating money.

Problem 2 – Acts of giving are rarely linked to ideas of justice

Linked to problem 1, our research also suggested in the vast majority of cases charitable engagement in schools is framed within a discourse of contribution and personal responsibility (Westheimer, 2015), with many children lacking opportunities for participative and/or critical engagement with the cause which sits behind the charitable need. For example, only around 15% of teachers reported that the issues behind the cause they were fundraising for are critically discussed with children (Body et al., 2023b). Previous research with children highlights that while most primary school children give to charity in schools, less than 20% knew who or what the charitable cause they were giving was trying to help, and less than 8% knew why that cause needed help (Body et al., 2020).

While the normalisation of acts of helping others and charity should be celebrated within schools, without agency and critical thinking, giving decisions are being imposed on children. Adopting a children's rights approach to participation in charitable giving, means we acknowledge children and young people as capable, social actors who are experts of their own lives and their own experiences – as current citizens who should be facilitated to help shape the world, they are part of and not simply viewed as future citizens to mould into existing systems and structures (Jerome, 2016; Nolas, 2015). Engaging children and young people in charitable and philanthropic decision-making, should not simply be about developing a rhetoric about how to grow children as future donors within these current systems and structures. Instead, it should question how we can support and facilitate children and young people to critically question these systems and structures and consider different ways of being; ways of being which foster ideas of equity and social justice and promote ideas of the interdependence of all parts of the philanthropic ecosystem in achieving social change, including the role of volunteering, advocacy, campaigning and lobbying governments. Furthermore, it is important we consider what we are teaching children about charity. Promoting giving for giving sakes without critical thinking potentially teaches charity as the response to social ills (Power & Taylor, 2018), negating to consider other responses, such as governmental responsibility. For example, as Westheimer (2015) points out, we can encourage people to support food banks, but without facilitating them to critically question and challenge the social injustices and wealth inequalities which lead to food poverty, we do little to help solve the wider issue.

Problem 3 – There is a risk that current approaches exacerbate inequalities

In our 'Educating for Public Good' project, we also found that while primary school educators are committed to facilitating children to engage in ideas of charity; distribution of opportunities is uneven, with children from more privileged backgrounds more likely to have access to opportunities to develop their civic skills and practice their civicness through charitable acts, such as volunteering, charitable giving, social action and advocacy.

Indeed, our research shows substantive differences in children's access to opportunities, particularly in relation to socio-economic status. This is perhaps most exaggerated when we look at private schools versus state schools, nonetheless, we also see stark differences based on the most affluent versus the least affluent school communities. Schools with the most disadvantaged communities are not only twice as likely to report experiencing multiple barriers, and therefore unsurprisingly offer fewer opportunities as a result, but they are also least likely to offer children the chance to engage in participatory and justice-orientated approaches to discussing charity (Body et al., 2023a). Given the multiple issues facing these schools and their communities, this is hardly surprising and should not be taken in any way as criticism of these schools, instead, if we really value children's civic education, additional efforts need to be made to support all schools facilitating these active civic engagement opportunities as part of a wider curriculum, which are inclusive for all children. Furthermore, using Free School Meal data as a proxy indicator of deprivation, the more deprived a school is the more likely the school is to offer no civic engagement opportunities (Body et al., 2024).

Considering the barriers teachers face in terms of engaging children in civic acts such as fundraising and charitable giving, when we analysed the responses by Free School Meal data, as a proxy indicator of levels of deprivation, findings show that schools within the most deprived communities face significantly more barriers than schools with more affluent communities, especially when it comes to aspects related to the socio-economic context of the families within their communities. Perhaps most concerning is that 57% of teachers within the most affluent primary schools reported concerns about financial constraints of families as a barrier to children's civic engagement, especially when it came to financial giving. This rises sharply to 75% of teachers in the most deprived school communities. Furthermore, while teachers report being concerned about children being beneficiaries of charities such as foodbanks is around 17% in the wealthiest three-quarters of schools, we find this figure more than doubles in the most deprived quartile of schools to 36% of teachers, with around 80% of schools supporting some children, and their families, within their school with food poverty.

Interestingly, however, bucking this trend, schools with the most deprived communities are both the least likely to report struggling to find the time to fit civic engagement into the curriculum, alongside the least likely to see teacher confidence in discussing issues of social justice as a barrier. Nonetheless, schools with the most deprived communities are twice as likely to report that they offer no active civic engagement opportunities, largely due to concerns about the financial situation of children and families. Thus, to encourage equity of access in philanthropic learning, framing civic engagement around the contributions of money is extremely problematic, marginalising vast numbers of children and families from participating. Yet, most active civic engagement activities across primary schools involves fundraising for the school, participating in large fundraising campaigns and/or funding for local charities. This highlights a call for resituating philanthropic engagement around participative action, rooted in ideas of social justice, facilitating all children to engage in issues they care about within the classroom, through activities such as campaigning, volunteering and advocacy.

This is not just an issue for education, but also for societal equality and democracy, both now and in the future. Children from the most privileged backgrounds are most likely to have early access to active civic engagement opportunities, where they are encouraged to critically discuss and debate and which extend beyond giving to charity, and thus are most likely to be equipped with the skills for active civic engagement pre-secondary school. The potential implications of this are that certain socio-economic groups are readied for participative civic engagement more than others, increasing the likelihood of these voices being more dominant, reproducing societal inequalities in citizenship engagement rather than seeking to redress them.

Possible Implications

The imperative of sustaining the long-term viability of nonprofit organisations hinges upon the proactive engagement of younger social actors, as supporters, volunteers, activists, campaigners, staff and leaders (Gorczyca & Hartman, 2017). Extensive scholarly inquiry has concentrated on strategies for involving upcoming generations of donors within the nonprofit sector (e.g., Goldseker & Moody, 2020). However, as posited within this chapter, insufficient attention has been directed towards understanding the socialisation processes through which younger children learn philanthropic behaviours. This discussion highlights how discourses concerning philanthropy shape children's experiences in philanthropy, which are grounded in individualistic, and often tokenistic experiences of charity. Consequently, I advocate for a transformative paradigm shift in philanthropy, leveraging principles of social justice to foster children's philanthropic citizenship. Adopting a children's rights perspective acknowledges children's inherent capabilities and agency as influential stakeholders deserving of active citizenship roles, wherein they contribute to shaping their social milieu. Rather than relegating children to the status of prospective citizens and donors within existing frameworks, this calls for us all to empower and integrate children into the decision-making processes of philanthropic endeavours. This approach transcends simply preparing children as future donors within current systems and structures, and instead invites them to critically examine established systems and fosters the exploration of alternative paradigms, which are more conducive to equity, social justice and a holistic understanding of the wider philanthropic ecosystem.

Addressing this challenge extends beyond children's experiences in education and is not the sole responsibility of educators; it necessitates concerted efforts across the philanthropic spectrum to enhance children's philanthropic citizenship through diverse strategies and initiatives. Nonetheless, while research underscores the capacity of even the youngest children to engage critically with various socio-political issues, initiatives must be thoughtfully tailored to accommodate evolving cognitive abilities and perspectives. Potential avenues for charities and funders to help cultivate children's philanthropic citizenship, can include (Body, 2024):

1 **Raising education and awareness**: Create educational programs that promote philanthropic citizenship, embracing the core components of active participation, collective action, empowerment, critical thinking and justice orientation (Westheimer, 2015), and help children learn about social issues and how to imagine and create different ways of being. This also involves raising awareness among children about the power of their actions in making a difference.

2 **Child-orientated activities**: Develop specific philanthropic initiatives and projects tailored with and for children and youth, offering age-appropriate opportunities for children to get involved in a range of philanthropic initiatives, connecting critical thinking with actions, such as charitable giving, social action, volunteering, fundraising, advocacy, campaigning and protesting activities (Body et al., 2020).

3 **Evaluation and learning**: Philanthropic institutions and nonprofits should continuously reflect on their initiatives to help cultivate children's philanthropic citizenship, working with children, as coproducers of knowledge, to help inform future activities. This should include open and honest critical reflection on philanthropic institutions themselves, for example, are activities orientated towards changing systems, or reproducing and retaining the status quo.

4 **Empower children's leadership**: Encourage children's engagement in leadership and involve children in decision-making processes. Participatory activities can include the creation of youth advisory boards or committees where children can meaningfully influence philanthropic strategies and grant allocations (see Patuzzi & Pinto, 2022).

5 **Inspiring role models**: Facilitate children to engage with positive role models and mentors who can collaborate with, and inspire, them on their philanthropic journey. Fostering interactions with community leaders, volunteers and successful philanthropists, who adopt collective and activist orientations, help encourage children to lead on philanthropic decision-making (Body et al., 2021).

6 **Collaborating with educational institutions**: Establish partnerships with schools to incorporate philanthropic citizenship into the curriculum. Body et al. (2023) highlight how partnerships between schools and justice-orientated nonprofits, support schools in adopting more justice-orientated approaches to philanthropic citizenship.

7 **Acknowledging children's contributions**: Recognise, commend and celebrate the philanthropic efforts and achievements of children, in ways that are meaningful to the children themselves. As research highlights, this increases philanthropic engagement long-term (Ongley et al., 2014; Weller & Lagattuta, 2013).

8 **Nurturing global perspectives**: Stimulate children to look beyond their local communities and comprehend global issues, as "citizens of the world" (Nussbaum, 1998). Expose them to diverse cultures and viewpoints, fostering a sense of global citizenship.

9 **Supporting skill development**: Provide resources and training opportunities to enhance children's philanthropic skills, leadership abilities and understanding of social issues. For example, even in the youngest of children aged 3–5-years old, Payne et al. (2020) through their research highlight that as children are given more agency to practice every day civicness, children's civic capabilities expand.

10 **Advocating child participation**: Promote policies and practices that respect and encourage children's right to participate in decision-making processes across the philanthropic ecosystem, shaping societal responses to social and environmental issues (Body et al., 2021).

In summary, nurturing children's philanthropic citizenship demands a multifaceted approach, intertwining educational, organisational and societal efforts to empower children as active agents of positive change within their communities and beyond.

Practice-Based Examples

The charity SuperKind is one example of a nonprofit organisation proactively working with schools to try and deliver philanthropic education differently, by providing a comprehensive platform to educate, inspire and empower children for social action and embed civic learning within the curriculum. They seek to do this in three ways:

1 **Educate**: 'Cause' pages offer child-safe coverage of the 17 UN Sustainable Development Goals (UN SDGs) and other global issues with lesson plans and charity recommendations.
2 **Inspire**: 'Change-Maker' pages showcase over 50 young activists, breaking stereotypes and demonstrating the impact of youth-driven change.
3 **Empower**: 'Take Action' pages guide children through 12 toolkits and a fundraising platform, allowing them to actively contribute to their chosen causes.

This threefold strategy not only equips children with the necessary knowledge but also instils confidence, fostering a generation of socially conscious and proactive individuals.

As a case study in action, Surrey Square Primary School, under the leadership of Headteacher Matt Morden, utilised SuperKind to empower children in their quest to build a better world. He stated, that by integrating the platform into their curriculum, every student became a proactive agent of change, tackling issues ranging from waste reduction to pest control. SuperKind streamlined the process of exploring global challenges and implementing solutions, fostering a culture of social responsibility among students. Through engaging with the UN SDGs, children not only gained awareness but also took tangible actions to address pressing issues in their community. Notable initiatives included campaigns to reduce disposable mask usage and advocate for pest control measures within social housing, showcasing the transformative impact of student-led advocacy and action. The introduction of SuperKind sparked a shift in the school's approach to community projects, with children at the forefront of decision-making and implementation. By empowering students to lead initiatives aligned with their interests and values, Surrey Square Primary School seeks to cultivate a generation of compassionate and proactive global citizens, embodying their commitment to "Building a Better World" for children and others (SuperKind, n.d.).

Another example would be the charity First Give. Since 2014, First Give has been working in partnership with schools to inspire and empower children and young people to take action to make a positive change in society. The core programme is designed to empower all classes in an entire school year group. A combination of lessons delivered by teachers, plus facilitated workshops delivered by First Give, help build understanding of the issues facing the local community, alongside the confidence and skills to take action in support of local charities they choose to support. At the conclusion of the programme, students advocate for their chosen charity to win a First Give grant of £1000, supplementing any support already given to the charities. In a similar way to SuperKind, the First Give programme structure seeks to go beyond fundraising, providing children with agency to choose the issues that matter most to them. Children are given the space to discuss, research and learn about social issues affecting their community, meeting with representatives from local charities. The agency they are given to lead on social action projects alongside the critical exploration of the issues they choose to address are two of the most critical elements of the programme (First Give, n.d.).

Conclusion

This chapter critically explores the socialisation of children and young people as philanthropic citizens within Western democracies, with a focus on primary education in England. It examines the prevalent virtues-based approach to teaching philanthropy, which emphasises individual benevolence and personal traits. While acknowledging the value of virtues in shaping children's philanthropic behaviour, the chapter argues that such approaches often reinforce the status quo and fail to address systemic inequalities effectively. Instead, within this chapter, I advocate for a justice-oriented approach to cultivating children's philanthropic behaviours, centred on principles of justice, activism and systemic change. Although this perspective may face criticism from proponents of more traditional, donor-centric forms of philanthropy or those sceptical of Western liberal ideology, the chapter aims to stimulate discussion and emphasises the importance of critically examining how children are engaged as philanthropic actors. I also seek to highlight the importance of understanding how our children are socialised into philanthropic ecosystems. Our understanding of children's roles as active social actors within this context remains under-researched and requires a greater focus from both research and practice in this area.

Education and nonprofit organisations, including philanthropic funders, have a critical role of empowering children with the knowledge and tools to engage in transformative philanthropy, which involves questioning systemic issues and promoting collective action. By adopting a transformative perspective, society can move towards greater justice and equity for all.

Discussion Questions

1 Considering the disparities in access to philanthropic opportunities among children from different socio-economic backgrounds, what measures do you think educational institutions and philanthropic organisations could implement to promote equity in philanthropic learning experiences?

2 Reflecting on the concept of 'philanthropic citizenship' and its integration into educational curricula, how do you envision incorporating critical thinking and discussions about systemic issues into philanthropy education, both within schools and the wider community?

3 What role do you think other institutions, such as universities, philanthropic foundations and fundraising organisations can play in preparing individuals to adopt more justice-oriented approaches to philanthropic citizenship?

References

Arthur J, Harrison T, Taylor-Collins E, & Moller F. (2017). *A Habit of Service: The Factors that Sustain Service. Jubilee Centre for Character and Virtues.* University of Birmingham Report.

Body, A. (2024). Raising philanthropic children: Moving beyond virtuous philanthropy, towards transformative giving and empowered citizenship. *Journal of Philanthropy and Marketing*, 29(1), e1833.

Body, A., Lau, E., Cameron, L. & Ali, S. (2021). Developing a children's rights approach to fundraising with children in primary schools and the ethics of cultivating philanthropic citizenship. *Journal of Philanthropy and Marketing*, e1730.

Body, A., Lau, E., Cameron, L., & Ali, S. (2023a). Developing a children's rights approach to fundraising with children in primary schools and the ethics of cultivating philanthropic citizenship. *Journal of Philanthropy and Marketing*, 28(4), e1730.

Body, A., Lau, E., Cameron, L., & Cunliffe, J. (2023b). *Educating for Social Good: Part 1 Mapping Children's Active Civic Learning in England*. University of Kent, Kent, UK.

Body, A., Lau, E., Cunliffe, J., & Cameron, L. (2024). Mapping active civic learning in primary schools across England—A call to action. *British Educational Research Journal*, 50(3), 1308–1326.

Body, A., Lau, E., & Josephidou, J. (2020). Engaging children in meaningful charity: Opening-up the spaces within which children learn to give. *Children & Society*, 34(3), 189–203.

Charities Aid Foundation (CAF). (2013). *Growing Up Giving: Insights Into How Young People Feel About Charity*. West Malling, Kent: Charities Aid Foundation.

Covell, K., & Howe, R.B. (2001). Moral education through the 3 Rs: Rights, respect and responsibility. *Journal of Moral Education*, 30(1), 29–41.

Daly, S. (2012). Philanthropy as an essentially contested concept. *VOLUNTAS International Journal of Voluntary and Nonprofit Organizations* 23(3), 535–557.

de Andreotti, V. (2014). Soft versus critical global citizenship education. In: McCloskey S (Ed.), *Development Education in Policy and Practice*. London: Palgrave Macmillan, pp. 21–31.

First Give (n.d.). Empowering young people; igniting a spark of social conscience. At https://firstgive.co.uk/about-us/ (accessed 12th February 2024).

Giridharadas, A. (2018). Beware rich people who say they want to change the world. *The New York Times*. Aug 24.

Goldseker, S., & Moody, M. (2020). *Generation Impact: How Next Gen Donors Are Revolutionizing Giving*. Hoboken, NJ: John Wiley & Sons.

Gorczyca, M., & Hartman, R. L. (2017). The new face of philanthropy: The role of intrinsic motivation in millennials' attitudes and intent to donate to charitable organizations. *Journal of Nonprofit & Public Sector Marketing*, 29(4), 415–433.

Jefferess, D. (2008). Global citizenship and the cultural politics of benevolence. *Critical Literacy: Theories and Practices* 2(1), 27–36.

Jerome, L. (2016). Interpreting children's rights education: Three perspectives and three roles for teachers. *Citizenship Social and Economics Education* 15(2), 143–156.

Jerome, L. & Kisby, B. (2019). *The Rise of Character Education in Britain: Heroes, Dragons and the Myths of Character*. London: Palgrave Macmillan.

Kisby, B. (2017). 'Politics is ethics done in public': Exploring linkages and disjunctions between citizenship education and character education in England. *Journal of Education & Social Sciences*, 16(3), 7–20.

Lau, E. & Body, A., (2021). Community alliances and participatory action research as a mechanism for re-politicising social action for students in higher education. *Educational Action Research*, 29(5), 738–754.

Martin, M. (1994). *Virtuous Giving: Philanthropy, Voluntary Service, and Caring*. Indianapolis, IN: Indiana University Press.

Nolas, S.M. (2015). Children's participation, childhood publics and social change: A review. *Children & Society* 29(2), 157–167.

Nussbaum, M. (1998). *Cultivating Humanity*. London: Harvard University Press.

Ongley, S. F., Nola, M., & Malti, T. (2014). Children's giving: Moral reasoning and moral emotions in the development of donation behaviors. *Frontiers in Psychology*, 5, 458.

Patuzzi, L., & Pinto, L. L. (2022). *Child and Youth Participation in Philanthropy: Stories of Transformation*. Philanthropy Europe Association. https://philea.issuelab.org/resource/child-and-youth-participation-in-philanthropy-stories-of-transformation.html

Paulus, M. & Moore, C. (2012). Chapter 8 – Producing and understanding prosocial actions in early childhood. In J. B. Benson (Ed.), *Advances in Child Development and Behavior*, JAI (Vol. 42), Elsevier.

Payne, K. A., Adair, J. K., Colegrove, K. S. S., Lee, S., Falkner, A., McManus, M., & Sachdeva, S. (2020). Reconceptualizing civic education for young children: Recognizing embodied civic action. *Education, Citizenship and Social Justice*, 15(1), 35–46.

Peterson, A. (2019). Character education, the individual and the political. *Journal of Moral Education* 49(2), 143–157. https://doi.org/10.1080/03057240.2019.1653270

Power, S., & Smith, K. (2016). Giving, saving, spending: What would children do with £1 million? *Children & Society*, 30(3), 192–203.

Power, S., & Taylor, C. (2018). The mainstreaming of charities into schools. *Oxford Review of Education*, 44(6), 702–715.

Reich, R. (2018). *Just Giving: Why Philanthropy Is Failing Democracy and How It Can Do Better*. Princeton, NJ: Princeton University Press.

Schervish, P. (2014). Beyond altruism: Philanthropy as moral biography and moral citizenship of care. In: Jeffries V (Ed.), *The Palgrave Handbook of Altruism, Morality, and Social Solidarity*. New York, NY: Palgrave Macmillan, pp. 389–405.

Simpson, J. (2017). 'Learning to unlearn' the charity mentality within schools. *Policy & Practice: A Development Education Review* 25(Autumn), 88–108.

Suissa, J. (2015). Character education and the disappearance of the political. *Ethics and Education* 10(1), 105–117.

SuperKind (n.d.) *Empowering Children to Make a Difference*. At https://superkind.org/ (accessed 12 February 2024).

Taylor-Collins, E., Harrison, T., Thoma, S.J. & Moller, F. (2019). 'A habit of social action: understanding the factors associated with adolescents who have made a habit of helping others', *Voluntas*, 30(1), 98–114

Vallely, P. (2020). *Philanthropy: From Aristotle to Zuckerberg*. London: Bloomsbury Publishing.

Van Deth, J. W., Abendschon, S., & Vollmar, M. (2011). Children and politics: An empirical reassessment of early political socialization. *Political Psychology*, 32, 147–173.

Weinberg, J. & Flinders, M. (2018). Learning for democracy: The politics and practice of citizenship education. *British Educational Research Journal*, 44(4), 573–592.

Weller, D., & Lagattuta, K. (2013). Helping the in-group feels better: children's judgments and emotion attributions in response to prosocial dilemmas. *Child Development*, 84(1), 253–268.

Westheimer, J., (2015). *What Kind of Citizen?: Educating Our Children for the Common Good*. New York: Teachers College Press.

Westheimer, J., & Kahne, J. (2004). What kind of citizen? The politics of educating for democracy. *American Educational Research Journal*, 41(2), 237–269.

Wörle, M., & Paulus, M. (2018). Normative expectations about fairness: The development of a charity norm in preschoolers. *Journal of Experimental Child Psychology*, 165, 66–84.

2

WHAT DRIVES INDIVIDUALS TO INITIATE DONATION-BASED CROWDFUNDING APPEALS? AN APPLICATION OF THE CHARITY DISINTERMEDIATION TYPOLOGY

Rita Kottasz, Ian MacQuillin and Claire van Teunenbroek

Introduction: Understanding the Disintermediation of the Charity Sector

Much of the scholarly literature concentrates on a specific type of disintermediated giving in the charitable sector, namely donation-based crowdfunding (DBC). This form of giving is facilitated through digital platforms like GoFundMe and JustGiving. However, not all DBC disintermediates charities from the process of giving (i.e., many charities raise funds on crowdfunding platforms themselves) and not all charity disintermediation happens on digital crowdfunding platforms.

The disintermediation typology devised by MacQuillin et al. (2023) uncovers the functions and processes of charity work that are being bypassed by many new technologies and actors. Many new players, including individuals, commercial fundraising entities, companies and newly formed charities have entered the markets for social purpose and philanthropy and are actively disrupting and re-shaping what we understand by the 'traditional charity model'. In the 'traditional charity model', a charity solicits voluntary income which it converts into goods and services for beneficiaries. Disintermediation poses challenges to the charity sector and raises questions of the utility of the traditional charity model as well as a variety of questions concerning ethics, regulation and accountability (MacQuillin et al., 2023). The typology is a first step to understanding the possible implications of disintermediation, aiming to help the charity sector adjust to the various disruptions, ensuring its continued relevance and survival.

DOI: 10.4324/9781003396802-2

In the for-profit world, disintermediation is understood as the elimination of the 'middleman' in business transactions, often via digital means (Tapscott, 2015). (Dis)intermediation in the charity sector is more complex, as a traditional business value exchange does not exist between two parties: here, the middleman is the charity that raises money (from donors) and uses this money to create products and services on behalf of a charity's target beneficiaries – a transfer process rather than exchange. In MacQuillin et al.'s (2023) typology, there are two loci for disintermediation in this transfer process: the first between donor and beneficiary in the market for resource acquisition (Sargeant, 2008); the second, less obvious locus, is in market for resource allocation (ibid), between charity and beneficiary.

Disintermediation at the first locus permits donors to give directly to beneficiaries. It is important to note here that the two loci exist, because DBC raises money for beneficiaries but does *not* provide any services that a charity would to the beneficiary. At this locus, fundraising charities are disintermediated from Chapman et al.'s (2022) triadic relationship of donors, fundraisers/charities and beneficiaries, and are replaced by a different type of intermediary such as a microlending platform in the triad, or a direct dyadic relationship between donor and beneficiary.

Traditional charities deliver their services directly to beneficiaries. However, other models or methods of service delivery could disintermediate (or substitute) charities in this function at the second locus, in the resource allocation market, for instance, commercial organisations that subscribe to and engage in corporate social responsibility programmes. Pressure for social purpose is growing and inevitably the providers of social purpose and its markets are growing in tandem. This latter locus for disintermediation would almost certainly require raising money to provide services, and thus would also include a large element of the disintermediation of the giving process.

MacQuillin et al.'s (2023) typology contains three main types of disintermediation where one or multiple charity functions are bypassed: (a) in full (i.e., the entire traditional charity model is disintermediated), with donations and support being given directly by donors to beneficiaries [Type A]; (b) partially, the charity's fundraising function is disintermediated [Type B]; and finally (c) partially, the charity's service provision to beneficiaries is disintermediated [Type C]. MacQuillin et al.'s (2023) typology is presented in Figure 2.1.

Classic examples of full Type A disintermediation include DBC platforms being used for direct donor-to-beneficiary transactions, but also organisations such as Kiva, the microlending site, which allows lenders to make loans directly to individuals as an investment in their business enterprise (Knudsen & Nielsen, 2013). This is lending-based crowdfunding rather than DBC. Indeed, Kiva's mission is to tackle global poverty as an alternative to traditional charity (Schwittay, 2019). Whereas Type A disintermediation is

	Who is doing the disintermediating?		
	Organisations operating an alternative to the 'Traditional Charity Model'	Individuals	Commercial fundraising organisations
What is disintermediated? 'Traditional Charity Model'	Ai (C)	Aii	NA
Charity/NPO fundraising function	NA	Bi	Bii
Service provision	C	NA	NA

FIGURE 2.1 Disintermediated giving typology.

Source: Taken from MacQuillin et al. (2023).

close to Tapscott's (2015) classic definition of disintermediation in commerce, Type B disintermediation in the charity sector extends the concept.

In a Type B scenario, it is just the professional fundraising arm of a traditional charity that is disintermediated from the giving process, to be replaced by a different intermediary, often without the knowledge or consent of the charity in whose aid an entity is raising funds. These disintermediating actors are free agents (Type Bi) or organisations (Type Bii) who set themselves up as an alternative to fundraising organised and run by a charity's fundraising function. An example of Type Bi disintermediation by free agents is the setting up of Twestival by Amanda Rose (Kanter & Fine, 2010), which raised US$1.84m for 312 charities between 2009 and its last annual event in 2013 (Sharman, 2014). Type Bii disintermediation includes platforms like Pennies, allowing donors to make microdonations during digital purchases. Although charities can register to receive funds raised by Type Bii organisations, they do not have control over the fundraising operation.

Finally, Type C sees a charity's service provision being disintermediated usually by commercial providers often via philanthrocapitalist initiatives and carried out by entities such as B-Corps and social enterprise (Bajde, 2013, p. 4; Bishop, 2007). Furthermore, companies are also increasingly establishing their own charities and charitable foundations (Coleman, 2013), which do the work that would otherwise have been done through a partnership with an established charity. So, in this latter example, whilst charities per se are not disintermediated (because organisations are constituted as charities), the end result of establishing these new breeds of charities is to replace existing charity structures. In some instances, Type C commercial entities that subscribe to a strong social purpose mission still partner with charities to carry out charitable acts, such is the case of clothing firm Patagonia, which donates profits to more than 700 charities. At other times, the line between nonprofit and for-profit becomes blurred, as is the example of Kenco's 'Coffee vs Gangs' campaign (Kemp, 2014) or Timberland's 'Nature Needs Heroes' campaign.

Recent philanthropic activity on the Airbnb portal is a straightforward example of Type A disintermediation at play. Shortly after the start of Russia's invasion of Ukraine in February 2022, individuals booked rooms on the Airbnb platform, without any intention of travelling to Ukraine, and transferring the booking fee to the owners of the rooms (perceived beneficiaries/victims of war by the donor) (Fong, 2022; Mukherjee & Gelb, 2022). Money was transferred directly to Ukrainian residents, without the aid or help of charities. Hundreds of thousands of rooms were booked in this way, transferring millions of pounds to Airbnb hosts living in Ukraine (Fong, 2022). This practice demonstrates how easily an individual can partake in a charitable act whilst completely bypassing the charity sector at the same time. Many people advocate for this type of direct giving as it is seen as a more meaningful and efficient way of giving, i.e., all the money goes to the beneficiaries rather than to a charity that also needs to cover its overheads (Fong, 2022). It is important to note, that the Airbnb initiative offers little guarantee that the right people are being helped (Mukherjee & Gelb, 2022).

The Airbnb example is a unique form of disintermediation as the giving pledge is happening on a business platform that does not have a philanthropy-focus. And in fact, the disintermediated charity space includes actors that have deliberately set up to disrupt the giving space (e.g., GoFundMe and Kiva), but also entities that operate within the 'sharing economy/social media space', but who have since diversified into fundraising and giving (e.g., Facebook Fundraising) and those that accidentally landed in it (e.g., Airbnb in facilitating donations to Ukrainian families).

The most well-known way of disintermediating a charity is via dedicated DBC platforms such as GoFundMe or JustGiving, where individuals set out to raise money to help beneficiaries directly, possibly because the experience of giving feels more personal and immediate than giving to a charity (Niles, 2023). We know from research that direct giving of this nature is popular partly because of a sense of immediacy, and a sense of transparency (knowing where the money is going). Also, direct giving tends to favour local beneficiaries over distant ones (Baron & Szymanska, 2011) and beneficiaries with whom the donors feel socially connected (Jones & Rachlin, 2006;

Knowles & Sullivan, 2017). A content analysis of crowdfunding platforms indicates a strong emphasis on the 'proximity' aspect of giving, with 6/9 of the most popular DBC sites (Crowdfunder, GoFundMe, Global Giving, Donors Choose, Just Giving and Fundly) emphasising the support of local communities on their platform.

Exploring Type Bi Disintermediation and the Motivations behind Donation-Based Crowdfunding

Despite the growing significance of DBC within today's society, scholarly attention predominantly centres on investigating the motivations to *donate* to crowdfunding campaigns (van Teunenbroek, Dalla Chiesa & Hesse, 2023) rather than explanations for initiating such appeals, resulting in an imbalance in our understanding of behaviours and motives of donors versus the motives of citizen fundraisers (Chapman et al., 2022).

Kottasz, van Teunenbroek and Wade (work in progress) have embarked on a study that aims to decipher the motivations behind Type Bi disintermediating actors, i.e., individuals who set up and run DBC appeals, without the aid of charity fundraisers (see MacQuillin et al., 2023). A vast body of inter-disciplinary literature (including organisational psychology, social psychology, behavioural economics, sociology and marketing) has been reviewed in trying to understand the citizen fundraiser who initiates the raising of funds and then subsequently donates this money to a charity. The literature review has arrived at three themes and five categories in this regard (see Figure 2.2).

It is important to note that an initiator of a DBC campaign may exhibit characteristics from multiple categories, thus, the themes should not be seen as mutually exclusive. The categories simply seek to uncover individuals' principal motivations for engaging in this type of activity. DBC individuals are highly motivated proactive agents (Wade, 2023) who are worth understanding: they take an alternative route to simply donating (which requires substantially less time and effort); they go the extra mile by proactively fundraising for a cause. Charities can learn from their activities and potentially partner with them in the future in a fundraising capacity.

Theme 1: Focus on stewardship

Stewardship in the DBC context encompasses ethical values that orientate around the responsible planning and management of resources on behalf of a charitable cause. Stewarding often serves a temporary purpose in overseeing specific projects, which have a relatively short time frame, and can be linked to the so-called *effective altruism* movement that advocates for the efficient

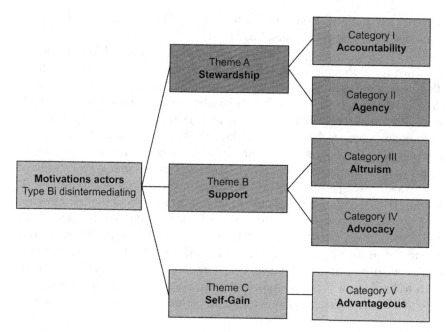

FIGURE 2.2 Motivations for Type Bi citizen fundraising.
Source: Taken from Kottasz and van Teunenbroek (work in progress).

management of charity resources and considers high overheads to be wasteful (Berman et al., 2018). Individuals who align with the stewardship theme may have a sense that by taking control of donation management, they are in effect buying into this movement. Empirical research has concluded that many potential donations are influenced by reported financial efficiencies (e.g., Caviola et al., 2014; Exley, 2020; Blackbaud Report, 2018), information that donors can consult and is readily available for free on charity ratings guides (e.g., Charity Navigator) which compares charities on efficiency ratios. Within the stewardship theme, accountability and agency are two unique (conceptual) profiles that were uncovered by the literature review.

Accountability category – these individuals take the responsible management of donation money very seriously. Rather than donating to a charity that is reputed for its financial management and transparency, they seek to take ownership for raising funds on behalf of a cause. Being personally involved in the fundraising side of things, they feel empowered to oversee the financial success of the DBC. A desire for control can stem from a general lack of trust in how charities raise and manage funds, but it can also manifest an individual's preference for restricted charity funding, or their deep connection with the cause. DBC's projectisation model (i.e., raising money for a concrete purpose) works in tandem with the principles of restricted funding, and appeals to some individuals because it signals transparency and impact (Niles, 2023).

Agency category – agency allows for a sense of control, a capacity to influence one's thoughts and behaviours and manage tasks and situations (Bandura, 1997). In the DBC scenario, individuals are agents, allowing choices over how they conduct their philanthropic activities, on what channels and with which crowds: they can dictate the terms and use of their gifts (Ostrander, Silver & McCarthy, 2005; van Teunenbroek & Smits, 2023). Undoubtedly, the generation of digital natives has grown up in a world where co-production and peer-production are a reality in just about every walk of life (Crawford & Jackson, 2019), including in the charity setting (Booth & Matic, 2011), so taking a proactive stance becomes second nature. Howson (2021) argued that digital technologies including crowdfunding, blockchain and crypto-giving platforms are designed to afford donors influence over nonprofits in an overt and restrictive manner, giving them more options, more control and an active stance over how their money is being allocated. Such technological design features offset and impact individual motivations and behaviours in an everyday setting and within the philanthropic sphere.

Theme 2: Focus on support

Individuals that fall within this theme are primarily focused on actively providing support for a cause: it can stem from a genuine dedication to the cause and an aim to collect funds for the alleviation of suffering and/or the betterment of society (arising from innate altruism), but it also connects with a drive to actively promote the cause (advocacy) to activate wider support on its behalf. Whilst both the altruist and the advocate deeply care about the cause, advocates may seek recognition for their efforts, whilst the altruist type is driven purely by selfless commitment. Moreover, altruists are primarily motivated by providing direct financial support, whilst advocates are primarily motivated by raising awareness and advocacy for the cause, using DBC to achieve this goal.

Altruist category – the empathy–altruism hypothesis by Batson (1987) provides a useful lens to describe the altruism category. It states that empathic concern produces altruistic motivation, which drives people to act in a way that benefits others. *Empathy* includes feelings of sympathy and compassion when another is perceived to be in need (Batson, Lishner & Stocks, 2015). Researchers have found that empathy motivates prosocial behaviours (Wilhelm & Bekkers, 2010) including donating money to crowdfunding projects (Lee, Winterich & Ross Jr, 2014; Liu, Suh & Wagner, 2018). DBC requires substantial effort from the citizen fundraiser, as it demands considerable time and energy (van Teunenbroek & Smits, 2023), but such an effortful stance may simply be more rewarding to an altruist type (see

Niles, 2023). Note also that initiators of projects do not receive financial compensation for collecting funds and may even get charged a starting fee by some of the platforms. According to the empathy–altruism hypothesis, this is reflected in a person's selflessness: an individual is willing to sacrifice their own resources (time, effort, money, etc.) to help others without the expectation of external reward or reciprocation (Batson, Lishner & Stocks, 2015; Gorczyca & Hartman, 2017).

Advocacy category – the process of undertaking active interventions to influence government policy is known as advocacy (Onyx, et al., 2010). Recently, the number of advocacy causes has dramatically increased (Cullerton, 2017). Starting a DBC project can serve to raise awareness and advocate for a cause. An individual may believe that a DBC appeal provides an opportunity to influence the public and subsequently influence stakeholders responsible for public policy change. A combination of networked visibility and financial support makes crowdfunding platforms powerful mediators in shaping public discourse and political action.

Advocates can be seen as innovators who are at the forefront of spreading awareness and inspiring support for their cause. Research within this sphere, for instance, has examined how journalists are using crowdfunding to support work that falls outside of the typical '*fair and balanced*' approach to news that dominates North American journalistic norms (Hunter, 2018). Effective advocacy requires entrepreneurial and communication skills (Cullerton, 2017), extensive social networks (Zhang et al., 2022) and needs clear insight into the rules of policy making and its power structures (Cullerton, Donnet & Lee, 2018). Platform owners and project sponsors often frame crowdfunding as an opportunity to join a movement of like-minded people (Davies, 2015) and to bring "*voice and visibility to efforts that would likely otherwise go unnoticed or unfunded*" (Hunter & di Bartolomeo, 2019). By intervening directly in areas that have traditionally been the preserve of government, large corporations and third-sector organisations, crowdfunding platforms give individuals the ability to create change in society that is meaningful to those individuals to raise awareness and advocate for a cause (Hunter, 2018; Crawford & Jackson, 2019).

Theme 3: Focus on self-gain

Part of philanthropy and giving happens for the purposes of self-gain and self-fulfilment rather than genuine altruism (Bekkers & Wiepking, 2011; Andreoni, 1990). We know this from the classic giving and the volunteering literature where many are impelled to dedicate time and money to a charity or a cause simply to build a resume, to make friends (Bennett & Kottasz, 2001) or to climb social ladders (Kocaman, 2024; Kottasz, 2004). Today's philanthropists are less loyal to charities (Bekkers & van Teunenbroek,

2020), and it is often an activity (e.g., skydiving) rather than a charity that propels individuals to engage in philanthropic endeavour (Saxton, 2020). The initiators of DBC campaigns often engage in adventure sports or similar initiatives to motivate others to contribute. Patterns indicate that younger people are more likely to give in a social manner (Kocaman, 2024), carry out with friends in a social setting and/or broadcast their charitable deeds on social media (Crawford & Jackson, 2019).

Driven by *"social pressure, social reward, and a higher social standing attained from charitable involvement"* (Graça & Zwick, 2021, p. 8), the strongest extrinsic motivators related to new generations of donors is social recognition (Fehrer & Nenonen, 2020; Graça & Zwick, 2021), and DBC donors are often younger and active via social media (van Teunenbroek & Hasanefendic, 2023). Some individuals may be looking for the cachet of being part of a new trend, or praise for the cleverness of a DBC idea (Niles, 2023). Crowdfunding networks are open and non-hierarchical (Ketonen-Oksi, Jussila & Kärkkäinen, 2016) and form spontaneously. Compared with networks of formal ties (e.g., between employers and employees), which have an upper limit for growth due to limited available resources, networks of informal ties are highly scalable (Dagnino et al., 2016) and if enough support is amassed via a DBC appeal, they have great potential to signify social capital (Granovetter, 2005), give credence to the creator of the campaign (Lin, Spence & Lachlan, 2016) and increase the likelihood of securing the target donations.

Technology as a Catalyst and the Crowdfunding Paradox

Technology plays a pivotal role in the discussed form of disintermediation by facilitating, growing and supporting it. A focus on exploring the technological impact on philanthropic decision-making is important (Christie, 2020). Innovation often disrupts existing systems, introducing new ways of working and thinking. DBC exemplifies this paradigm shift in how ideas are funded and brought to market. It has democratised the innovation process by empowering individuals, startups and communities, and re-defined the relationship between creators and their audience. Below, we argue that introducing a technology-supported platform like DBC is a catalyst for restricted funding, donor involvement and even donor-controlled philanthropy (see Figure 2.3).

Implications for charities – The landscape of philanthropy is evolving, and charities can leverage this change. The disruption caused by DBC could attract new contributors who were previously disengaged (van Teunenbroek & Hasanefendic, 2023). DBC empowers donors by allowing them to choose the projects they fund, amplifying their voices. This shift could broaden the reach of charities and enhance their visibility. Furthermore, DBC underscores the interplay between individual actions and societal frameworks in the digital age. Donor-centred philanthropy has been on the rise for a while (Ostrander, 2007), and DBC pushes it towards donor-controlled philanthropy and helps it to professionalise further.

Emphasis on transparency – The DBC model, emphasising restricted funding and transparency, could lead to more careful monitoring and evaluation of how charitable funds are used. Transparency, in this context, refers to the openness and honesty of the charity in showing donors how their funds are being used. This could potentially improve accountability and effectiveness in the sector.

Regulation and oversight – The increased focus on DBC also calls for regulation and oversight. As platforms develop further, increasing their market share

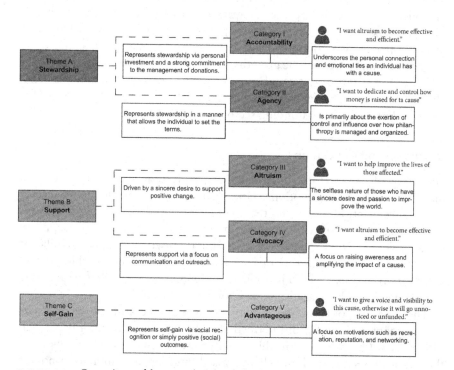

FIGURE 2.3   Overview of how technology facilitates disintermediation, supports donation-based crowdfunding (DBC) and innovates the sector.

Notes: DBC serves as a catalyst for several implications for charities, like donor-controlled philanthropy. DBC also increases the emphasis on transparency. The DBC paradox is that, at the same time, there is also a call for increased regulation and oversight. This paradox could deter donors and put further innovations on hold.

Source: Authors' own work.

and adding new features, their power and responsibilities grow. Currently, these platforms are hardly monitored, and voices are arising that they should abide by the same rules and regulations as charities. Most forms of disintermediated fundraising fall outside of established regulatory regimes and frameworks (Mayer, 2022).

The paradox of DBC – We have identified a significant paradox in the realm of DBC: the tension between its emphasis on transparency and trust (Bunger, 2013), and the lack of regulation and oversight in the sector (Alter, Strachwitz and Unger, 2021). On one hand, DBC platforms emphasise transparency and trust, fostering a sense of accountability. On the other hand, the lack of regulation and oversight in the crowdfunding sector can pose challenges, potentially undermining the trust essential to the functioning of DBC platforms.

This paradox highlights the need for a balance between the freedom and innovation that DBC allows and the need for some level of regulation to protect donors and ensure the integrity of projects (Adena et al., 2019). This paradox could have significant implications for the future development of DBC. If trust is undermined due to a lack of regulation, it could deter potential donors and limit the growth of DBC. On the other hand, if stringent regulations are imposed, it could stifle the innovation and freedom that DBC allows. Therefore, navigating this paradox will be a crucial challenge for stakeholders in the crowdfunding sector.

Discussion and Conclusion

For nonprofit marketeers and managers, it is crucial to stay ahead of industry trends and disruptions. One such disruption in the charity sector is disintermediation, driven by the rise of DBC. Understanding the reasons behind this disruption will empower nonprofit organisations to adapt and remain relevant. DBC is gaining traction and is poised to become a significant alternative to traditional fundraising methods. The extent to which it will substitute traditional methods is currently unknown. Regardless, embracing this change could be a strategic move for future success.

The type of crowdfunding initiative that we discuss in the second part of this chapter (Type Bi) disintermediates the professional fundraising arm of a charity. On the face of it, this activity may be seen to work in favour of the nonprofit sector, as ultimately the raised funds are disseminated amongst charities. However, the loss of control could pose a challenge for charities. Understanding why citizen fundraisers want to control the fundraising function is therefore paramount and may provide valuable inputs into new strategies to engage these individuals as potential partners. Individuals who want to bypass the charity sector altogether (i.e., Type Aii according to the disintermediation typology) are likely to possess very different motivations to Type Bi fundraisers, such as a concern for more personal connection

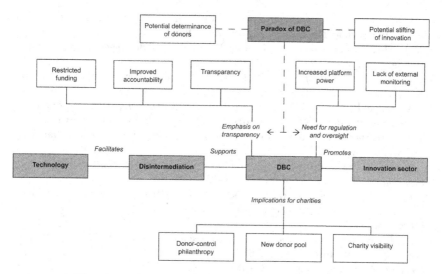

FIGURE 2.4 The three themes and five profiling categories of Type Bi citizen fundraisers.

Source: Taken from Kottasz and van Teunenbroek (work in progress).

with beneficiaries (Pierce, O'Driscoll & Coghlan, 2004) or a wish for swift beneficiary funding (Karimi & Kelly, 2022).

The five profiling categories of Type Bi citizen fundraisers are not mutually exclusive, are conceptual at this stage and need to be tested empirically. However, they will hopefully provide some insight into philanthropic attitudes that are apparent in the digital age and may become a useful segmentation tool for DBC platforms. Figure 2.4 provides a summary.

Future research may wish to explore the selection process behind chosen crowdfunding sites, i.e., why individuals select JustGiving versus GoFundMe, for instance. Charities will want to also understand how citizen fundraisers decide which charities they donate the raised funds to, whether this is to do with charity branding (Gregory, Ngo & Miller, 2020), or charities that 'match' the identity, ideology and/or values of the initiator of the campaign (Chapman, Louis & Masser, 2018) or something entirely different.

References

Adena, M., Alizade, J., Bohner, F., Harke, J., & Mesters, F. (2019). Quality certification for nonprofits, charitable giving, and donor's trust: Experimental evidence. *Journal of Economic Behavior & Organization*, 159, 75–100.

Alter, R., Strachwitz, R. and Unger, T. (2021). Trust in philanthropy: A report on the Philanthropy Insight project 2018–2021. Available at www.ssoar.info/ssoar/bitstream/handle/document/77556.2/ssoar-2022-alter_et_al-Trust_in_Philanthropy_a_Report.pdf [Accessed 24 01 2024.]

Andreoni, J. (1990). Impure altruism and donations to public goods: A theory of warm glow giving. *The Economic Journal*, 100(401), 464–477.

Bajde, D. (2013). Marketized philanthropy: Kiva's utopian ideology of entrepreneurial philanthropy. *Marketing Theory*, 13(1), 3–18.

Bandura, A. (1997). *Self-Efficacy: The Exercise of Control.* New York, NY: Freeman.

Baron, J., & Szymanska, E. (2011). Heuristics and biases in charity (215–235). In D.M. Oppenheimer, & C.Y. Olivola (Eds.), *The Science of Giving: Experimental Approaches to the Study of Charity.* London: Psychology Press. Available at https://creativescience.co/wp-content/uploads/2018/08/Heuristics-and-Biases-in-Charity.pdf [Accessed 24 01 2024.]

Batson, C. D. (1987). Prosocial motivation: Is it ever truly altruistic? *Advances in Experimental Social Psychology*, 20, 65–122.

Batson, C. D., Lishner, D. A., & Stocks, E. L. (2015). The empathy–altruism hypothesis. *The Oxford Handbook of Prosocial Behavior*, 259–268, Oxford Library of Psychology.

Bekkers, R., & van Teunenbroek, C. (2020). Generatieverschillen in geefgedrag en vrijwilligerswerk. In R. Bekkers, B. M. Gouwenberg, & T. N. M. Schuyt (Eds.), *Geven in Nederland 2020* (pp. 22–48). Amsterdam: Lenthe.

Bekkers, R., & Wiepking, P. (2011). A literature review of empirical studies of philanthropy: Eight mechanisms that drive charitable giving. *Nonprofit and Voluntary Sector Quarterly*, 40(5), 924–973.

Bennett, R., & Kottasz, R. (2001). Advertisement style and the recruitment of charity volunteers. *Journal of Nonprofit & Public Sector Marketing*, 8(2), 45–63.

Berman, J. Z., Barasch, A., Levine, E. E., & Small, D. A. (2018). Impediments to effective altruism: The role of subjective preferences in charitable giving. *Psychological Science*, 29(5), 834–844.

Bishop, M. (2007). What is philanthrocapitalism? Alliance, March 1, www.alliancemagazine.org/feature/what-is-philanthrocapitalism/ [Accessed 24 01 2024.]

Blackbaud Report (2018). How giving performed in 2018, Blackbaud Institute, Available at https://institute.blackbaud.com/asset/2018-charitable-giving-report/ [Accessed 24 01 2024.]

Booth, N., & Matic, J. A. (2011). Mapping and leveraging influencers in social media to shape corporate brand perceptions. *Corporate Communications: An International Journal*, 16(3), 184–191.

Bunger, A. C. (2013). Administrative coordination in nonprofit human service delivery networks: The role of competition and trust. *Nonprofit and Voluntary Sector Quarterly*, 42(6), 1155–1175.

Caviola, L., Faulmüller, N., Everett, J. A., Savulescu, J., & Kahane, G. (2014). The evaluability bias in charitable giving: Saving administration costs or saving lives? *Judgment & Decision Making*, 9(4), 303–315.

Chapman, C. M., Louis, W. R., & Masser, B. M. (2018). Identifying (our) donors: Toward a social psychological understanding of charity selection in Australia. *Psychology & Marketing*, 35(12), 980–989.

Chapman, C. M., Louis, W. R., Masser, B. M., & Thomas, E. F. (2022). Charitable Triad Theory: How donors, beneficiaries, and fundraisers influence charitable giving. *Psychology & Marketing*, 39(9), 1826–1848.

Christie, A. (2020). Can distributed ledger technologies promote trust for charities? A literature review. *Frontiers in Blockchain*, 3, 31.

Coleman, A. (2013). Why setting up a charity makes good business sense. *The Guardian*, July 17. Available at www.theguardian.com/small-business-network/2013/jul/17/setting-up-charity-good-business [Accessed 24 01 2024.]

Crawford, E. C., & Jackson, J. (2019). Philanthropy in the millennial age: Trends toward polycentric personalized philanthropy. *The Independent Review*, 23(4), 551–568.

Cullerton, K. (2017). *An exploration of the factors influencing public health nutrition policymaking in Australia* (Doctoral dissertation, Queensland University of Technology).

Cullerton, K., Donnet, T., Lee, A., & Gallegos, D. (2018). Effective advocacy strategies for influencing government nutrition policy: A conceptual model. *International Journal of Behavioral Nutrition & Physical Activity*, 15(1), 1–11.

Dagnino, G. B., Levanti, G., & Mocciaro Li Destri, A. (2016). Structural dynamics and intentional governance in strategic interorganizational network evolution: A multilevel approach. *Organization Studies*, 37(3), 349–373.

Davies, R. (2015). Three provocations for civic crowdfunding. *Information, Communication & Society*, 18(3), 342–355.

Exley, C. L. (2020). Using charity performance metrics as an excuse not to give. *Management Science*, 66(2), 553–563.

Fehrer, J. A., & Nenonen, S. (2020). Crowdfunding networks: Structure, dynamics, and critical capabilities. *Industrial Marketing Management*, 88, 449–464.

Fong, A. (2022). Airbnb cash transfers to Ukrainians can help, but they're disrupting charities. *The Conversation*, March 27, Available at https://theconversation.com/amp/airbnb-cash-transfers-to-ukrainians-can-help-but-theyre-disrupting-charities-179189 [Accessed 24 01 2024.]

Gorczyca, M., & Hartman, R. L. (2017). The new face of philanthropy: The role of intrinsic motivation in millennials' attitudes and intent to donate to charitable organizations. *Journal of Nonprofit & Public Sector Marketing*, 29(4), 415–433.

Graça, S. S., & Zwick, H. C. (2021). Perceived value of charitable involvement: The millennial donor perspective. *Journal of Philanthropy and Marketing*, https://onlinelibrary.wiley.com/doi/pdfdirect/10.1002/nvsm.1705

Granovetter, M. (2005). The impact of social structure on economic outcomes. *Journal of Economic Perspectives*, 19(1), 33–50.

Gregory, G., Ngo, L., & Miller, R. (2020). Branding for non-profits: explaining new donor decision-making in the charity sector. *Journal of Product & Brand Management*, 29(5), 583–600.

Howson, P. (2021). Crypto-giving and surveillance philanthropy: Exploring the trade-offs in blockchain innovation for nonprofits. *Nonprofit Management & Leadership*, 31(4), 805–820.

Hunter, A. (2018). "It's like having a second full-time job": Crowdfunding, journalism, and labour. In Entrepreneurial Journalism, 77–92, Abingdon, UK: Routledge.

Hunter, A., & Di Bartolomeo, J. (2019). "We're a movement": Crowdfunding, journalism, and feminism. *Feminist Media Studies*, 19(2), 273–287.

Jones, B., & Rachlin, H. (2006). Social discounting. *Psychological Science*, 17(4), 283–286.

Kanter, B. and Fine, A.H. (2010). *The Networked Nonprofit*. San Francisco, CA: Jossey Bass.

Karimi, F. & Kelly, S. (2022). People around the world are booking Airbnb's in Ukraine: They don't plan to check in. March 5, *CNN Travel*. Available at https://edition.cnn.com/travel/article/ukraine-airbnb-donations-cec/index.html [Accessed 24 01 2024.]

Kemp, N. (2014). Why Kenco is taking on gang culture. *Campaign*, August 14, Available at www.campaignlive.co.uk/article/why-kenco-taking-gang-culture/1307805 [Accessed 24 01 2024.]

Ketonen-Oksi, S., Jussila, J. J., & Kärkkäinen, H. (2016). Social media-based value creation and business models. *Industrial Management & Data Systems*, 116(8), 1820–1838.

Knowles, S., & Sullivan, T. (2017). Does charity begin at home or overseas? *Nonprofit & Voluntary Sector Quarterly*, 46(5), 944–962.

Knudsen, B. T., & Nielsen, A. E. (2013). Acts that matter–an analysis of Kiva. *Social Responsibility Journal*, 9(4), 603–6221.

Kocaman, R. (2024). Exploring the underpinnings of why millennials engage in charitable activities: Empirical evidence from Türkiye. *Journal of Philanthropy and Marketing*. https://doi.org/10.1002/nvsm.1831

Kottasz, R. (2004). How should charitable organisations motivate young professionals to give philanthropically? *International Journal of Nonprofit and Voluntary Sector Marketing*, 9(1), 9–27.

Lee, S., Winterich, K. P., & Ross Jr, W. T. (2014). I'm moral, but I won't help you: The distinct roles of empathy and justice in donations. *Journal of Consumer Research*, 41(3), 678–696.

Lin, X., Spence, P. R., & Lachlan, K. A. (2016). Social media and credibility indicators: The effect of influence cues. *Computers in Human Behavior*, 63, 264–271.

Liu, L., Suh, A., & Wagner, C. (2018). Empathy or perceived credibility? An empirical study on individual donation behavior in charitable crowdfunding. *Internet Research*, 28(3), 623–651.

MacQuillin, I., Kottasz, R., Locilento, J., & Gallaiford, N. (2023). A typology of disintermediated giving and asking in the non-profit sector. *Journal of Philanthropy and Marketing*, https://onlinelibrary.wiley.com/doi/pdf/10.1002/nvsm.1820

Mayer, L. H. (2022). Regulating charitable crowdfunding. *Indiana Law Journal*, 97, 1375.

Mukherjee, A., and Gelb, A. (2022). People around the world are booking Airbnb's in Ukraine to help people in need. Will it work? *Centre for Global Development*, March 8, Available at www.cgdev.org/blog/people-around-world-are-booking-airbnbs-ukraine-help-people-need-will-it-work [Accessed 24 01 2024.]

Niles, M. (2023). Recasting the "middleman": The role of charities in the age of disintermediation. *Journal of Philanthropy and Marketing*, 28(1), https://doi.org/10.1002/nvsm.1779

Onyx, J., Armitage, L., Dalton, B., Melville, R., Casey, J., & Banks, R. (2010). Advocacy with gloves on: The "manners" of strategy used by some third sector organizations undertaking advocacy in NSW and Queensland. *VOLUNTAS: International Journal of Voluntary and Nonprofit Organizations*, 21, 41–61.

Ostrander, S. A. (2007). The growth of donor control: Revisiting the social relations of philanthropy. *Nonprofit and Voluntary Sector Quarterly*, 36(2), 356–372.

Ostrander, S. A., Silver, I., & McCarthy, D. (2005). Mobilizing money strategically: Opportunities for grantees to be active agents in social movement philanthropy. *Foundations for Social Change: Critical Perspectives on Philanthropy and Popular Movements*, 271–290.

Pierce, J. L., O'Driscoll, M. P., & Coghlan, A. M. (2004). Work environment structure and psychological ownership: The mediating effects of control. *The Journal of Social Psychology*, 144, 507–534.

Sargeant, A. (2008). Marketing for nonprofit organizations, in Baker, M.J., and Hart, S. *The Marketing Book*, 6th edition, pp. 526–550. Oxford: Butterworth-Heinemann.

Saxton, J. (2020). The impact, the successes, and the failures of the charity sector and the Covid pandemic, December 3, *nfp Research*. Available at https://nfpresea rch.com/blog/impact-successes-and-failures-charity-sector-and-covid-pandemic [Accessed 24 01 2024.]

Schwittay, A. (2019). Digital mediations of everyday humanitarianism: the case of Kiva.org. *Third World Quarterly*, 40(10), 1921–1938.

Sharman, A. (2014). Twestival to end after five years. *Civil Society*, February 17, www.civilsociety.co.uk/news/twestival-to-end-after-five-years.html [Accessed 24 01 2024.]

Tapscott, D. (2015). *The Digital Economy*. 20th Anniversary Edition. New York, NY: McGraw-Hill.

van Teunenbroek, C., Dalla Chiesa, D., & Hesse, L. (2023). The contribution of crowdfunding for philanthropy: A systematic review and framework of donation and reward crowdfunding. *Journal of Philanthropy and Marketing*, 28(3), 1–15.

van Teunenbroek, C., & Hasanefendic, S. (2023). Researching the crowd: Implications on philanthropic crowdfunding and donor characteristics during a pandemic. *Journal of Philanthropy and Marketing*, 28(1), e1773.

van Teunenbroek, C., & Smits, R. (2023). Four lessons learned: Employees' perceptions of crowdfunding for cultural institutions. *Journal of Philanthropy and Marketing*, 28(3), 1–9.

Wade, M. (2023). 'The giving layer of the internet': A critical history of GoFundMe's reputation management, platform governance, and communication strategies in capturing peer-to-peer and charitable giving markets. *Journal of Philanthropy and Marketing*. https://doi.org/10.1002/nvsm.1777

Wilhelm, M. O., & Bekkers, R. (2010). Helping behavior, dispositional empathic concern, and the principle of care. *Social Psychology Quarterly*, 73(1), 11–32.

Zhang, X., Liu, X., Wang, X., Zhao, H., & Zhang, W. (2022). Exploring the effects of social capital on crowdfunding performance: A holistic analysis from the empirical and predictive views. *Computers in Human Behavior*, 126, 107011.

3

CHOICE, IMPACT, FUN, REPEAT!

Exploring the Current State and Future Opportunities of Youth Volunteering

Sarah-Louise Mitchell and Irene Garnelo-Gomez

Introduction

Are Gen-Z the long-awaited 'agents of change'? Those who will help us reverse climate change and advance social justice? Early indicators show Gen-Z are a strongly cause-orientated generation who actively participate in addressing societal problems such as climate change, homelessness and inequality (YouGov, 2021), with Edelman (2021) identifying that 70% of Gen-Z globally are involved with a social or political cause. The Youth Futures Report (Future Laboratory, 2018) labelled this cohort as 'rebels with a cause' who are 'intent on a new activism-inspired agenda'. Labelled as 'Philanthroteens' by Kanter (2015), Gen-Z contributes money and/or time to making a difference. Globally, the UN State of Volunteering Report (2022) puts the value of hours volunteered by young people each year at $35 billion and finds that 70% of 18–24-year-olds report volunteering at some point.

The act of volunteering not only leads to support for a specific social or environmental cause, but also contributes to society as a whole (EESC, 2021) and benefits the volunteers themselves. Volunteering helps both create and satisfy a sense of belonging (Dallimore et al., 2018) and makes salient aspects of our social identity (Thoits, 2021). It also helps our mental health and wellbeing (Appau and Awaworyi Churchill, 2019; Haski-Leventhal et al., 2020), and has proven to positively influence self-confidence and self-esteem (Haski-Leventhal et al., 2020). While these benefits are important to any volunteer, they are perhaps more significant amongst young volunteers, who are developing a sense of personal identity and building habits that will likely continue later in life (Hart et al., 2006).

DOI: 10.4324/9781003396802-3

Despite evidence highlighting the benefits of volunteering, the decline in the number of volunteers engaging with charities is putting their survival at risk. The most recent Community Life Survey (Gov.uk, 2023) highlights a significant drop in both formal and informal volunteering in England. For example, formal volunteering amongst 16–24-year-olds fell from 23% (2019/2020) to 17% (2020/2021). Likewise, Volunteer Scotland found a decline from 49% in 2019 to 37% in 2022 amongst young people in the country participating in formal volunteering (Volunteer Scotland, 2023). Statistics are even more alarming when considering reluctant individuals, as the number of young people in the UK who were unlikely to participate or had no intention of participating in volunteering, increased from 17% to 25% between 2016 and 2019 (Bratsa et al., 2020). These trends highlight the fundamental need for effective marketing communication by charities to engage young people to participate (Mitchell, 2021; Mitchell & Clark, 2020).

Drivers and barriers of youth volunteering

Motivations behind youth volunteering are both altruistic and egocentric, based on self-interest (Haski-Leventhal et al., 2009; Bocsi et al., 2017). Research has shown that altruistic motives could relate to factors such as being useful to others (Jardim & Marques da Silva, 2018), achieving something positive for others (Rehberg, 2005), caring for others (Hart & Fegley, 1995) and helping the community (Nursey-Bray, 2020). Considering more individualistic and instrumental reasons, young people might engage in volunteering driven by practical gains, such as the opportunity of learning new skills (Khasanzyanova, 2017) and enhancing their career profiles (Dávila & Díaz-Morales, 2009). This is more salient across groups who volunteer as a pre-condition of a Higher Education (HE) course application such as midwifery or teaching. Volunteering helps young people develop their own sense of self, in particular, in relation to their social identity (Thoits, 2021), and helps them build self-confidence and a sense of belonging (Dallimore et al., 2018). A recent study suggests that even though most young people engage in this type of programmes as a requirement or to get work experience, one of the key benefits gained is increased self-confidence, which empowers them and allows them to feel more comfortable with themselves and others (Plunkett Foundation, 2023; Buelens et al., 2015). This is of particular importance when considering how to engage young people in volunteering, as while older adult volunteers are focused on service, younger volunteers are more relationship-oriented, and they are more likely to volunteer if their friends also do it (Haski-Leventhal et al., 2008). According to Cho et al. (2018) traditional collective motivations to volunteer, such as helping others or contributing to a cause, are becoming secondary for Gen-Z volunteers; a motivational shift that was already highlighted by academics in relation to precedent generations (e.g., Hustinx, 2001). While Gen-Z might be strongly cause-oriented (YouGov, 2021), and still motivated to volunteer by both the willingness to help others and the desire of achieving individual benefits, egocentric reasons (i.e., making friends, having fun, learning new skills) seem to be the most important motivations behind their behaviour.

So, what is holding them back? Some of the classic barriers to engagement with charities through volunteering include lack of time, while lack of awareness about volunteering opportunities is also quite prominent amongst some segments of the youth (Sundeen & Raskoff, 2000). External factors also hinder the adoption of volunteering behaviours. The lack of integration of social issues in schools' curricula (Lin et al., 2015), again more prominent in areas of disadvantage (Body et al., 2024), negatively affects volunteering practice. Young people living in lower socio-economic communities are also impacted by the limited volunteering opportunities available (Davies, 2018), and by different social norms, as volunteering might not be a common behaviour practised in their area (Dean, 2016). The decline in faith groups, particularly amongst Gen-Z (PRRI, 2023), also acts as a barrier to engagement, as religious groups used to be a classic route into volunteering (Sundeen & Raskoff, 2000). Likewise, the economic environment is also a barrier, negatively impacting volunteers and volunteering. For instance, volunteers suffering the cost-of-living crisis in the UK believe they cannot afford to volunteer, as they are experiencing rising costs and the current situation is affecting their mental health, making it difficult to find time to volunteer (Volunteer Scotland, 2024). Young people (in particular, students) who previously volunteered are now using that time to get part-time jobs to support themselves financially.

Why engaging young people in volunteering is important?

Three core reasons underpin why engaging the next generation in civic society matters? Firstly, society is increasingly relying on charities to be the front-line response to social issues (Ferrell-Schweppenstedde, 2023), as seen recently with the cost-of-living crisis through food banks and community warm spaces (warmwelcome.uk, 2024). With the reduction in both central and local funding of charities, attracting donations, volunteering time and goods-in-kind are key to their sustainability: put another way, without the resources to enable them to deliver their charitable missions, charities will be unable to help. Thus, charity survival strongly depends on their capacity to recruit and maintain young volunteers (Shields, 2009).

Secondly, if patterns of civic engagement at a global, national and/or local community level are established now, they are more likely to endure through changes in life-stage (Brodie et al., 2011). We know people are more likely to volunteer if their parents volunteered (Grimm et al., 2005; Perks &

Knoecny, 2015). If they volunteer, they are more likely to feel they belong to their local community (Dallimore et al., 2018; Wakefield et al., 2022), whilst volunteering also helps young people develop positive attitudes towards society and acquire social responsibility (Haski-Leventhal et al., 2008). By communicating effectively with younger people now, and attracting them to volunteering, for example, there is a chance that habits can be established which last a lifetime.

Finally, there is an increasing risk for charities that younger people bypass them when they do engage with causes and social/environmental issues. Traditionally, charitable organisations have played an important role in enabling individuals to fulfil a desire to make a difference. Charities highlight important causes, present options for engagement and, crucially, provide effective means to enact change, by marshalling expertise, resources, networks and strategies to ensure the operational efficiency needed to achieve high impact. However, the growth of direct digital engagement, for example, through crowdfunding campaigns by individuals and the growth of online movements such as #BlackLivesMatter and #ReclaimTheStreets, are early indicators of sector-wide service disintermediation (Kottasz et al., 2023).

The future of volunteering, therefore, is somehow uncertain. While we are seeing a decline in volunteering amongst the youth (Gov.uk, 2023), reports suggest that one in six young people aged 18–34 living in the UK plan to start volunteering (Jemal et al., 2022). But, will those intentions translate into actual behaviour? Will we see Gen-Z closing the attitude–behaviour gap seemingly affecting their generation? While COVID-19 has, in some cases, aggravated power dynamics between volunteers and organisations, the pandemic has also highlighted the role of volunteers as 'agents of change', and the capacity of volunteering in creating hope and building resilience. The pandemic has also accelerated the transition towards online forms of volunteering, providing new opportunities and improving accessibility (Chadwick El-Ali, 2022). Digital platforms are also proving to be a good aid when recruiting young volunteers. Sites such as 'Reach Volunteering' or 'Volunteering Matters' make volunteering programmes possible by bringing together volunteers and charitable organisations. Social media and 'altruistic influencers' (Bagley, 2023) are nowadays one of the main channels to target young volunteers. For example, in November 2020, a volunteer used TikTok to gain 100,000 new volunteers for the 'Be My Eyes' app, an application which aims to help blind and visually impaired individuals cope with everyday situations. Recent research by Kılıç et al. (2024) also found that volunteering information shared by travel influencers positively influences attitudes and intentions towards volunteer tourism (i.e., when individuals travel to volunteer in less affluent countries). As of February 2024, the hashtag #volunteer has more than 246,000 posts on TikTok, and more than

9.4 million posts on Instagram. Capitalising on these new ways of recruiting volunteers could help charities increase their attractiveness to young people.

When developing marketing strategies for the future, charities are also acknowledging the shifts in motivations mentioned above. The British Heart Foundation, for example, released a new volunteering strategy in 2023, which highlights the need to make volunteering "Easy, Flexible and Inclusive" (British Heart Foundation, 2023). It focuses on improving the volunteering experience, so volunteers help the cause while maximising the benefits they get out of their participation. These initiatives align with the future trends suggested by previous reports, which signal the importance of creating experiences and providing rewards (Rochester, 2021). In the future, charities might rely more on 'episodic volunteers', those who volunteer as a one-off or for a short period of time (Cnaan & Handy, 2005; Handy et al., 2006). This type of volunteering includes volunteering at specific events (e.g., a festival) or during a specific period of time (e.g., help developing a new community garden for a week). Importantly, episodic volunteers might still be committed to volunteering, by *sustaining* their volunteer behaviour over time, volunteering to participate in the activity every year (Hyde et al., 2016). They might also be episodic volunteers within the same organisation or other organisations, participating in different short-term activities regularly (Handy et al., 2006). The trends in volunteering explored by Rochester (2021) also highlight the growing importance of micro-volunteering (i.e., signing a petition), which could reduce barriers (in particular time and mobility), but that also bring challenges, mainly in terms of ethics and relationships dynamics between organisations and volunteers (Heley et al., 2022).

Attracting a new generation of volunteers requires amplifying the pockets of excellence we glimpse today, to enable young people to step forward and contribute in a way that is meaningful for them. This is highly unlikely to look like the traditional models of the past, with their formal interviews, contracts, set days and minimum service commitments. Looking forward to how volunteering might develop in the future, we identify seven distinct approaches aimed at encouraging young people in particular to engage with volunteering, all with important implications for charity marketing. In the next section, best practice examples of different types of volunteering are explained.

Volunteering Best Practice Typologies

Type 1: Recognition programmes

Positioning: 'Stand out from the crowd'

The UK's Duke of Edinburgh Award Programme provides a blueprint for voluntary formal programmes to engage young people (DofE, 2024). In

2022/2023, over half a million young people participated, and through the volunteering section of the programme, 3.5 million hours were given to local communities (estimated value £17 million). Although usually organised through secondary schools, this voluntary programme enables the experience to be completely personalised, in terms of level of commitment (progressing from Bronze to Silver to Gold Awards) and choice of ways to meet the requirements including compulsory volunteering. The fact that the scheme is highly recognised and respected by employers and universities alike is a strong attraction, demonstrating extra-curricular personal achievements (Campbell et al., 2009). Community engagement through volunteering has been identified as enjoyable; young people can choose something they are passionate about, it teaches them how to get along with different people and, crucially, they feel rewarded through seeing the contribution they make. For many, it represents their first experience of civic participation. Research based on in-depth interviews with past participants showed that over half carried on volunteering after the DofE commitment was completed (Campbell et al., 2009). Significant attempts have been made to increase access to the programme, and shift it from a predominantly white, middle-class stereotype to current day, where 25% participants are from ethnic backgrounds, 15% are experiencing poverty and 7% have special needs (DofE, 2024).

This type of voluntary, individualised, formal programme can also be seen in HE. For example, the RED Award at the University of Reading, which has seen over 14k students registering to take part since it started in 2010 and over 35% completing the 40 hours commitment required. It is positioned as "An opportunity to gain experience and stand out from the crowd in an increasingly competitive job market" (Reading.ac.uk, 2024). It is anchored in harnessing extra-curricular activity to enhance the employability of Reading graduates. Across the UK, this approach can also be seen throughout many other Universities including Goldsmiths (The Gold Award), Manchester (Stellify), Bristol (Bristol Plus) and Glasgow (HEAR). However, with the HE context, these tend to be one-off awards rather than having progressive levels and based on a set number of extra-curricular hours spent on a wide range of recognised activities, of which one of the options is volunteering: the minimum requirement to complete the RED Award, for example, is only one hour of volunteering.

Type 2: Immersive taster

Positioning: 'Give it a go!'

The National Citizenship Service (NCS) started as a one-off civic engagement experience, positioned as an opportunity for personal growth for young people with the call to "Boost your confidence. Nurture new skills. Grow your resilience. Be a force for good. Make a whole new set of friends" (wearencs. com, 2024). Over three-quarters of a million young people have completed NCS since it started in 2011 by (then) UK Prime Minister David Cameron. Originally, a 3–4-week programme that included a one-week residential away from home plus a week spent on a community action project, this represented a one-off immersive and accessible experience, that included participation within local communities at its heart. Interestingly, research by University College London and the Behavioural Insights Team (Taylor, 2021), found that participation in NCS increased subsequent political participation by 12%, demonstrating its impact on broader civic consciousness and engagement.

With the policy shift within the UK government towards funding ongoing youth groups/centres and away from one-off experiences, the funding for NCS has been cut from £180 million to £57 million (2022). Post-COVID, young people can now choose an NCS experience from online skill development (free), taking in a local community project (free) or gaining an away from home adventure experience (£95 but with some bursaries to broaden access). Therefore, we argue that the NCS experience is no longer an immersive, rounded experience with civic engagement at its heart, and as a result, unfortunately its power to feed forward to life-long patterns of volunteering in young people has diminished.

However, the idea of giving young people a one-off taste of volunteering through charities in their local community remains interesting, particularly for people lacking family volunteer role models. It needs to be a direct engagement in a specific project where the young person can see that through their efforts, working with others, they made a difference (Nordstrom et al., 2022). For example, through the weekend experience of joining a 'Trees for Cities' planting day in their local area (treesforcities.org), results are clearly visible, and effort is collegiate. The 'Big Help Out' initiative raises the profile of volunteering and provides direct links to one-off volunteering opportunities in your area (thebighelpout.org.uk). This provides a potential future blueprint for other organisations; time-bound local community-based opportunities with low barriers to participation, that enables the young person (and those of all ages) to experience first-hand the social and rewarding nature of the activity which potentially might lead to them stepping forward again in the future.

Type 3: Social change movements

Positioning: 'Make a difference: Join the movement'

The social consciousness of young people is well documented (Deloitte, 2023). Leading causes for concern are climate change, mental health, income inequality and diversity and inclusion. This is reflected in the choice of companies to work for, as social conscious, values-based organisations appeal to those seeking purpose-driven work. It can also drive individual purchase behaviour as young people say they want companies to commit to social causes and take a stand and are willing to alter their purchases to reward those that do (Edelman, 2021).

However, it is a cohort level where things become interesting. Mobilisation for transformative movements, particularly across Western Europe, reflects a passionate concern for the future and a willingness to rebel against the status quo (Europa.Eu, 2023). Charitable organisations that authentically harness this sense of being part of a movement for change, tap into the need to be part of something bigger, something transformative (European Union, 2024). A strong example of this is the UK marine charity 'Surfers Against Sewage' (sas.org.uk). Their appeal is "We raise awareness of plastic pollution through mobilising hundreds of thousands of Ocean Activists, UK-wide, to clean their local environment. And the data we gather supports our campaigns against the polluters". SAS use the language of change, of practical local action, to make a difference and political campaigning to encourage especially young people to become 'part of the movement'. This positioning of volunteering as a coming together for something important is now permeating into charity discourse, as a way to resonate with young people and others, including recent marketing from #iwill, Parkinsons UK and Extinction Rebellion.

Type 4: National requirement

Positioning: 'You know you have to'

To facilitate a step change in volunteering participation by young people in the future, one model worth considering is the compulsory requirement across many districts in Canada that students complete at least 40 hours of community involvement in order to graduate. In addition, much higher levels, such as 300–400 hours service, are expected in order to apply for the top University scholarships (Volunteer FDIP, 2023). This creates a culture where volunteering is the norm (Ain, 2003), and indeed 79% of Canadians volunteer (aged 15+), contributing 2.5 billion hours and valued at $55 billion for 2018. On average, that equates to every Canadian volunteer contributing 206 hours each year, which is almost 26 eight-hour working days. Their primary motivation (for 93% volunteers) is to make a difference to their local communities (Bush, 2024).

However, there is an argument that the graduation requirement undermines the sense of volunteering as a choice. Indeed, the United Nations defines volunteering as:

Undertaken of one's own free will. The decision to volunteer may be influenced by peer pressure or personal feelings of obligation to society but, in essence, the individual must be in a position to choose whether or not to volunteer

(UN General Assembly, 2001)

Canada is not alone in trying to mandate volunteering in order to kickstart a lifetime of civic participation. France launched its Civic Service in 2010 and so far, more than 200,000 young people have taken part (Europa.eu, 2023). Civic Service has a positive image amongst 9 out of 10 young French people and is "seen first as a way to gain experience and then as a way to become socially involved" (Gouv.fr, 2022). This has provided the foundation for the introduction of Universal National Service, aimed at all young people, starting with a pilot in 2019 and gradually being extended throughout France. By 2022, 32,500 young people took part, and it is on course to become compulsory for all 15–17-year-olds. The programme consists of a compulsory one-month commitment that aims to enable young participants to acquire a set of knowledge and skills, both practical and behavioural, around three major issues: strengthening the resilience of the nation, developing social cohesion and promoting a culture of commitment. The idea is this will provide a springboard for each young person (16–25) to make a subsequent voluntary volunteering commitment, from 3 to 12 months. This could take the form of tutoring, helping the environment or supporting national defence and security via army, police or civil security. Clearly, as a pathway for future volunteering, compulsory mandates require national governmental commitment and funding to implement.

Type 5: Direct reciprocity

Positioning: 'Give and take'

A focus on sustainable living, especially amongst younger people, has led to the increasing popularity of selling clothes no longer needed through sites such as Vinted[1] or Depop[2], and buying second-hand ('vintage') to save money, discover unique finds but also to help reduce the significant land waste from fast fashion. Likewise, buying/selling through Amazon Marketplace or buying/donating through charity shops have become mainstream retail channels in Europe, a way of sharing resources. It is interesting to consider how this will evolve for sharing time and skills, not just material objects.

The babysitting circles of 1970s Britain can still be found in some communities, where time spent looking after someone else's children, often toddlers, earns tokens which can be exchanged when you need the reciprocal arrangement, that is a night out without paying for a babysitter. This model of volunteering is anchored in reciprocity. Babysitting is like-for-like, but a broader model is helping someone who needs something specific, skills you happen to have such as book-keeping or gardening. In the future, when you need something else, you ask who has those skills in the community, for example, mending a bicycle. On one hand, this can be seen as just being a good neighbour, offering episodic and informal mutual aid. However, more formalised programmes can raise awareness of which skills people have within a community and overcome any reticence in asking for help. For example, TimeBanking UK, founded in 2002, has seen 6.68 million hours exchanged so far and currently has nearly 25,000 members. The principles of the organisation included advocating that every person is valuable and has something to offer other people in the community (timebanking.org). Social capital is generated through these mutual social and support networks (Goodwin & Cahn, 2018; Naughton-Doe et al., 2021). This model of volunteering resonates with those wanting to live a more sustainable life, where mutual support rather than money makes the world go round. On paper, this should appeal to more environmentally conscious young people (Calane, 2015), but so far, the traction amongst this cohort just has not been there, perhaps due to a lack of awareness or a misguided perception that it is a scheme for the retired.

A similar model exchanges time for specific rewards, for example, the Tempo Time Credits programme. This recognises and rewards people for volunteering for community organisations or national charities with 'credits' that they can then spend on a range of rewards such as local or national days out, using leisure facilities or on groceries. Over 10,000 volunteers currently take part in the programme and 14% of people taking part in the Tempo programme had never volunteered before (wearetempo.org). For the participating charities/community groups, the impact of being part of Tempo is the ability to recruit and retain volunteers. Given the rising cost of living, the attraction of taking part in Tempo through giving time and earning extras such as theatre visits or children's' outings, feels strong and something that is likely to grow despite commentators who argue this is not 'true volunteering' as it involves a 'payment' of sorts.

Type 6: Reciprocal community

Positioning: 'One for all and all for one'

A different model of volunteering with important implications for future approaches is the one used by parkrun (parkrun.org). Started in 2004, parkrun is a 5-km run or walk every Saturday morning in communities around the world, plus a Junior 2-km happening on Sundays in a few countries also. In the UK alone, 816 communities currently host parkruns and over 3.1 million people have completed the run/walk. It is free and easy to participate and so far. Every week almost 40,000 people volunteer in 22 countries around the world to enable these events to happen: for the UK over the 20 years since it started, 430k volunteers have taken part. What is ground-breaking about this as an approach to volunteering is how flexible it is: you can choose a specific volunteering role (such as marshalling the course, tail walking, uploading results) or just do what is required. You can change roles each time you do it or stick with the same one. You can do as much or as little as you want. The level of flexibility baked in significantly reduces the barriers to people stepping forward to volunteer (Mitchell, 2023). It is indirect reciprocity at its finest: research has shown that people very much feel part of a brand community, that it is part of their self-identity ("I am a parkrunner") and social identity within their community (Mitchell, 2023), encouraged by the post-parkrun coffee shop meetups and local social media groups. This emotional connection to the big idea of parkrun, connection within their local community and the impact it has on them personally provides three reinforcing layers of engagement. 99% of parkrun volunteers would recommend the experience to other people (parkrun.org).

Type 7: Online support

Positioning: 'It's an online world'

Currently, 31% of people who volunteered in the last 12 months did some of it online or over the phone (NCVO, 2023). The impact of the COVID-19 pandemic meant charity use of digital technology for staff or volunteers rose from 42% to 83% (NCVO, 2021). Despite the lockdown, 45% charities reported increased accessibility of their services as a result of their online operations, with only 17% reporting a decline in service accessibility. Despite the advantages of convenience, accessibility and flexibility, virtual volunteering can be isolating, lacking a sense of team, and it can also weaken the connection to the mission as the difference you make is harder to spot. However, overall, no difference has been found in motivation levels between those who volunteered online/by phone versus those who only volunteered face to face (NCVO, 2023).

Through the Bookmark Reading Charity, you can help a child to read (online), with two half-hour sessions per week for a six-week period (bookmarkreading.org). Becoming a virtual buddy through Sense, committing to a one-hour chat a week, helps reduce the social isolation and loneliness of disabled people (sense.org.uk). Food poverty charity the Trussell Trust has a programme of online volunteers as Social Media Advocates, who use their existing social media profile to talk about the work being done by the charity. This could include sharing their news stories, liking a message from a local Trussell Trust food bank or encouraging their network to take one of the charity's campaign actions (trusselltrust.org). For charities with the resources and skills to be able to effectively harness online volunteering, the future is bright. For example, the United Nations Online Volunteering service was launched in 2000 and now reports engaging 12,000 volunteers per year (unv. org). The challenge is to ensure that the sense of community, engagement with the mission and personal satisfaction from having made a difference are felt as strongly by online volunteers as traditional, in person volunteers.

Conclusion

This deep dive into types of volunteering best practice helps inform how volunteering can develop in the future to engage more people, reduce barriers and build stronger societies. It is by no means exhaustive. Corporate volunteering, either through specific days, team building activities or allowances for individual efforts, is another route, as are social outreach programmes through faith groups. Volunteering as a travel experience (e.g., gap year programmes or VSO) or leisure activity (e.g., fundraising through half marathons or Movember) remains popular. Everyone is different, and at different stages in their life. Volunteering choices need to include commitment levels (taster, episodic, regular), locality (community, national, international), context (individual vs group, in person vs online) and especially the positioning (reciprocity, brand communities, movements).

How Can Charities Market Themselves to Attract Young Volunteers?

After reviewing the current state of youth volunteering, and analysing seven case studies of best practice, we argue charities should focus on the following 'success factors' when designing their programmes and communication strategies aimed at recruiting young volunteers.

1 **Make it fun!** Making the experience enjoyable and social is important for young volunteers. Enjoying the task will lead to positive emotions, which will allow volunteers to gain personal benefits (i.e., satisfaction, identification with the group/cause), but will also increase the intentions to continue volunteering (Barraza, 2011).
2 **Allow flexibility.** Time is one of the main barriers of volunteering. Charities could capitalise on the growth of online volunteering, and either offer volunteering opportunities in both offline and online formats (when possible), making it more accessible to those struggling with time or currently in the pre-contemplation or contemplation phases. We believe that by allowing flexibility, charities could build volunteering habits, as some young people might start with the online option (perceived as 'easier' and less time-consuming) to then continue volunteering through

offline activities, once they perceive the value of volunteering and a habit is created.

3 **Offer 'episodic' and micro-experiences.** We believe charities could also add episodic and micro-experiences as part of their volunteering offering portfolio. By allowing young volunteers to commit to volunteering for a short period of time, or by performing tasks that do not require a big effort, charities will be able to target those potential volunteers that experience some of the barriers mentioned in this chapter and would not engage in more formal volunteering opportunities. We believe these opportunities could be a good starting point for those currently non-engaged in volunteering and would favour the creation of volunteering habits. The more they engage in this type of volunteering, the greater the chances for them to 'come back' and to engage in other volunteering tasks (that would require more time and effort).

4 **Focus on 'us' but also on rewards.** Younger volunteers are motivated by both the feeling that 'we are in this together' and a willingness to get something in return (a combination of altruistic and egocentric motives). Charities should therefore highlight both aspects when communicating about their volunteering opportunities. This is an approach recently used by Oxfam, on a communication focused both on individual and collective benefits, while also signalling the 'fun' part of the job (which would make the opportunity more appealing). In the campaign, including an image of a young person at one of their charity shops, Oxfam used the following message: "Make a difference; Build new skills; Join our team; Drink tea; Eat cake; Change the world; Help beat poverty; Volunteer with Oxfam" (oxfam.org.uk). Importantly, charities should then ensure young volunteers get these benefits, which would favour retention.

5 **Make their impact visible.** Charities should understand that their efforts do not end once volunteers have been recruited. Young people want to see the consequences of their effort and understand how their commitment is making a difference to the cause they are contributing to. Whilst in some types of volunteering (e.g., planting a tree, litter picking), the impact of their volunteering is immediate, in others (e.g., donating to a cause, volunteering at a charity shop), the consequences of their work are not as clear. Despite young volunteers being driven by both the desire to help the cause and the willingness to get a reward (i.e., build skills, make friends), research has shown that altruistic motives lead to higher levels of commitment to volunteering (Clary & Orenstein, 1991). By making the impact of their work more visible, charities could appeal to those more altruistic motives, and make volunteers feel more valued, which will help organisations increase retention rates.

These five factors could work as a roadmap for charities to follow when designing volunteering programmes and the marketing strategies attached to them. We believe these 'success factors' are interconnected, and organisations should look at them holistically. Importantly, we believe these factors should not only be acknowledged when recruiting new volunteers, but also while aiming to maintain current ones (recognising their work, congratulating them, offering rewards). By recognising the importance of each of these factors, charities will allow 'agents of change' from Gen-Z to flourish as volunteers, which will contribute to them becoming a vital resource to enable charities to survive and thrive.

Discussion Questions

1 Why is it that every country that hosts the Olympics struggles to create a permanent legacy of increased volunteering once the event is over?
2 If you wanted to design a campaign to recruit young people who had never volunteered to give it a go, what would be your lead motivational message?
3 Do you think charities should pay volunteers their travel expenses? If they do so, what are the implications for both the volunteer and the charity?

Notes

1 www.vinted.co.uk
2 www.depop.com

References

Ain, S. (2003). *New York Times*, Available at: www.nytimes.com/2003/03/23/nyregion/the-logic-of-mandatory-volunteerism.html (Accessed 10th October 2023).

Appau, S. and Awaworyi Churchill, S. (2019). 'Charity, volunteering type and subjective wellbeing'. *VOLUNTAS: International Journal of Voluntary and Nonprofit Organizations*, 30, pp. 1118–1132.

Bagley, S. R. (2023). *Green Lighting the Altruistic Influencer*. (Doctoral dissertation, Brigham Young University).

Barraza, J. A. (2011). 'Positive emotional expectations predict volunteer outcomes for new volunteers'. *Motivation and Emotion*, 35, pp. 211–219.

Bocsi, V., Fényes, H. and Markos, V. (2017). 'Motives of volunteering and values of work among higher education students'. *Citizenship, Social and Economics Education*, 16(2), pp. 117–131.

Body, A., Lau, E., Cameron, L. and Cunliffe, J., (2024). 'Mapping active civic learning in primary schools across England–a call to action'. *British Educational Research Journal*, 00, pp 1–19.

Bratsa, Y., Mollidor, C. and Stevens, J. (2020). National Youth Social Action Survey 2019, Summary Report. Available at: https://assets.publishing.service.gov.uk/government/uploads/system/uploads/attachment_data/file/931216/National_Youth_Social_Action_Survey_2019_-_Summary_Report-c.pdf (Accessed: 24 January 2024).

British Heart Foundation (2023). *From Goodwill to Great Impact: Maximising the Benefits of Volunteering.* Available at: www.bhf.org.uk/-/media/files/what-we-do/policy-and-public-affairs/volunteering-report-1805co.pdf. (Accessed 1 February 2024).

Brodie, E., Hughes, T., Jochum, V., Miller, S., Ockenden, N. and Warburton, D. (2011). *Pathways Through Participation.* London: NCVO, Involve, IVR.

Buelens, E., Theeboom, M., Vertonghen, J. and De Martelaer, K. (2015). 'Socially vulnerable youth and volunteering in sports: Analysing a Brussels training program for young soccer coaches'. *Social Inclusion*, 3(3), pp.82–97.

Bush, O. (2024). *Made in Canada*, Available at: https://madeinca.ca/volunteer-work-statistics-canada/ (Accessed 2nd February 2024)

Calane, C. (2015). *The Guardian*, Available at: www.theguardian.com/voluntary-sector-network/community-action-blog/2015/mar/30/time-banking-encouraging-new-volunteers (Accessed 10th October 2023)

Campbell, J., Bell, V., Armstrong, S., Horton, J., Mansukhani, N., Matthews, H., Pilkington, A. (2009). *The Impact of the Duke of Edinburgh's Award on Young People. Centre for Children and Youth School of Social Sciences.* Northampton: The University of Northampton. Available at: http://nectar.northampton.ac.uk/2447/. (Accessed 2 February 2024).

Chadwick El-Ali, A. (2022). *Future Trends in Volunteering - Exploring Synergies Across Research from IAVE, Forum and UN Volunteers.* Available at: https://leadership4vol.iave.org/wp-content/uploads/2022/02/Future-Trends-in-Volunteering-Briefing-Paper.pdf (Accessed 1 February 2024).

Cho, M., Bonn, M. A. and Han, S. J. (2018). 'Generation Z's sustainable volunteering: Motivations, attitudes and job performance'. *Sustainability*, 10(5), pp. 1400.

Clary, E. G. and Orenstein, L. (1991). 'The amount and effectiveness of help: The relationship of motives and abilities to helping behavior'. *Personality and Social Psychology Bulletin*, 17, pp. 58–64.

Cnaan, R. A. and Handy, F. (2005). 'Towards understanding episodic volunteering'. *Vrijwillige Inzet Onderzocht*, 2(1), pp. 29–35.

Dallimore, D. J., Davis, H., Eichsteller, M. and Mann, R. (2018). 'Place, belonging and the determinants of volunteering'. *Voluntary Sector Review*, 9(1), pp. 21–38.

Davies, J. (2018). '"We'd get slagged and bullied": understanding barriers to volunteering among young people in deprived urban areas'. *Voluntary Sector Review*, 9(3), pp. 255–272.

Dávila, M. C. and Díaz-Morales, J. F. (2009). 'Age and motives for volunteering: Further evidence'. *Europe's Journal of Psychology*, 5(2), pp. 82–95.

Dean, J. (2016). 'Class diversity and youth volunteering in the United Kingdom: Applying Bourdieu's habitus and cultural capital'. *Nonprofit and Voluntary Sector Quarterly*, 45(1_suppl), pp. 95S–113S.

Deloitte (2023). *Gen Z and Millennial Survey 2023*, Available at: www.deloitte.com/global/en/issues/work/content/genzmillennialsurvey.html (Accessed 1 February 2024)

DofE (2024). *'What Is the DofE'*. Available at: www.dofe.org/do/what/ (Accessed 31 January 2024)

Edelman (2021). *The Power of Gen Z*, Available at: www.edelman.com/sites/g/files/aatuss191/files/2022-04/Edelman%20The%20Power%20of%20Gen%20Z%20Report.pdf (Accessed 1 March 2024).

EESC (2021). *Volunteering Empowers Society as a Whole and Each One of Us as Individuals.* www.eesc.europa.eu/en/news-media/news/volunteering-empowers-society-whole-and-each-one-us-individuals (Accessed 9 January 2024).

Europa.Eu (2023). *National Programmes for Youth Volunteering*, Youth Wiki, Available at: https://national-policies.eacea.ec.europa.eu/youthwiki/chapters/france/24-youth-volunteering-at-national-level#:~:text=Universal%20National%20Service,-Universal%20national%20service&text=It%20is%20currently%20being%20generalised,ages%20of%2018%20and%2025 (Accessed 1 February 2024)

European Union (2024). *Youth and Social Movements*, Available at: https://pjp-eu.coe.int/en/web/youth-partnership/youth-and-social-movements (Accessed 1 March 2024)

Ferrell-Schweppenstedde (2023). Charities Aid Foundation. Available at: www.cafonline.org/about-us/blog-home/charities-blog/challenges-and-opportunties-facing-charity-sector (Accessed 1 March 2023).

Future Laboratory (2018). *Youth Futures Report*, Available at: www.thefuturelaboratory.com/youth-futures-2018-report (Accessed 1 March 2024).

Goodwin, N. and Cahn, E., (2018). 'Unmet Needs and Unused Capacities: Time Banking as a Solution'. *Interdisciplinary Journal of Partnership Studies*, 5(1), pp. 3–3.

Gouv.fr (2022). *Civil Service*, Available at: www.service-civique.gouv.fr/api/media/assets/document/ifop-2022.pdf (Accessed 1 February 2024)

Gov.uk (2023). Volunteering and Charitable Giving – Community Life Survey 2020/21. Available at: www.gov.uk/government/statistics/community-life-survey-202122/community-life-survey-202122-volunteering-and-charitable-giving (Accessed 1 October 2023).

Grimm Jr, R., Dietz, N., Spring, K., Arey, K. and Foster-Bey, J. (2005). *Building Active Citizens: The Role of Social Institutions in Teen Volunteering. Youth Helping America. Corporation for National and Community Service. School K-12* (55).

Handy, F., Brodeur, M. and Cnaan R. (2006). 'Summer on the Island: Episodic volunteering'. *Voluntary Action*, 7(3), pp. 31–46.

Hart, D., Atkins, R. and Donnelly, T. M. (2006). Community service and moral development. In *Handbook of Moral Development* (pp. 651–674). London: Psychology Press.

Hart, D. and Fegley, S. (1995). 'Altruism and caring in adolescence: Relations to self-understanding and social judgment'. *Child Development*, 66, pp. 1346–1359.

Haski-Leventhal, D. (2009). 'Altruism and volunteerism: The perceptions of altruism in four disciplines and their impact on the study of volunteerism'. *Journal for the Theory of Social Behaviour*, 39(3), pp. 271–299.

Haski-Leventhal, D., Paull, M., Young, S., MacCallum, J., Holmes, K., Omari, M. and Alony, I. (2020). 'The multidimensional benefits of University Student Volunteering: Psychological contract, expectations, and outcomes'. *Nonprofit and Voluntary Sector Quarterly*, 49(1), pp. 113–133.

Haski-Leventhal, D., Ronel, N., York, A. S. and Ben-David, B. M. (2008). 'Youth volunteering for youth: Who are they serving? How are they being served?'. *Children and Youth Services Review*, 30(7), pp. 834–846.

Heley, J., Yarker, S. and Jones, L. (2022). 'Volunteering in the Bath? The Rise of Microvolunteering and Implications for Policy'. *Policy Studies*, 43(1), pp. 76–89.

Hustinx, L. (2001). 'Individualization and new styles of youth volunteering: an empirical exploration'. *Voluntary Action*, 3, 2, pp. 57–77.

Hyde, M. K., Dunn, J., Bax, C. and Chambers, S. K. (2016). 'Episodic volunteering and retention: An integrated theoretical approach'. *Nonprofit and Voluntary Sector Quarterly*, 45(1), pp. 45–63.

Jardim, C. and Marques da Silva, S. (2018). 'Young people engaging in volunteering: Questioning a generational trend in an individualised society'. *Societies*, 8(1), p. 8.

Jemal, J., Larkham, J., King, D., Mainard-Sardon, J., Nguyen, H. D., Rossiter, W., Sykes, N. and Wakefield, J. (2022). *Hands in the Air Like You Just Do Care. An analysis of the VCSE Sector Barometer, in partnership with Nottingham Trent University VCSE Data and Insights Observatory*. Available at: www.probonoec onomics.com/Handlers/Download.ashx?IDMF=8cbe598c-8788-4fad-a554-721965404e37 (Accessed 1 February 2024).

Kanter, B. (2015). *Hey Nonprofits: Here Comes Gen Z Donors*, Available at: https://bethkanter.org/hey-nonprofit-here-comes-gen-z-donors/ (Accessed 1 March 2024).

Khasanzyanova, A. (2017). 'How volunteering helps students to develop soft skills'. *International Review of Education*, 63, pp. 363–379.

Kılıç, İ., Seçilmiş, C. and Özdemir, C. (2024). 'The role of travel influencers in volunteer tourism: An application of the cognitive response theory'. *Current Issues in Tourism*, 27(2), pp. 200–216.

Kottasz, R., MacQuillin, I. and Bennett, R. (2023). 'Non-profit and charity marketing: Navigating amidst the growing markets for 'social conscience and pressure for purpose''. In *The Routledge Companion to Marketing and Society* (pp. 306–315). Abingdon: Routledge.

Lin, A.R., Lawrence, J.F. and Snow, C.E. (2015). 'Teaching urban youth about controversial issues: Pathways to becoming active and informed citizens'. *Citizenship, Social and Economics Education*, 14(2), pp.103–119.

Mitchell, S. L. (2021). 'Marketing charities to attract volunteers: Time for B2V', In Hyde F. and Mitchell, S-L. (Eds) *Charity Marketing: Contemporary Issues, Research and Practice*. Abingdon: Routledge, pp. 59–76.

Mitchell, S. L. (2023). 'Reframing the practice of volunteering as a collective endeavour through a focal brand community'. *European Journal of Marketing*, 57(10), pp. 2683–2712

Mitchell, S. L. and Clark, M. (2020). 'Volunteer choice of nonprofit organisation: an integrated framework', *European Journal of Marketing*, 55(1), pp. 63–94.

Naughton-Doe, R., Cameron, A. and Carpenter, J., (2021). 'Timebanking and the co-production of preventive social care with adults; what can we learn from the challenges of implementing person-to-person timebanks in England?' *Health & Social Care in the Community*, 29(5), pp.1285–1295.

NCVO (2021). *Covid-19 Voluntary Sector Impact Barometer. National Council of Voluntary Organisations*. Available at: www.ncvo.org.uk/news-and-insights/news-index/new-survey-digital-technology-during-the-pandemic/ (Accessed 2 February 2024).

NCVO (2023). *Time Well Spent 2023. National Council of Voluntary Organisations*. Available at: www.ncvo.org.uk/news-and-insights/news-index/time-well-spent-2023/ (Accessed 2 February 2024).

Nordstrom, O., Tulibaski, K. L. and Peterson, T. O. (2022). 'Bridging the gap: A qualitative analysis of what it takes to inspire youth to engage in volunteering', *Nonprofit and Voluntary Sector Quarterly*, 51(2), pp. 350–368.

Nursey-Bray, M. (2020). The ART of Engagement Placemaking for Nature and People in Cities. In: Hes, D., Hernandez-Santin, C. (eds) *Placemaking Fundamentals for the Built Environment*. Palgrave Macmillan, Singapore.

Perks, T. A. and Konecny, D. (2015). 'The enduring influence of parent's voluntary involvement on their children's volunteering in later life', *Canadian Review of Sociology/Revue Canadienne de Sociologie*, 52(1), pp. 89–101.

Plunkett Foundation (2023). '*Young People in Community Business: A legacy report from the #iwill programme*'. Available at: https://eprints.icstudies.org.uk/id/eprint/449/1/Legacy-report-from-the-iwill-programme.pdf (Accessed 31 January 2024).

PRRI (2023). American Values Survey 2023. Available at: www.prri.org/research/threats-to-american-democracy-ahead-of-an-unprecedented-presidential-election/ (Accessed 31 January 2024).

Reading.ac.uk (2024). *The Red Award*, www.reading.ac.uk/essentials/Careers/Gaining-experience/RED-Awards/RED (Accessed 1 March 2024).

Rehberg, W. (2005). 'Altruistic individualists: Motivations for international volunteering among young adults in Switzerland'. *Voluntas: International Journal of Voluntary and Nonprofit Organizations*, 16, pp. 109–122.

Rochester, C. (2021). 'Trends in volunteering'. In *The Routledge Handbook of Volunteering in Events, Sport and Tourism* (pp. 460–472). Abingdon: Routledge.

Shields, P. O. (2009). 'Young adult volunteers: Recruitment appeals and other marketing considerations'. *Journal of Nonprofit & Public Sector Marketing*, 21(2), pp. 139–159.

Sundeen, R. A. and Raskoff, S. A. (2000). 'Ports of entry and obstacles: Teenagers' access to volunteer activities'. *Nonprofit Management and Leadership*, 11(2), pp. 179–197.

Taylor, P. (2021). *Getting Young People into Politics Through Service Learning*. London: Behavioural Insights Team. Available at: www.bi.team/publications/getting-young-people-into-politics-through-service-learning/ (Accessed 2 February 2024).

Thoits, P.A. (2021). 'Motivations for Peer-Support Volunteering: Social identities and role-identities as sources of motivation'. *Nonprofit and Voluntary Sector Quarterly*, 50(4), pp.797–815.

UN General Assembly (2001). Support for volunteering, Available at: chrome-extension://efaidnbmnnnibpcajpcglclefindmkaj/www.un.org/webcast/events/iyv/a56288.pdf

United Nations (2001). *Support for Volunteering: Report of the Secretary General*, Available at: www.un.org/webcast/events/iyv/a56288.pdf (Accessed 1 February 2024)

Volunteer FDIP (2023). Available at: www.volunteerfdip.org/college-or-university-admissions-and-scholarships (Accessed 2 February 2024)

Volunteer Scotland (2023). *Young People in Scotland Survey 2022*. Available at: www.volunteerscotland.net/wp-content/uploads/2023/05/Young-People-in-Scotland-2022.pdf. (Accessed 1 January 2024).

Volunteer Scotland (2024). '*Cost of Living and Practice*'. Available at: www.volunt eerscotland.net/volunteer-practice/cost-of-living-and-practice   (Accessed   31 January 2024).

Wakefield, J.R.H., Bowe, M. and Kellezi, B. (2022). 'Who helps and why? A longitudinal exploration of volunteer role identity, between-group closeness, and community identification as predictors of coordinated helping during the COVID-19 pandemic', *British Journal of Social Psychology*, 61(3), pp. 907–923.

Warmwelcome.uk (2024). *Warm Welcome Spaces Campaign*. Available at www. warmwelcome.uk (Accessed 1 January 2024)

YouGov (2021). *Being Purpose Driven Can Attract Gen-Z*, Available at: https://you gov.co.uk/topics/resources/articles-reports/2021/06/09/being-purpose-driven-can-attract-gen-z, (Accessed 1 March 2023).

Websites cited

bighelpout.org.uk: Volunteering Programme (UK)
bookmarkreading.org: Bookmark Reading Charity (UK)
Oxfam.org.uk: Oxfam (UK/International)
parkrun.org: parkrun (UK/International)
reading.ac.uk: University of Reading (UK)
sas.org.uk: Surfers Against Sewage (UK)
sense.org.uk: Sense (UK)
timebanking.org: Timebanking UK(UK/International)
treesforcities.org: Trees for Cities (UK)
trusselltrust.org: Trussell Trust (UK)
warmwelcome.uk: Warm Welcome Spaces (UK)
wearencs.com: National Citizenship Service (UK)
wearetempo.org: Tempo Time Credits Ltd. (UK)
unv.org: United Nations Volunteering (International)

4

PREPARING FOR GEN-Z PHILANTHROPY

Walter Wymer

Overview

Charities are beginning to take note of the next generation of potential supporters emerging into adulthood, Generation Z (Gen-Z). Gen-Z (born 1997–2012) are considerably different from prior generations with respect to their use of social media and its influence on their behavior (Goldring & Azab, 2021). Gen-Z is less likely to use newspaper or radio as an information source than prior generations (Ravula et al., 2023). Another way in which Gen-Z differs is their attitudes toward influencers and traditional media. They relate to influencers less like idols and more like peers and have less trust in traditional institutional sources like the media and government, and make greater use of social media (Beaupre, Alfaro-Barrantes & Jacobs, 2020). With respect to charity marketing, many in Gen-Z give to charities that provide compelling social media campaign appeals (Conlin & Bauer, 2021).

Gen-Z is a socially networked cohort (Rai, 2012). Suwana et al. (2020) reported that their sample of Gen-Z individuals used social media more than four hours daily. This generation heavily uses and depends upon social media and their social media usage influences their behaviors (Prakash Yadav & Rai, 2017). YouTube is now the number one platform for teens, with almost eight in ten using it to stream video content (Agius, 2023).

Gen-Z prefers social media as the channel through which to conduct their charitable giving. Gen-Z wants to feel personally connected to the charities and causes they support. Social media is a major influence. Peer influences are also important (Konstantinou & Jones, 2022). Not only is social media a communication channel for motivating Gen-Z philanthropy, but it is also a necessary communication channel for maintaining engagement. Buntz

DOI: 10.4324/9781003396802-4

(2022) reported that poor social media presence is a major reason Gen-Z discontinues their giving to a cause.

Future fundraising will increasingly rely on reaching young adults through social media (Conlin & Bauer, 2021; Yousef et al., 2022). For example, in one study of social media fundraising, Bhati and McDonnell (2020) reported that fundraising success—as measured by the number of donors and value of donations—is positively associated with a nonprofit's Facebook network size (number of likes), activity (number of posts) and audience engagement (number of shares), as well as organizational factors like budget size, age and program service area.

Successful online fundraising, especially to Gen-Z, is dependent on the ability of an appeal to go viral (Silver & Small, 2023). Going viral refers to the appeal's characteristics that inspires individuals to share the appeal within and between their social networks. A sufficient chain-reaction of user sharing of a fundraising appeal can have a substantial multiplier effect (Priante et al., (2022).

The social media channel will become more important in the future

Just as the commercial sector is relying more heavily on social media to present their messages to priority audiences, the charity sector will also rely more on social media to reach priority audiences, especially Gen-Z. Social media is well-suited for project-oriented fundraising campaigns (Wymer & Najev Čačija, 2023). It is well-suited for fundraising campaigns asking for small contributions from a large audience. Hence, fundraisers should view social media fundraising as a low involvement context (Saxton & Want, 2014). Factors that concern major donors include the charity's reputation, the charity's trustworthiness, and the charity's transparency and effectiveness (The Center on Philanthropy at Indiana University, 2011). However, in appealing to Gen-Z using social media, since it is a low involvement context (the charity is asking for small donations), the ability of the appeal to evoke an emotional response in the audience and the degree to which others in one's social network are supporting the campaign exert greater influence (Bhati & McDonnell, 2020).

Charity social media marketing success factors

Charity marketers and fundraisers will need to excel at effectively using social media to attract and retain support. This is a truism in general, but especially relevant for cultivating support from Gen-Z. Several factors will determine the degree to which charities can succeed.

Charities need to develop skills in motivating the sharing of social media content. The determinant to effective social media marketing is the ability of a charity appeal to be virally shared within and across social networks and social media channels. A chain reaction of sharing a charity's message has a leveraging effect for two reasons. First, the message is disseminated to many more people when virally shared. Hence, a mass audience will view the message. Second, since the message is sent from one social media friend to another, there is a de facto in-group endorsement of the fundraising appeal. Hence, the message is given more credibility and is accompanied by social influence.

One motivation individuals have for sharing information on social media is to give others a sense of who they are and what they care about (Ham et al., 2019). In effect, sharing information on social media is a means of managing others' impressions of themselves (Hayes & King, 2014). Hence, sharing a charity appeal would signal one's concern for the issue or cause inherent in the appeal (Kang & Schuett, 2013).

Perhaps the greatest motivation individuals have for sharing on social media is to maintain a social conversation. That is, people wish to share their thoughts and feelings with others by sharing content. When a charity appeal is evocative and interesting, people can share the appeal and add their own comments (John, 2012; Wittel, 2011). This enables the continuation of social media conversations and social expressions on social media. It enables individuals to have a way to stay connected with others (Youn & Lee, 2005).

Avoiding alienating other cohorts

A charity's tactics to cultivate support from Gen-Z must not alienate other supporter groups. Social media appeals especially for Gen-Z audiences may select projects of interest to Gen-Zers and may use images and language to engage Gen-Zers more effectively (Wymer & Najev Čačija, 2023). However, when other groups see the appeals, their perceptions of the charity should not be negatively impacted. The best way to avoid alienating other cohorts is to maintain a consistent brand image. A charity's values are tactically communicated to audiences when they have experiences with the charity (brand experiences), when they encounter comments and information about the charity, and when they view charity appeals and other communications. Therefore, brand management becomes even more important when a charity cultivates support from multiple audiences.

Charity Brand Management

Charities are discovering the benefits of having a brand management orientation as a guiding managerial mindset. Managing an organization as a brand is especially important if the organization must attract and retain support from donors. Brand refers to the way in which the organization is perceived by priority audiences. The strategic objective of brand management is to make the organization a strong brand and to maintain that strong brand position. Hence, brand strength is a latent psychological construct. It exists in the minds of priority audience members (Wymer, 2013).

Becoming a strong brand has a favorable moderating influence on an organization's marketing and fundraising efforts. This explains why a strong brand, like the Red Cross, attracts the preponderance of donations when fundraising in the aftermath of a disaster, compared with charities that are weaker brands (Wymer, 2015). This also explains why prior research finds that organizations that are well-known and enjoy favorable reputations are better able to attract donations (Bennett & Gabriel, 2003).

The best way to cultivate and retain support from multiple cohorts, including Gen-Z, is for a charity to become and remain a strong brand. To make a charity a strong brand, the organization must increase its brand strength to a high level. Brand strength has three dimensions: brand familiarity, brand remarkability and brand attitudes. Brand familiarity refers to the degree to which priority audiences are knowledgeable about the organization. Brand remarkability refers to the degree to which priority audiences perceive the organization to be exemplary, outstanding and extraordinary. Brand attitudes refer to the degree to which the organization is favorably perceived by priority audiences (Wymer, Gross & Helmig, 2016).

Figure 4.1 depicts the way in which the brand strength dimensions interact to form brand strength. The organization should practice continuous improvement to attain perceptions of organizational exceptionalism and excellence by priority audiences. Then, the organization should engage in regular communications to become well-known by priority audiences. Brand

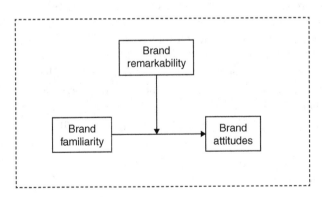

FIGURE 4.1 Brand strength.

familiarity is developed from exposure to information about the organization and experiences with the organization. As priority audiences become more familiar with the organization, they become more able to form perceptions about the organization's remarkability. Becoming more aware of how remarkable an organization is, leads to favorable attitudes. It is important to manage priority audiences' experiences with the organization (brand experiences). Brand experiences are influential in forming brand attitudes (Wymer & Casidy, 2019).

A charity that is well-known and enjoys an exemplary reputation is best positioned to attract broad support and to weather economic downturns (Meijer, 2009). A charity may choose fundraising projects and design fundraising campaigns to be especially appealing to Gen-Z. However, if the appeal to Gen-Z does not alter priority audiences' perceptions of its brand, the charity should not have to sacrifice one priority audience for another.

Another benefit of being a strong brand with respect to cultivating Gen-Z supporters is brand strength's influence on perceived donor risk. Perceived donor risk refers to the degree to which a prospective donor believes that a donation may be used in an undesirable manner. Risk is inversely associated with trust. As perceived donor risk increases, donor trust in the charity decreases, which has an inhibiting effect on donor's motivation to contribute (Stötzer, Martin & Broidl, 2023).

In the context of crowd-fundraising on social media, fundraising goals are attained by asking large numbers of people for small donations. This is why, as discussed previously, it is important for social media fundraising campaigns to achieve viral status. The influence of perceived donor risk is reduced on the donation decision when the amount of donation being considered is small. The context is more complex than this, however. A social media appeal usually wants supporters to make favorable comments on the fundraising appeal page as well as re-posting the appeal on their own social media pages. Hence, the risk is greater than the likelihood of a small donation being misused (financial risk). When someone makes favorable comments on the fundraising appeal's page and then re-posts the appeal of their own page, they are, in effect, endorsing the campaign and vouching for the charity. If something untoward happens, the endorser risks social embarrassment and guilt. In the social media context, there may be less financial risk because the donation amounts are relatively low, but there is increased social risk (Kietzmann et al., 2012). We discussed earlier that Gen-Zers spend a lot of time on social media and that managing their social images and connections is a motivation for their social media engagement. Hence, strong charity brands reduced perceived donor risk because strong brand enjoy higher levels of trust.

Example of Innovative Practice

Gen-Z for Change

This innovative charity, launched in 2020, was specifically founded by Gen-Z activists to appeal to Gen-Zers. Gen-Z for Change engages Gen-Zers by appealing to their values and using social media. Gen-Z for Change supports progressive causes and appeals to politically active, progressive Gen-Zers. While Gen-Zers are diverse and only a portion of this generation are politically active progressives (Burdie, 2023; THINQ Media, 2020), Gen-Z for Change has a clear purpose, mission and brand image (brand clarity).

Gen-Z for Change collaborates with content creators and organizations to create campaigns that will appeal to Gen-Z audiences. They cultivate Gen-Z supporters at the grassroots community level, engage Gen-Z supporters to support content development, computer programming and graphic design to create compelling social media campaigns.

Gen-Z for Change thrives because it operates in ways that engage its priority Gen-Z priority audience. Gen-Z for Change is an example of doing things right, according to Uong (2023). First, Gen-Z for Change's purpose and projects are congruent with the values of its priority audience. Gen-Z for Change is authentic, transparent and clear with respect to its political views. Its values are explicitly stated and implicitly communicated through its social media messaging and storytelling.

Second, Gen-Z for Change understands that 79% of Gen-Z donors learn about new causes through social media (Uong, 2023). Hence, Gen-Z for Change reaches Gen-Z through social media. Gen-Z for Change mobilizes a network of influencers across TikTok, Twitter, Instagram and YouTube, reaching an audience of over 500 million people (see https://genzforchange.org/about).

Third, Gen-Z for Change uses its influencers to engage its priority Gen-Z audience. Its influencers inspire their social media followers to support and disseminate messages and stories throughout their social networks. This is an effective way of communicating, and also a way to leverage social influence and value expressive benefits.

As an example of one of Gen-Z for Change's initiatives, in the 2022 midterm (i.e., not a presidential election year) US elections, Gen-Z for Change mobilized and educated Gen-Z voters about issues and candidates. It communicated through social media channels to reach Gen-Z audiences. Gen-Z for Change encouraged voting participation, volunteering to advocate for issues and candidates, and fundraising for specific candidates. It hosted a twenty-two-hour Livestream two weeks before the election to engage Gen-Z voters. The Livestream hosted panel discussions, and hosted Gen-Z candidates running for office. In addition to the Livestream, it hosted live interviews on TikTok and Instagram with celebrities who are popular with Gen-Zers. Gen-Z for Change also released lists of candidates it endorsed as well as lists of candidates it opposed for their anti-youth or objectionable positions.

Looking Forward

Much of the practitioner advice to charities for appealing to Gen-Zers is consistent, if simplistic. They view Gen-Zers as generally pro-social and engaged in their world. Gen-Zers are good donor prospects and motivated to give by aligning their values with relevant projects and causes. Gen-Zers get most of their information from social media, which they tend to use heavily. They are also influenced by others on social media and need to express their social identifies on social media (GiveRise, 2023; Jones, 2023). Hence, charities need to reach Gen-Zers through social media and social media influencers with compelling stories that evoke value-expressive motivations.

While using social media is essentially a communication channel choice, future research would be helpful in adding to our knowledge of how more effectively to use this channel. How can charity marketers segment a Gen-Z audience to identify a priority audience who will be the best prospects? How can charity marketers be effective in selecting and using social media influencers to reach a priority audience with a compelling appeal? How can fundraising appeals be crafted more effectively to engage a Gen-Z audience and stimulate the audience to support the appeal with donations, favorable comments and re-postings? Which projects and causes are most important to Gen-Z audiences?

In many ways, the current advice is tactical in nature. There is often excitement with a new emergent market segment and commentators tend to exaggerate their prosocial proclivities. Gen-Z is an important cohort, to be sure. They are entering adulthood as Baby Boomers are declining in number. Gen-Zers are heavy users of social media and are, thus, influenced by information on this communication channel. Social media is a powerful communication channel. It has multimedia capabilities. It allows for social influence and social distribution. With these changes, charities should not, however, forget about their marketing strategies. A tactical advantage in using social media is negated by a weak marketing strategy. We will review the elements of a strong charity marketing strategy next (See Figure 4.2).

Effective charity marketing requires the charity to be managed with a marketing orientation. The purpose of charity marketing is to assist the charity in attracting and retaining support (donations, volunteers, etc.). A marketing orientation is a managerial mindset that is manifested in a tendency to predominately view organizational issues from a marketing perspective.

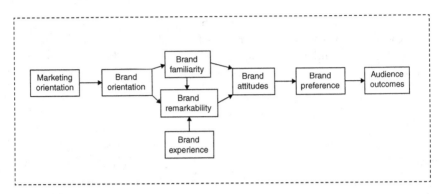

FIGURE 4.2 Charity brand management.

A marketing-oriented charity uses marketing thinking (a marketing mindset or perspective) not as a specialized area of the organization but as a general management orientation.

A brand orientation refers to a type of marketing orientation that emphasizes the achievement of organizational goals through successfully managing the charity as a brand. The charity is the brand object. The charity brand is the way in which priority audiences perceive the charity and how it compares to other charities. A brand orientation implies an emphasis on attracting and retaining supporters by: (1) continuously improving the charity in ways that are meaningful to priority audiences and (2) by increasing the charity's brand strength. The charity cannot be improved in ways that are meaningful to priority audiences unless its decision makers are aware of what priority audiences think about the charity. A brand orientation requires an emphasis on communicating with priority audiences. Effective communication requires an understanding of priority audiences that an internally focused manager (not marketing-oriented) lacks.

The objective of brand management is to make the charity brand stronger or, if it already is a strong brand, to keep it strong. (Since brand strength was discussed previously, it will only be addressed briefly in this section.) This is accomplished through increasing brand remarkability and brand familiarity. Brand remarkability refers to the degree to which priority audiences perceive the charity to be exceptional and extraordinary and how it compares with other charities. Brand familiarity refers to how knowledgeable priority audiences are with the charity. Brand remarkability is enhanced by a program of continual improvement in ways that are valued by priority audiences. Brand familiarity is enhanced by a program of continual communication to priority audiences. Priority audiences develop their perceptions, attitudes and opinions about a charity through information they receive from all sources about the charity and especially by their own experiences with the charity (brand experiences). Brand experiences are important in shaping enduring perceptions of a charity and, hence, brand experience is depicted in Figure 4.2 as an antecedent of brand remarkability.

As brand familiarity and brand remarkability increase, so do brand attitudes (discussed previously). As brand attitudes for the charity increase, brand preference increases. As charity brand preference increases, so does the desired outcomes, like donation frequency, favorable WOM, donor retention, among others. Hence, making the charity a strong brand provides a strong foundation that can leverage effective social media communications. All other things being equal, a charity that is a strong brand will attract and retain more support than a charity that is a weaker brand.

Summary

As more of Gen-Z enters adulthood and progresses into their careers, charities will need to place greater emphasis on cultivating support from this cohort. Gen-Z is a socially networked cohort that prefers social media as their primary communication and information channel. Hence, charities will need to use social media to reach and engage Gen-Zers. Fortunately, charities will find that social media is well-suited for project-oriented fundraising campaigns, appealing to large audiences for small donations.

To be effective in using social media, charities must adapt to the low involvement, low risk donation context for these audiences. The relative success of fundraising appeals delivered on social media will depend on their ability to viral. Charities will have to encourage user-generated content and develop skills in inspiring Gen-Zers to share charities' social media content. Charities will have to understand and engage with Gen-Z supporters to develop fundraising campaigns that are compelling to Gen-Zers.

Gen-Z is not a monolithic cohort, but a diverse one. Charities will have to identify Gen-Z subgroups whose values align with those inherent in a charities mission and operations. Charities will also have to identify and cultivate Gen-Zers who can serve as influencers, leaders with large followings who can serve as ambassadors for their favored charities.

While appealing to Gen-Z, charities will have the added challenge of not myopically attracting Gen-Zers, risking becoming less attractive to their other supporters.

Discussion Questions

1 What types of charities, causes and projects are most likely to appeal to Gen-Zers and why?
2 Should a charity fundraise on social media to Gen-Zers to support the charity or a specific charity project? Why?

3 Which subgroup of Gen-Zers are most likely to donate to charities?
4 How would you develop an effective social media fundraising appeal to a Gen-Z audience?

References

Agius, N. (2023, Aug 29). *Majority of Gen-Z Teens Watch YouTube Ads—Almost Half Can Recall Campaigns*. Online at https://searchengineland.com/gen-z-teens-youtube-ads-recall-431301

Beaupre, J. G., Alfaro-Barrantes, P., & Jacobs, B. (2020). Professional athletes and Gen-Z: A commentary on social media influence during the COVID-19 pandemic. *The Journal of Social Media in Society*, 9(2), 381–392.

Bennett, R., & Gabriel, H. (2003). Image and reputational characteristics of UK charitable organizations: An empirical study. *Corporate Reputation Review*, 6(3), 276–289.

Bhati, A., & McDonnell, D. (2020). Success in an online giving day: The role of social media in fundraising. *Nonprofit and Voluntary Sector Quarterly*, 49(1), 74–92.

Buntz, L. A. (2022). Diversity and philanthropy—Engaging women of color and the next generation of donors. In *Generosity and Gender: Philanthropic Models for Women Donors and the Fund Development Professionals Who Support Them* (pp. 193–214). Cham: Springer International Publishing.

Burdie (2023) Types of People in Gen-Z. [online video] Available at: https://youtu.be/w2Zif3p9qK4?si=P7gRdlBkXvfRVJcw [Accessed 2-Jan-2024]

Conlin, R., & Bauer, S. (2021). Examining the impact of differing guilt advertising appeals among the Generation Z cohort. *International Review on Public and Nonprofit Marketing*, 1–20.

GiveRise (2023). *5 Actionable Tips for Engaging the Next Generation of Donors*. CharityVillage. Available at: https://charityvillage.com/5-actionable-tips-for-engaging-the-next-generation-of-donors/ [Accessed Jan 3, 2024]

Goldring, D., & Azab, C. (2021). New rules of social media shopping: Personality differences of US Gen-Z versus Gen X market mavens. *Journal of Consumer Behaviour*, 20(4), 884–897.

Ham, C. D., Lee, J., Hayes, J. L., & Bae, Y. H. (2019). Exploring sharing behaviors across social media platforms. *International Journal of Market Research*, 61(2), 157–177.

Hayes J. L., King K. W. (2014). The social exchange of viral ads: Referral and coreferral of ads among college students. *Journal of Interactive Advertising*, 14, 98–109.

John N. A. (2012). Sharing and web 2.0: The emergence of a keyword. *New Media & Society*, 3, 1–16.

Jones, I. (2023). How charities can engage younger generations. *Charity Digital*. Available at: https://charitydigital.org.uk/topics/topics/how-charities-can-engage-younger-generations-10297 [Accessed Jan 3, 2024]

Kang, M., & Schuett, M. A. (2013). Determinants of sharing travel experiences in social media. *Journal of Travel & Tourism Marketing*, 30(1–2), 93–107.

Kietzmann, J. H., Silvestre, B. S., McCarthy, I. P., & Pitt, L. F. (2012). Unpacking the social media phenomenon: Towards a research agenda. *Journal of Public Affairs*, 12(2), 109–119.

Konstantinou, I., & Jones, K. (2022). Investigating Gen-Z attitudes to charitable giving and donation behaviour: Social media, peers and authenticity. *Journal of Philanthropy and Marketing*, 27(3), e1764.

Meijer, M. M. (2009). The effects of charity reputation on charitable giving. *Corporate Reputation Review*, 12, 33–42.

Prakash Yadav, G., & Rai, J. (2017). The Generation Z and their social media usage: A review and a research outline. *Global Journal of Enterprise Information System*, 9(2), 110–116.

Priante, A., Ehrenhard, M. L., van den Broek, T., Need, A., & Hiemstra, D. (2022). "Mo" together or alone? Investigating the role of fundraisers' networks in online peer-to-peer fundraising. *Nonprofit and Voluntary Sector Quarterly*, 51(5), 986–1009.

Rai, S. (2012). Engaging young employees (Gen Y) in a social media dominated world–Review and retrospection. *Procedia-Social and Behavioral Sciences*, 37, 257–266.

Ravula, U., Chunchu, S. R., Sanagapati, P. R. R., & Mooli, S. (2023). Social media usage and strategies in motivating various generations of blood donors. Are we doing it right?. *Transfusion and Apheresis Science*, 62(1), 103519.

Saxton, G. D., & Wang, L. (2014). The social network effect: The determinants of giving through social media. *Nonprofit and Voluntary Sector Quarterly*, 43(5), 850–868.

Silver, I., & Small, D. A. (2023). Put your mouth where your money is: A field experiment encouraging donors to share about charity. *Marketing Science*. Online at https://doi.org/10.1287/mksc.2023.1450

Stötzer, S., Martin, S., & Broidl, C. (2023). Using certifications to signal trustworthiness and reduce the perceived risk of donors–An exploratory investigation into the impact of charity labels. *Journal of Nonprofit & Public Sector Marketing*, 35(3), 265–289.

Suwana, F., Pramiyanti, A., Mayangsari, I., Nuraeni, R., & Firdaus, Y. (2020). Digital media use of Gen-Z during COVID-19 pandemic. *Jurnal Sosioteknologi*, 19(3), 327–340.

The Center on Philanthropy at Indiana University. (2011). Review of literature on giving and high net worth individuals. *Report*, available online at https://scholarworks.iupui.edu/server/api/core/bitstreams/e6538a57-3b9f-4450-ae40-f11729aa8304/content

THINQ Media (2020) *Mark Matlock: The Diversity of Gen-Z.* [online video] Available at: https://youtu.be/R2E2VaQOVo0?si=L7Sj6HagbxR6gw8t [Accessed Jan 2, 2024]

Uong, A. (2023). *3 Ways Nonprofits Can Engage Zen A; From Our Latest Report, Classy Blog.* Available at: www.classy.org/blog/nonprofits-engage-gen-z/ (Accessed: Jan 3, 2024).

Wittel A. (2011). Qualities of sharing and their transformations in the digital age. *International Review of Information Ethics*, 16(9), 3–8.

Wymer, W. (2013). Deconstructing the brand nomological network. *International Review on Public and Nonprofit Marketing*, 10(1), 1–12.

Wymer, W. (2015). Nonprofit brand strength's moderational role. *Ekonomski Vjesnik / Econviews – Review of Contemporary Entrepreneurship, Business and Economic Issues*, 28(1), 155–166.

Wymer, W. & Casidy R. (2019). Exploring brand strength's nomological net and its dimensional dynamics. *Journal of Retailing and Consumer Services*, 49(3), 11–22.

Wymer, W., Gross, H., & Helmig, B. (2016). Nonprofit brand strength: what is it? How is it measured? What are its outcomes? *VOLUNTAS: International Journal of Voluntary and Nonprofit Organizations*, 27(3), 1448–1471.

Wymer, W. & Najev Čačija, L. (2023). Online social network fundraising: Threats and potentialities. *Journal of Philanthropy and Marketing*, 28(4), e1782. http://doi.org/10.1002/nvsm.1782.

Youn, S., & Lee M. (2005). Advergame playing motivations and effectiveness: A "uses and gratifications" perspective. In Stafford M. R., Faber R. J. (Eds.), *Advertising, Promotion, and New Media* (pp. 320–347). Armonk, NY: M.E. Sharpe.

Yousef, M., Dietrich, T., Rundle-Thiele, S., & Alhabash, S. (2022). Emotional appeals effectiveness in enhancing charity digital advertisements. *Journal of Philanthropy and Marketing*, 27(4), e1763.

5

NAVIGATING UNCERTAINTY

Social Media Marketing in an Ever-Changing Landscape

Luan Wise

Introduction

There is no doubt that social media presents a hugely powerful tool for charities to achieve their marketing objectives. As a marketing channel, platforms such as Facebook, Instagram, X (Twitter) and TikTok offer charities the opportunity to reach new audiences, raise funds and showcase the impacts of their work. This not only strengthens donor relationships but also inspires social action and garners support from influencers.

No other media channel evolves quite as rapidly as social media, as new platforms launch and disappear, and established platforms change their features, algorithms and policies. Alongside this, we witness corresponding shifts in user behaviours. From demographic preferences for a platform to the role it plays in someone's personal and professional lives, social media remains an ever-shifting entity. This brings both opportunities and challenges.

Access to, and use of, social media continues to grow. In January 2024, 5.04 billion people across the world are active on social media. That is, 52.3% of the global population. Active users of social media spend an average of 2 hours 23 minutes a day, accessing 6.7 different social media platforms. These figures are skewed higher towards younger age groups, i.e., greater use of social media, more time on the platforms and a greater mix of different platforms (DataReportal, 2024).

Notably, 18–34-year-olds are recognised as the most frequent donors to charitable organisations (Barclays, 2022). They are tech-savvy, digitally native and eager to make an impact in today's world. Increasingly, they are turning to social media for search (versus search engines) making it important for information discovery. For Generation Z, social media platforms provide

DOI: 10.4324/9781003396802-5

much more than entertainment; they are becoming the number one source of news.

Challenges and Opportunities

The perpetual state of flux in social media has profound implications for all organisations, including charities – large and small – who seek to leverage social media to support their marketing objectives. A media channel that is available 24/7 is well-suited to an organisation that requires consistent communication with audiences including donors, beneficiaries, supporters, employees, volunteers and more.

While, as charity marketers, we have no control over the feature changes platforms introduce (or remove) or the changes in behaviours by social media users, we can learn how to embrace them to maximise our opportunities for success with social media.

For example, the growth in short-form video content, shown by the rise of TikTok and Reels (the name for short-form videos on Facebook and Instagram) has shifted the paradigm of social media content consumption significantly. Over half of the content viewed on Instagram is now video content (Social Media Today, 2023). Our chapter case studies from Spotlight YOPD and Pancreatic Cancer UK both shared the importance of video for storytelling, working with key stakeholders to understand and share their stories, which in turn support awareness and support for the charity.

The growing power of user-generated and collaborator content on social media can be harnessed to amplify the reach, and impact of a charitable mission. Influencers have become instrumental in shaping the landscape of charity marketing, leveraging their online presence and devoted follower base to champion philanthropic causes. These individuals, often with a substantial social media following, utilise their platforms to raise awareness and funds for charitable initiatives. The authentic and personal connection that influencers establish with their followers enhances the credibility and impact of charity marketing campaigns. Giovanna Fletcher's fundraising activities for CoppaFeel! (https://coppafeel.org/support-get-involved/fundraise-for-coppafeel/join-a-trek/coppatrek-challenge/) provide a useful example. Each year she and a team of celebrity team captains lead a 5-day trek challenge raising millions of pounds to end the late diagnosis of breast cancer. The presence on social media is significant, with content made more visible by using the campaign hashtag #TeamBoobs.

Engagement is a key metric for social media. By engagement, we mean interaction with a post such as a like, comment and share. Engagement plays a crucial role in achieving visibility of content when it is shared to a user's own network, plus it shapes how the platforms serve content to its users. We can measure visibility in terms of reach and impressions. Reach, defined as the total number of unique users who have viewed the content, quantifies the actual audience size. Impressions, on the other hand, represent the total number of times the content has been displayed, irrespective of whether it was viewed by unique users or multiple views by the same user. Platform algorithms utilise engagement signals to tailor the display of future content, ensuring that users see posts most aligned with their interests. Optimising social media content to achieve engagement is key; not only do we need to capture attention and stop social media users scrolling to read our messaging (or watch our video), but we also need to include clear calls to action to guide a user's next steps (and help achieve our objectives).

Social media managers regularly report drops in engagement, often attributing it to 'algorithm changes'. An alternative viewpoint, which I share, would attribute changes to user behaviours. For example, a December 2023 post from the Head of Instagram, Adam Mosseri, responding to a *Wall Street Journal* report (The Wall Street Journal, 2023) that explored why people are not posting as much on social media as they used to, said:

> People are sharing to feeds less, but to stories more and (even photos and videos) in messages even more still. On Instagram notes have quickly become a big thing, particularly for young people. So, it's not so much that people are sharing less, but rather that they're sharing differently.

Another notable change in the social media landscape is how the platforms generate income. Historically, this has been via advertising revenue, allowing users to access services free of charge. However, X (Twitter) are experimenting with different tiers of subscription services, offering differing levels of premium features. Meta too has introduced Meta Verified, a subscription bundle including verified bade, proactive account protection and more exclusive features. These monetisation models may or may not be connected to regulatory changes impacting social media platforms and the extent to which they can use data for advertising.

Changes to social media advertising models are not only impacted by regulation but also by user behaviours. In turn, these have an impact on marketing, beyond any control. The removal of health-related advertising criteria on some social media platforms has presented significant hurdles for charities seeking to promote their causes.

On 19th January 2022, Meta (for Facebook and Instagram advertising) removed detailed targeting options that "relate to topics people may perceive as sensitive, such as options referencing causes, organizations or public figures that relate to health, race or ethnicity, political affiliation, religion or sexual orientation". This included health causes, e.g., 'lung cancer awareness', 'World Diabetes Day' and key terms such as 'chemotherapy'. Their announcement (Meta, 2022) shared that the decision relates not to personal characteristics, but to how people interact with content on the platforms' and because of "concerns from experts that targeting options like these could be used in ways that lead to negative experiences". Such restrictions, in addition to platform content policies concerning the spread of misinformation and false health claims, which were prevalent during the COVID-19 pandemic, present many challenges. Not just for charities, but also for their business supporters who used relevant targeting criteria to amplify the reach of their own supporter activities.

The Emotive Requirements for Charity Marketing

While navigating uncertainty in the world around us and the tactical facets of an evolving marketing channel, the emotive requirement for charity marketing content emerges as a consistent requirement and factor in achieving engagement. According to Giving research (Barclays, 2022), emotive messaging with a personal connection is cited as the biggest driver of consumer support for a charity.

Guidance from the Charity Commission (2023) regulating charities in England and Wales supports engagement in emotive topics on social media, "if it is a way of achieving its charitable objectives and is in the charity's best interest". However, platforms like Meta continue to place restrictions on content in line with local laws and their own Community Standards that focus on keeping people safe. Restrictions are in place to remove hate speech, for example, and Meta also requires enhanced transparency from advertisers on social issues, elections or politics. There is an additional authorisation process, which can vary by country, for ads related to these topics.

Charities might find themselves impacted by these restrictions when their work includes raising awareness about key issues. The Charities Commission confirms that charities can use social media to engage in political activity and campaigning, provided they follow the rules as set out in the Campaigning and Political Activity guidance (Gov.UK, 2022).

While recognised as an important protection for social media users, these restrictions can pose challenges for charities who grapple with the need to disseminate information, provide support and raise awareness about sensitive topics, and healthcare-related issues.

So how do we, as charity marketers stay in-the-know about changes, and manage potential restrictions of using social media while embracing potential new opportunities? Answer: it is a significant information-gathering task that requires taking a strategic and adaptive approach.

Building Firm Foundations

Building a diversified social media marketing plan is crucial. Diversification includes embracing organic content creation, engaging with influencers and exploring emerging features or platforms that align with the charity's mission and values. Relying solely on one aspect, such as paid advertising, can become precarious when platforms change their targeting criteria.

Fostering a deep understanding of the platforms and their dynamics is also essential. Regularly monitoring updates, algorithm changes and emerging trends allow charities to anticipate shifts in the digital landscape and adjust their strategies accordingly. It is not difficult to find news of changes, as they are regularly reported by social media platforms via their own newsroom pages. The challenge is the frequency and pace of change; it is overwhelming for anyone working in social media to keep up. Finding the relevant resources and subscribing to email updates is extremely useful.

Collaboration and knowledge-sharing within the charity sector can also be instrumental in navigating uncertainty. Establishing networks and participating in industry discussions facilitate the exchange of insights and best practices. Learning from the experiences of peer organisations, especially those with similar objectives, can provide valuable perspectives on effective strategies and potential pitfalls. Additionally, investing in data analytics and insights is paramount. Understanding the metrics that matter allows charities to gauge the effectiveness of their campaigns, identify trends and make informed decisions. Utilising data-driven insights enhances the ability to tailor content, optimise engagement and refine targeting, ensuring that resources are allocated efficiently.

Applying Core Marketing Frameworks to Social Media

Charity marketers can apply core marketing frameworks to help understand and monitor the ever-changing landscape around us, factors that impact the tasks required for social media marketing and the messaging shared on social media profiles.

A PESTLE analysis, encompassing Political, Economic, Social, Technological, Legal and Environmental factors, aids in understanding external influences shaping the social media environment.

Let's consider an economic example – many UK households have seen reductions in their disposable income due to the cost of living crisis; for the moment, charity donation levels have remained steady (Barclays, 2022), however, this could easily change. An interesting social trend noted within the Barclays research suggests that consumers are seeking ways to give to charity that do not depend on monetary donations, instead opting for practical involvement. Common activities include signing a petition, sponsoring an activity and volunteering unpaid time.

A SWOT analysis, focusing on Strengths, Weaknesses, Opportunities and Threats, provides a comprehensive view of internal and external factors impacting charitable initiatives on social platforms. Strengths could include a dedicated and engaged online community, while weaknesses may involve limited resources for consistent content creation. Opportunities might arise from emerging social media trends or collaborations with influencers, whereas threats could stem from negative public perceptions or competition for attention within the crowded digital space.

A marketing funnel illustrates the path taken by prospective customers to make a buying decision, with the shape (of the funnel) signifying that more people start the journey than convert to a sale.

The same concept can be used for nonprofits to illustrate the path taken to become a donor/supporter. In a commercial context, marketers identify and find prospective customers who need a solution to their own (or their organisation's) problem. In a nonprofit world, we often need to get people to think and care about other people's problems.

According to a paper by the ESRC Centre for Charitable Giving and Philanthropy (CGAP), 'How donors choose charities' (Breeze, 2010), there are four non-needs-based criteria that commonly influence donors' decision-making:

1 Donors' tastes, preferences and passions, acquired as a result of an individual's social experiences.
2 Donors' personal and professional backgrounds, which shape their 'philanthropic autobiographies' and influence their choice of beneficiaries.
3 Donors' perceptions of charity competence, notably the efficiency with which they are believed to use their money.
4 Donors' desire to have a personal impact, such that their contribution makes a difference and is not 'drowned out' by other donors and government funding.

The Nonprofit Marketing Funnel

By understanding the stages of the nonprofit marketing funnel and the associated social media marketing tasks, charities can align their activities and message with the journey of their supporters, create content that will resonate with the criteria that influence decision-making, and overcome any barriers to charitable support. This is illustrated in Figure 5.1.

- **Awareness: Attracting audiences**
  At the 'top of the funnel', we are raising awareness. We are helping our prospective supporters identify a problem and cause that resonates with them. One of the greatest advantages of social media is its ability to reach vast audiences. Platforms like Facebook, Instagram, X (formerly Twitter) and TikTok have billions of active users.

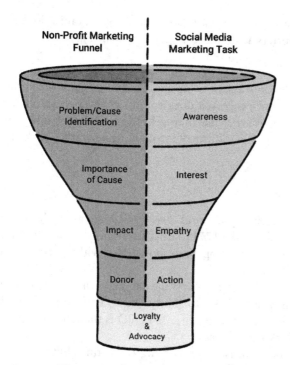

FIGURE 5.1 The nonprofit marketing funnel and social media marketing tasks.

- **Interest: Highlighting the importance of the cause and sharing impacts**
  Moving beyond the initial awareness, the social media task is to build interest in the charity and its work, by highlighting the importance of the cause that drives its mission and work. The Barclays research highlighted that a 'lack of trust' was the main factor preventing them from supporting charities. Consumers seek re-assurance that their donations are going to a worthwhile cause and that lack of knowledge about how donations are being used could be a deterrent. At this stage of the funnel, charities are building meaningful relationships with their audiences through both visibility and compelling content. Demonstrating the impact of the work, including how donations are spent, is key.
- **Action: Stimulating a call to action**
  As the relationship deepens, we need to encourage calls to action. This could be a donation, or as we have seen, it could be about support in other ways such as volunteering time.
- **Loyalty: Building sustainable support**
  The final stage of the marketing funnel involves retaining supporters, with a goal of converting one-time donors into advocates. Social media has become a powerful tool for advocacy campaigns in the charity sector.

By harnessing the viral nature of platforms, charitable organisations can quickly mobilise supporters around pressing issues, sparking conversations and catalysing action when required.

Good fundraising is all about relationships, and social media is the perfect tool to build them. A two-way process, it does not just give people the chance to get to know you, it gives you the chance to get to know your people – and to use that learning to improve their journey through the nonprofit marketing funnel.

Case Study: Spotlight YOPD

Spotlight YOPD (www.spotlightyopd.org) was registered as a charity in January 2016 (charity number 1165177) to raise awareness of Young Onset Parkinson's disease and to provide support to those living with the condition, via online and offline resources.

The charity name is also the mission – to shine a light on the largely hidden rare conditions classed as Young Onset (or Early Onset) Parkinson's Disease that can happen to people under the age of 50. YOPD is thought to account for around 10% of all Parkinson's cases.

A diagnosis of Parkinson's disease is devastating at any time, but for young people, it can be extremely challenging with greater impacts than those diagnosed later in life. YOPDers also often experience significantly different symptoms compared to later-onset Parkinson's.

Open Health worked with Spotlight YOPD to create the 'YOPD Glitch' campaign. The work was driven by data insights and aimed to challenge the misconceptions that Parkinson's is a disease that only affects older people with symptoms of shaky limbs and memory problems.

The programme of work began by gaining a deep understanding of life with YOPD and what the moments are that matter most to patients and their loved ones. Once creative ideas were generated, an online survey of a diverse group of people (from those with YOPD through to healthcare professionals and the public) was carried out to get feedback. Although there was a clear winner from the survey analysis, variations of the campaign were live-tested to identify which version was most effective so that the campaign could be refined and adapted for longevity.

The result was a bold omnichannel campaign that captured public attention, raising awareness using content that shared 'real person' stories. In 'Drew's Story' (https://spotlightyopd.org/drews-story/), we hear his mum, Lyn, talking about a Parkinson's diagnosis. A viewer might have assumed she was talking about herself, but it was revealed to be about her 35-year-old son.

Open Health used social media listening to identify the most relevant platforms to use for the campaign; platforms where conversations were happening around the topic, with a positive sentiment.

Video content and text/image posts with patient stories were shared on social media (Facebook, LinkedIn and Twitter), overachieving on expectations for post impressions, video views, click-throughs to the campaign website and new followers. The campaign was supported by digital banners and posters, out-of-home posters in both public and media settings, plus support articles and volunteer information were prepared and available for follow-up. It was widely talked about at industry conferences and the campaign has supported recruitment of both employees as well as supporters.

Case Study: Pancreatic Cancer

Pancreatic cancer is one of the toughest cancers – it is tough to diagnose, treat, research and survive. More than half of people diagnosed with pancreatic cancer die within 3 months. Despite being a common cancer and having the poorest survival rates, only 3% of the annual UK cancer research budget goes into pancreatic cancer.

Pancreatic Cancer UK (charity number 1112708) provides expert, personalised support and information via a Support Line and through a range of publications. They fund innovative research to find the breakthroughs that will change how we understand, diagnose and treat pancreatic cancer. The charity campaigns for change; for better care, treatment and research and for pancreatic cancer to have the recognition it needs.

Social media content about pancreatic cancer, such as communicating how to spot symptoms, is predominately organic. Through previous experience, they identified the importance of not putting a 'gate' on content that provides information about the disease to those who are seeking support, and therefore this needs to be easily available on the page.

Pancreatic Cancer UK uses social media advertising, particularly on Meta platforms to acquire new supporters by asking people to sign a petition. From a donor perspective, advertising has been used to grow their regular giving program, and support community and challenge event fundraising that encourages both participation and sponsorship. Advertisements have also been used for events hosted for healthcare professionals. They have been most successful when the objectives in terms of the expected return have been made clear, and when a call to action can be included – for example, petition signatures, donations and event attendees. Advertising is most likely to be used for middle and bottom-of-funnel marketing activity, with organic content used for top-of-funnel awareness.

The biggest advertising challenge has been when platform features change, without notice. This has included payment options and targeting criteria.

Overcoming these changes requires ongoing monitoring of data to identify impacts as soon as possible and to allow amends to advertising copy or set-up to be made as quickly as possible.

Find out more about pancreatic cancer campaigns at www.pancreaticcan cer.org.uk/get-involved/make-a-difference/join-our-campaigns/

The Future of Social Media Marketing

The future for charities using social media marketing holds both exciting possibilities and challenges. The case studies from Spotlight YOPD and Pancreatic Cancer UK are just two examples of using social media successfully.

With younger demographic groups being core to the future of charity giving, the fit with increasing use of social media platforms is a natural fit.

The rise of new and immersive technologies is set to revolutionise how charities tell their stories. Virtual and augmented reality, for instance, can transport supporters into the heart of a charitable initiative, creating a more profound emotional connection.

For those managing social media, the rise of generative AI features within the platforms, and tools such as ChatGPT for copywriting and Dall-E for image creation is valuable for both creativity support and productivity.

However, as social media algorithms continue to evolve and privacy concerns become more prominent, charities may find it challenging to navigate the intricacies of digital platforms. Ensuring ethical and transparent use of data while complying with evolving regulations will be crucial. Additionally, the competition for attention in an increasingly crowded digital space poses a significant challenge. Charities will need to innovate and diversify their content to cut through the noise and capture the attention of online audiences.

The potential for misinformation and the spread of false narratives on social media continues to pose reputational risks for individuals and organisations, particularly for charities related to healthcare. Navigating this landscape will require robust fact-checking measures and a proactive approach to address and counter any inaccuracies promptly. Following best practice advice by The Charities Commission for setting out a social media policy and planning to manage risk is essential.

Conclusion

Core marketing frameworks such as PESTLE, SWOT and the marketing funnel provide a structure for collecting, analysing and strategising based on the broader external environment and internal resources for social media marketing.

By understanding the nonprofit marketing funnel and adapting to the challenges posed by an ever-changing landscape, charities can continue to leverage the power of social media to achieve their marketing objectives. Staying agile, creative and informed is the key to navigating uncertainty and building a robust online presence that resonates with supporters and other stakeholders.

Cultivating resilience and agility is a mindset crucial for charity marketers. Acknowledging that change is constant in the social media landscape helps in embracing challenges as opportunities for innovation. By fostering a culture of adaptability, charities can turn uncertainties into strategic advantages, allowing them to pivot swiftly and maintain a meaningful presence.

Discussion Questions

1 Select a stage of the nonprofit marketing funnel. How could a charity best use social media to communicate with its target audience at that stage?
2 How could a charity manage the economic impact of the cost-of-living crisis on charity support, particularly where younger givers prefer to offer practical involvement versus financial donations?
3 What approach would you take to find suitable influencers to be an ambassador for a charity?

References

Barclays (2022). *Giving: A New Landscape. How Technology Is Changing the Charity Sector.* Available at: www.barclayscorporate.com/content/dam/barclaysco rporate-com/documents/insights/Industry-expertise-22/Barclays-Giving-a-new-landscape-charity-report.pdf

Breeze. B. (2010) *How Donors Choose Charities: Findings of a Study of Donor Perceptions of the Nature and Distribution of Charitable Benefit.* UK, Centre for Charitable Giving and Philanthropy. Available at: www.cgap.org.uk/uploads/repo rts/HowDonorsChooseCharities.pdf

DataReportal (2024). *Digital 2024: Global Overview Report.* Available at: https:// datareportal.com/reports/digital-2024-global-overview-report

Gov.UK (12 October 2022). *Political Activity and Campaigning by Charities.* Available at: www.gov.uk/guidance/political-activity-and-campaigning-by-charities

Meta (2022). *Removing Certain Ad Targeting Options and Expanding Our Ad Controls.* Available at: www.facebook.com/business/news/removing-certain-ad-targeting-options-and-expanding-our-ad-controls

Social Media Today (13 November 2023). *Instagram Updates Reels Composer UI to Provide More Creation Options.* Available at: www.socialmediatoday.com/news/ instagram-updates-reels-composer-ui-provide-more-creation-options/699672/

The Wall Street Journal (23 December 2023). *We Aren't Posting on Social Media as Much Anymore. Will We Ever?* Available at: www.wsj.com/tech/personal-tech/soc ial-media-nobody-posting-f6c2fd3e

6

A GUIDE TO UTILISING ARTIFICIAL INTELLIGENCE TO INCREASE PRODUCTIVITY AND EFFICIENCY

Transforming Keyword Analysis and SEO

Alan Shaw

Introduction

History has many examples of technology disrupting established working practices and business models. A notable instance is the Swing Riots of the 1830s, triggered by the introduction of threshing machines, which radically altered agricultural labour (Caprettini & Voth, 2018). Another is the decline of Blockbuster in 2014, marking a significant shift in the entertainment industry as Netflix revolutionised the way we consume films and television (Griffiths et al., 2019). More recently, the launch of OpenAI's ChatGPT (Chat Generative Pre-trained Transformer, a large language model (LLM)-based chatbot) reached 100 million monthly active users just 2 months after its launch. It has become the fastest-growing consumer application in history (Gordon, 2023). Generative artificial intelligence (AI) is likely to be the next big technology disruptor; Goldman Sachs (a global management consultancy firm) predicts that its impact could potentially displace 300 million knowledge workers in the next few years (Hatzius et al., 2023).

In terms of charities, The Business Research Company (2023) has predicted that the global charity and NGO sector will grow from \$329 billion to \$528 billion by 2025. However, there is still some concern; the UK's Charities Aid Foundation (2023) identified that financial sustainability is the primary concern, with many charities planning to use their reserves to cover income shortfalls. This is compounded by the fact that more than 50% of not-for-profit organisations also struggle to attract skilled staff (Poulter, 2023). A potential solution to this dilemma is the adoption of Generative AI to help bridge skills gaps and increase productivity and efficiency, which will help reduce costs.

DOI: 10.4324/9781003396802-6

The Boston Consulting Group believe that Generative AI is best used to revolutionise content creation (BCG, 2023). They also believe that the application of Generative AI is endless. With this in mind, I have taken guidance from Sheffield (2020). He identified that search engine optimisation (SEO) is a valued process within the marketing domain, but requires specially trained staff. It is the ideal example for demonstrating Generative AI's capabilities as it addresses the two main concerns discussed earlier, i.e., the skills gap and saving money by removing the need to outsource the process.

This guide starts by defining Generative AI. It then demonstrates how Generative AI (and other digital tools) can be used to enhance the keyword analysis, SEO and content creation process. A single case study, X-PERT Health, is used; they are a small UK-based charity providing education and information about improving and preventing long-term health conditions such as diabetes (www.xperthealth.org.uk).

Generative AI

What is generative AI? Before answering this question I must first define AI:

> It is the science and engineering of making intelligent machines, especially intelligent computer programs. It is related to the similar task of using computers to understand human intelligence, but AI does not have to confine itself to methods that are biologically observable.
>
> *(McCarthy, 2007, p. 2)*

To be more succinct, it is the result of combining data with computer algorithms to provide solutions. Generative AI refers to AI systems that can generate new content (text, images, videos, code or audio), based on the input they receive in the form of text, speech or other data. Generative AI platforms are built on LLMs which are also known as Foundational Models. These models can be considered a subset of AI, machine learning (ML) and deep learning (DL): Figure 6.1 is a graphical representation of the concepts.

ML is the field of study that allows computers to learn without explicitly being programmed (Brown, 2021). The developments in ML have helped advance AI. There are three categories of ML: supervised, unsupervised and reinforcement. Unsupervised ML is when the computer reviews a corpus of data and makes a judgement based on the algorithms it has been programmed with; an example could be the classification of a dataset of Tweets into specific themes. Supervised ML is when the training data have been given a label signifying a proposed category or theme for the data. An example is assessing a dataset of Tweets to identify positive, negative or neutral

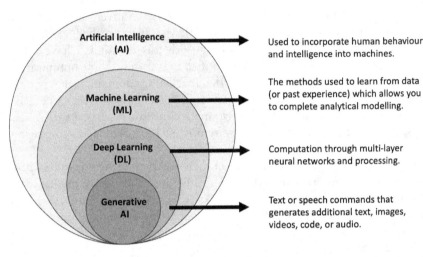

Artificial Intelligence (AI) → Used to incorporate human behaviour and intelligence into machines.

Machine Learning (ML) → The methods used to learn from data (or past experience) which allows you to complete analytical modelling.

Deep Learning (DL) → Computation through multi-layer neural networks and processing.

Generative AI → Text or speech commands that generates additional text, images, videos, code, or audio.

FIGURE 6.1   A graphical representation of the concepts associated with generative AI.

Source: Adapted from Zhuhadar and Lytras (2023).

sentiment by comparing it with a labelled dataset. Finally, reinforcement ML is when the programme solves a problem through an iterative process: think of a rat in a mini-maze trying to get some food placed in the centre. Like the rat, the programme will continually assess the situation until it reaches the desired solution.

DL technology involves a particular type of AI algorithms called neural networks, which are inspired by the structure and function of the human brain. These neural networks consist of layers of interconnected nodes, and each layer transforms the input data in some way to learn from it (Sarker, 2021). Unlike ML, where specific rules are written, DL algorithms learn directly from large amounts of data. DL models can improve themselves automatically through a process called training. During training, the model makes predictions, compares them against the correct answers and adjusts its internal parameters to improve its accuracy (Vasilev, 2019).

ML and DL both function by employing a variety of mathematical concepts (Janiesch et al., 2021). Unlike an internet search, where the results are presented to you as snippets of a page with together with its URL, Generative AI platforms create the desired output by calculating the probability of each subsequent word to make up the complete sentence (see Figure 6.2).

The LLMs encode complex 'patterns of words' into parameters. Parameters are components of the LLM that are adjusted during the training process. These 'patterns of words' are not stored in the traditional sense (like a database). Instead, the LLM learns patterns in the data. It means that

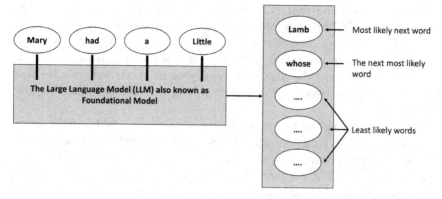

FIGURE 6.2 A schematic overview of an LLM being asked to complete the sentence, "Mary had a little...".

Source: Author.

the model picks up on statistical relationships between words and phrases, learning the likelihood of a word following a given sequence of words. As such, LLMs can be prone to hallucinations (i.e., giving you the wrong output).

An LLM with a higher parameter value will have better general knowledge than a lower one. As of January 2024, there were 236 different LLMs available for use (Thompson, 2023). If your objective is to use the LLM on a specific task, i.e., to answer 'Frequently Asked Questions', then you could embed your data to an LLM with a low parameter value because it only needs to focus on the 'Frequently Asked Questions'. LLMs are either open-sourced (available to anyone) or closed/proprietary. Closed/proprietary LLMs keep their source code and training methodologies private. It is still unclear which will dominate, although we can see that Google and OpenAI have opted for the closed system with Meta opting for the open-source option.

The rest of this chapter will focus on how Generative AI can be used to help you identify keywords and SEO. My initial research has shown that LLMs with a high number of parameters tend to perform better.

Using Generative AI in SEO and Keyword Analysis

Identifying keywords

Every charity should know its keywords, i.e., the search terms used online to find it. Most will not realise there will be an additional list of long-tail keywords: a concept introduced by Anderson (2006) in his book, *The Long Tail*. He demonstrated that there is a market for virtually any product, no matter how small the niche. The hypothesis was adopted by search engine marketers who found that individuals use various phrases (keywords) to search for their desired item/service online. As such, charities should develop a strategy of creating content that is 'search engine optimised' (SEO) for all keywords. This can be done by publishing articles on the charity's blog (or equivalent webpage). The idea is to repurpose or create new articles that focus on a given keyword or its associated long tail without looking overtly similar.

Before embarking on this strategy, the charity must first identify what keywords it should focus on. The process must include long-tail keywords. The best way to start this is to initiate a 'brain-storming' session with the team and your chosen LLM platform. Using the X-PERT Health case study, the following prompt was used to identify the primary keywords (note: Appendix 1 gives you more guidance on how to formulate a prompt):

The Prompt: You are an SEO expert and you have been given the task of identifying potential keywords for a charity, look at the following website, www.xperthealth.org.uk and identify a list of 12 keywords they should be focusing on. It should not include the brand name, I.e., XpertHealth.

The response: Based on the content of the X-PERT Health website, here are 12 potential keywords for SEO purposes:

1. *Diabetes Education*
2. *Weight Loss Programmes*
3. *Type 2 Diabetes Remission*
4. *Health Coaching*
5. *Diabetes Management*
6. *Digital Health Programmes*
7. *Prediabetes Education*
8. *Weight Management Solutions*
9. *Personalised Health Solutions*
10. *Diabetes Prevention*
11. *Health and Wellbeing Coaching*
12. *Behaviour Change Support*

This prompt assumes that your chosen LLM can browse a webpage: ChatGPT 3.5 does not have this capability, but ChatGPT 4 can interact with the web in a limited and controlled manner. ChatGPT 4 can retrieve and provide information based on the latest content available on the internet within the constraints of the browsing tool. The prompt also assumes that the website's homepage has been designed to include the keywords. The results can be tested against your brain-storming results. You should also use the LLM to test similar or competitor charities. Readers will note that the prompt states that the analysis should not include the brand name; this is because the objective is to target individuals unfamiliar with the brand. Once you have completed this phase, you must identify the long-tail keywords for each primary keyword. You now have two options: continue with the chat by including the following prompt:

> **The Prompt:** *Thank you for the response. Can you now focus on "Diabetes Education" and identify what long-tail keywords I should use to help with my SEO? Remember, the focus is on a charity that provides diabetes education and resources. Please suggest keywords that encompass various aspects of diabetes education, including program types, target audiences, and additional educational features.*

Alternatively, you can start with a brand-new prompt; this requires the context again:

> **The Prompt:** *You are an SEO expert, and you have been given the task of identifying potential long-tail keywords for a charity that provides diabetes education and resources. Please suggest a list of long-tail keywords that build on the term "diabetes education". It should encompass various aspects of diabetes education, including program types, target audiences, and additional educational features.*

Your chosen Generative AI platform will provide you with a definitive list of options. If you think it is too short, ask it to continue with additional responses. You must never take the final output as a *fait accompli* (i.e., irreversible); a human must always have the final say. To help with this reflection, you could ask the Generative AI platform to also explain the logic of its answer, example:

> ***At the end of each Prompt include the following:*** *To help me understand the logic of your answer please explain the reason why you presented me with the keywords.*

Another option is to use Google's keyword planner[1]; Figure 6.3 illustrates the output for a search for additional keywords associated with 'Diabetes Education'. In this example, the planner has identified 758 alternative ideas. My advice is not to go for all the 758 options; narrow the range using the 'Avg. Monthly Searches' (higher values) and 'Competition' (marked as low) columns as a guide. These are likely to yield a better success rate.

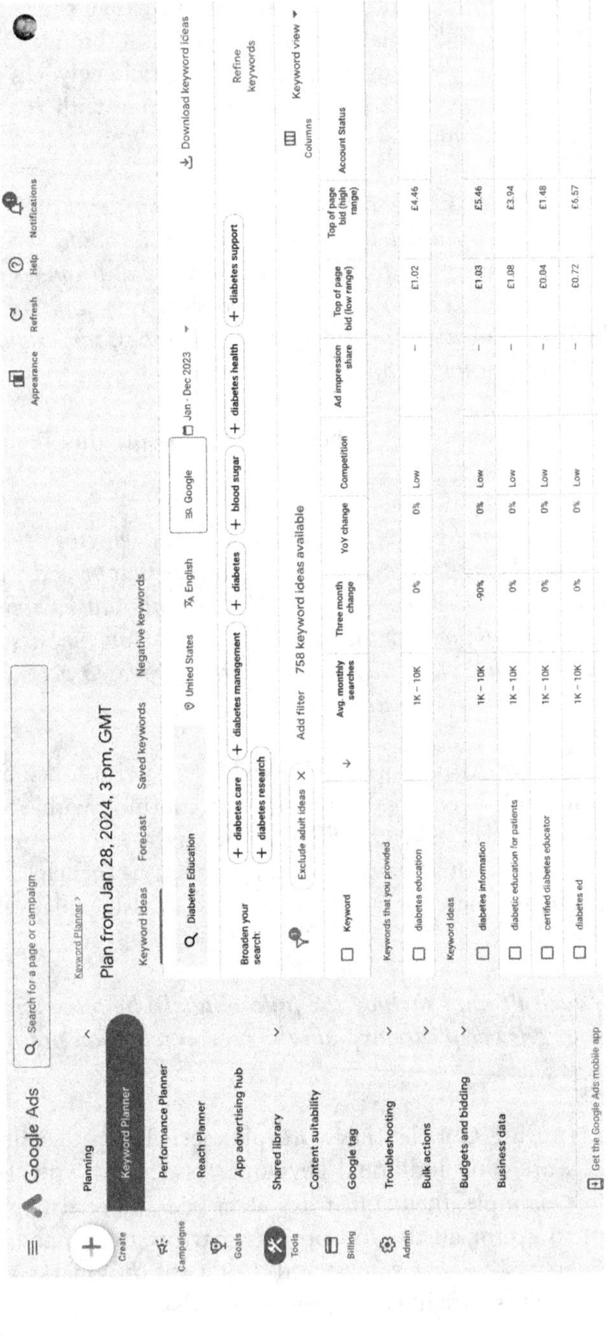

FIGURE 6.3 Google's keyword planner.

Source: Google.

Assessing your SERP

Having identified the primary and long-tail keywords, you now need to identify if the keywords are included on any of your website pages and, more importantly, what the SERP (search engine result position) is, i.e., its position in the list of searches. This is an important performance indicator because van Deursen & van Dijk (2009) identified that users tend to stay within page one (under a SERP value of 11) when using Google.

My suggestion is to use Neil Patel's Ubersuggest (https://neilpatel.com/uber suggest/) to do this. It is an SEO research tool that operates using a freemium model. It provides keyword and content planning features, competitor analysis, backlink data and site audits. Sign-up as a free user and create your first project (i.e., linking Ubersuggest to the charity's website). Once this is complete, click on the Keyword Research tab, then select Keywords by Traffic (see Figure 6.4). Enter the website's URL, then click search.

Ubersuggests will list all the keywords (see Figure 6.4) within your website. You must now compare the list (which can be downloaded as a CSV) with your chosen keywords (including long tails). Any keyword with a position of 10 or less (see point 4 in Figure 6.5) will be on page one of the Google results. Any keywords not listed or with a position of 11 or more will need new content created to help with the site's SEO: these should be added to your priority list.

Generating content

Having developed a priority list, you can now either rework or generate new content for the website. The prompts below, which builds on the SEO guidance of Neil Patel (2020) and Yoast, an SEO company that provides resources for digital marketers (see van de Rakt, 2020):

The Prompt for reworking: *You are a Search Engine Optimisation (SEO) expert, and you have been tasked with reviewing a webpage that has a poor SERP. You need to rewrite the content in the text below. The keywords to focus on are 'your keyword'. When producing the answer you must take into account the following:*

On-Page SEO:

> 1. *Optimize Title Tags: Include the target keyword in your page titles.*
> 2. *Meta Description: Write compelling meta description with your keyword.*
> 3. *Headings and Subheadings: Use H1, H2, H3 tags effectively. Include keywords in at least one subheading.*

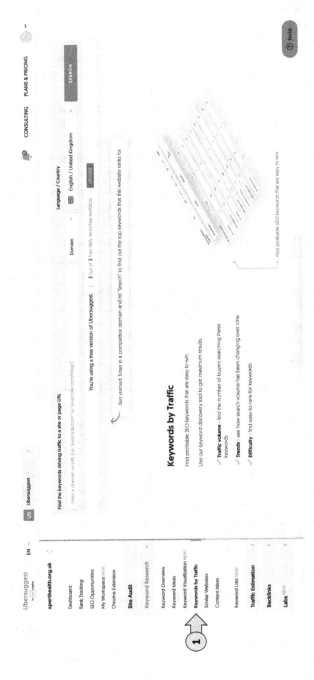

FIGURE 6.4 Neil Patel's Ubersuggest – keywords by traffic.
Source: Neilpatel.com.

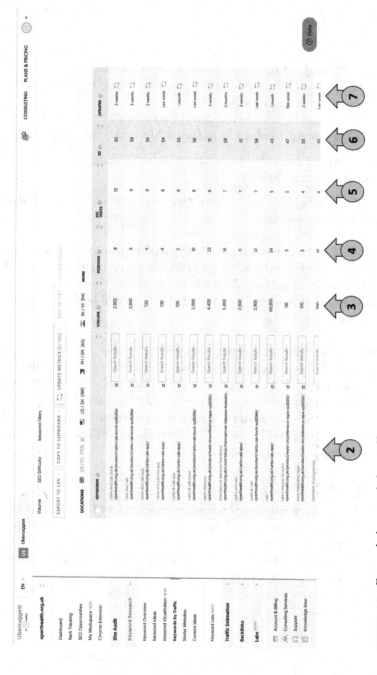

FIGURE 6.5 Example keywords by traffic output.
Source: Neilpatel.com.

4. *Keyword Placement: Use your target keyword in the first 100 words of your content.*

Content Quality:

5. *Valuable and Relevant Content: Create content that is thorough, useful, and answers the user's query.*
6. *Keyword Density: Avoid keyword stuffing. Use natural language and synonyms.*
7. *Regular Updates: Keep content up-to-date and relevant.*
8. *The article needs to be at least 300 words long, ideally longer.*

Please also explain to me how you have addressed the eight points I asked you to take into consideration.

Text "" Copy and paste the body of text you want the LLM to rewrite within the double quotes"".

Do not ask the LLM to browse a given webpage: the results are much better if you copy the data from the webpage in question and include it as text to review within the prompt. If you do not have any existing text to use, you can ask the LLM to create new content for you, which should be done in smaller excerpts of work.

The Prompt for generating new content: *You are a Search Engine Optimisation (SEO) expert, and you have been tasked with creating an article for a website that is 900 words long and is search engine optimised. The article's keyword is 'your keyword', and the context of the article should relate to ..... (**you need to provide relevant context**). Please provide your answer in 300 word chunks. When producing the answer you must take into account the following:*

On-Page SEO:

1. *Optimize Title Tags: Include the target keyword in your page titles.*
2. *Meta Description: Write compelling meta description with your keyword.*
3. *Headings and Subheadings: Use H1, H2, H3 tags effectively. Include keywords in at least one subheading.*
4. *Keyword Placement: Use your target keyword in the first 100 words of your content.*

Content Quality:

5. *Valuable and Relevant Content: Create content that is thorough, useful, and answers the user's query.*

6. *Keyword Density: Avoid keyword stuffing. Use natural language and synonyms.*
7. *Regular Updates: Keep content up-to-date and relevant.*
8. *The article needs to be at least 300 words long, ideally longer.*

Please also explain to me how you have addressed the eight points I asked you to take into consideration.

When asking the LLM to produce the output in smaller excerpts, you should review each stage, acknowledge it is good and then ask it to continue. We do this because the LLMs have a finite context window, meaning they can only 'remember' or 'see' a certain amount of text at a time. Breaking down a long article into smaller chunks will ensure that the model can maintain a coherent narrative and logical consistency throughout the article. It also means you can provide more frequent user interaction (i.e., feedback). Even though 300 words were stipulated in the prompt, you may get slightly less or more in the output. With the new content created, you can now post it on your website. This needs to happen at least weekly: Google will identify that the Charity is a frequent poster and crawl it more often. You will need to keep checking the SERP results (use Neil Patel's Ubersuggest – Keywords by Traffic); it may take several weeks before any benefits are seen. Figure 6.6 has been produced to summarise the stages explained above.

Generative AI's Impact on X-PERT Health

X-PERT Health employs eight individuals; there is no trained marketing professional. In the past, they relied on paying marketing agencies to provide the critical services they needed. Since the training in Generative AI, an administrator working two and half days a week has embedded the above process into her routine. Spending just a morning a week, she can now create new content for the website. In addition to this, she uses the same concept to create social media posts. I have yet to assess the impact on the keyword SERPs, as the project has only just been completed. However, the whole team have stated that they can see the benefits of Generative AI as a critical friend.

Final Thoughts: How Generative AI Will Evolve

Generative AI is still in its infancy, and many issues need resolution. These include but are not limited to: were copyrights infringed when building the LLMs, what new legislation will be introduced to regulate its use, the ethics of using it and how to manage hallucinations. Readers should note that anything produced in its entirety by Generative AI is unlikely to receive complete copyright protection; however, if it is reworked by a 'human', then

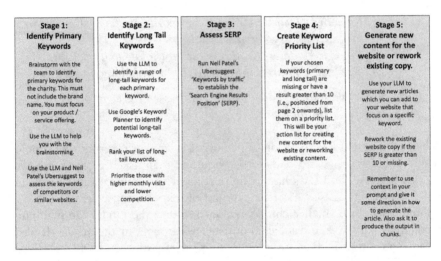

Stage 1: Identify Primary Keywords	Stage 2: Identify Long Tail Keywords	Stage 3: Assess SERP	Stage 4: Create Keyword Priority List	Stage 5: Generate new content for the website or rework existing copy.
Brainstorm with the team to identify primary keywords for the charity. This must not include the brand name. You must focus on your product / service offering. Use the LLM to help you with the brainstorming. Use the LLM and Neil Patel's Ubersuggest to assess the keywords of competitors or similar websites.	Use the LLM to identify a range of long-tail keywords for each primary keyword. Use Google's Keyword Planner to identify potential long-tail keywords. Rank your list of long-tail keywords. Prioritise those with higher monthly visits and lower competition.	Run Neil Patel's Ubersuggest 'Keywords by traffic' to establish the 'Search Engine Results Position' (SERP).	If your chosen keywords (primary and long tail) are missing or have a result greater than 10 (i.e., positioned from page 2 onwards), list them on a priority list. This will be your action list for creating new content for the website or reworking existing content.	Use your LLM to generate new articles which you can add to your website that focus on a specific keyword. Rework the existing website copy if the SERP is greater than 10 or missing. Remember to use context in your prompt and give it some direction in how to generate the article. Also ask it to produce the output in chunks.

FIGURE 6.6 Using generative AI in keyword analysis and SEO.

there is an argument that it could be protected by copyright, although this has not been tested in court. The project is now developing a transparent policy to explain how the charity uses Generative AI. This is something that all organisations should do if they commence this journey.

I believe the 'genie is now out of the bottle', and there will be no turning back. Microsoft (2023) have just introduced Microsoft Copilot 365 which is an AI-powered feature integrated into the Microsoft 365 applications. It combines LLMs with your data to assist users in tasks such as creating, summarising and analysing content within programs like Word, Excel and PowerPoint.

The key objective of this chapter is to demonstrate how a charity can become more productive and efficient by exploiting Generative AI. ChatGPT became the fastest-growing technology platform because of its ease of use, so I suggest using it daily within your work routine. Start with the free version and see it as a mentor. Use the prompt guidance I have provided (see Appendix 1) to set your questions, and remember, do not be afraid to challenge the answer, i.e., ask it to do it again. Also, never incorporate sensitive data within the prompt. If you wish to create your own LLM or start using sensitive data, then external help will be required. One option is to think about a Knowledge Transfer Partnership with a University.

Discussion Questions

1 What is the best way to check that the keywords you want to optimise are the most important for your business?

2 There are many different Generative AI platforms that you could adopt; how will you know that your selection will be correct?

3 Do you think Generative AI is just hype and will disappear from the business agenda anytime soon?

4 What could you do if you believe that your team is not ready to use the tools mentioned in this chapter?

Funding: This study was funded by the Productivity Institute and the Economic and Social Research Council, grant number: ES/V002740/1.

Acknowledgement: The author, who is also the Chair of Trustees for X-PERT Health, would like to thank the team at X-PERT Health for helping him with this research.

Note

1 See https://ads.google.com/home/tools/keyword-planner/

References

Anderson, C. (2006). *The Long Tail: Why the Future of Business is Selling Less of More.* New York, NY: Hachette Books

BCG (2023). *Generative AI.* [Online]. Boston Consulting Group. Available from: www.bcg.com/capabilities/artificial-intelligence/generative-ai [Accessed 14 January 2024].

Brown, S. (2021). *Machine Learning Explained.* [Online]. MIT Sloan School of Management. Available from: https://mitsloan.mit.edu/ideas-made-to-matter/machine-learning-explained [Accessed 14 January 2024].

Caprettini, B., & Voth, H. J. (2018). *Rage Against the Machines: New Technology and Violent Unrest in Industrializing England.* Zurich, Switzerland: UBS International Center of Economics in Society, University of Zurich.

Charities Aid Foundation (2022). *Charities Aid Foundation Charity Landscape 2022.* Available from: www.cafonline.org/docs/default-source/about-us-research/charity_landscape_report_2022.pdf [Accessed 14 January 2024].

Gordon, C. (2023). *ChatGPT Is The Fastest Growing App In The History Of Web Applications.* Forbes Media LLC. [Online]. Available at: www.forbes.com/sites/cindygordon/2023/02/02/chatgpt-is-the-fastest-growing-ap-in-the-history-of-web-applications/?sh=51a74f1678ce [Accessed: 11 November 2023].

Griffiths, M., Fenton, A., & Fletcher, G. (2019). Horizon scanning: cautionary tales. In Fenton, A., Fletcher, G., & Griffiths, M. Eds. *Strategic Digital Transformation: A Results-Driven Approach.* New York, NY: Routledge, pp. 65–72

Hatzius, J., Briggs, J., Kodnani, D. & Pierdomenico, G. (2023). *The Potentially Large Effects of Artificial Intelligence on Economic Growth.* New York, NY: Goldman Sachs & Co. LLC.

Janiesch, C., Zschech, P., & Heinrich, K. (2021). Machine learning and deep learning. *Electronic Markets,* 31(3), 685–695. https://doi.org/10.1007/s12525-021-00475-2

McCarthy, J (2007). *What Is Artificial Intelligence?* Stanford University. [Online]. Available at: http://jmc.stanford.edu/articles/whatisai/whatisai.pdf [Accessed: 10 January 2024].

Microsoft (2023). Introducing Microsoft 365 Copilot – Your Copilot for Work. Microsoft. [Online]. Available at: https://blogs.microsoft.com/blog/2023/03/16/introducing-microsoft-365-copilot-your-copilot-for-work/ [Accessed: 12 January 2024].

Open AI (2023). *Prompt Engineering.* Open AI. [Online]. Available at: https://platform.openai.com/docs/guides/prompt-engineering [Accessed: 13 December 2023].

Patel, N. (2020). *What is SEO? Your complete step-by-step guide.* https://neilpatel.com/what-is-seo/ [Accessed: 13 December 2023].

Poulter, R. (2023). *Charities Struggling to Attract and Retain Skilled Staff, Global Study Finds.* Third Sector UK. [Online]. Available at: www.thirdsector.co.uk/charities-struggling-attract-retain-skilled-staff-global-study-finds/management/article/1848016#:~:text=Charities%20struggling%20to%20attract%20and%20retain%20skilled%20staff%2C%20global%20study%20finds,-17%20November%202023&text=More%20than%20half%20of%20not,a%20global%20survey%20has%20revealed. [Accessed: 10 December 2023].

Sarker, I. H. (2021). Deep learning: a comprehensive overview on techniques, taxonomy, applications and research directions. *SN Computer Science*, 2(6), 420. https://doi.org/10.1007/s42979-021-00815-1

Sheffield, J. P. (2020). Search engine optimization and business communication instruction: interviews with experts. *Business and Professional Communication Quarterly*, 83(2), 153–183. https://doi.org/10.1177/232949061989033

The Business Research Company (2023). *NGOs and Charitable Organisations Market 2022.* The Business Research Company. [Online]. Available at: www.thebusinessresearchcompany.com/report/ngos-and-charitable-organizations-market [Accessed: 15 December 2023].

Thompson, A.D. (2023). *Inside language models (from GPT-4 to PaLM).* Life Architect [Online]. Available at: https://lifearchitect.ai/models [Accessed: 20 December 2023].

van de Rakt, M. (2020) Word count and SEO: how long should a blog post or page be? Yoast BV [Online]. Available at: https://yoast.com/blog-post-word-count-seo/#:~:text=Yoast%20SEO's%20content%20analysis%20checks,should%20be%20over%20200%20words. [Accessed: 15 January 2024].

van Deursen, A. J. A. M., & van Dijk, J. A. G. M. (2009). Using the Internet: Skill related problems in users' online behavior. *Interacting With Computers*, 21, 393–402. https://doi.org/10.1016/j.intcom.2009.06.005

Vasilev, I. (2019). *Advanced Deep Learning with Python: Design and Implement Advanced Next-Generation AI Solutions Using TensorFlow and PyTorch.* Birmingham, UK: Packt Publishing Ltd.

Zhuhadar, L. P., & Lytras, M. D. (2023). The application of auto ML techniques in diabetes diagnosis: current approaches, performance, and future directions. *Sustainability*, 15(18), 13484. https://doi.org/10.3390/su151813484

Appendix 1: Guidance on Creating Better Prompts

The key to creating effective prompts within an LLM is striking the right balance of providing enough guidance while allowing the model flexibility to generate useful responses. With practice and iteration, you can learn to craft effective prompts that get the most out of your AI assistant. Here are some rules that build on OpenAI's (2023) advice on prompt design.

1 **Be specific and clear:** LLMs respond best to clear, specific prompts. The more detailed your request, the more accurate and relevant the response will be. Avoid ambiguity and be explicit about what you are asking for.
2 **Context:** Start by giving some context, example who is the output for.
3 **Data description:** Now describe the data set. Mention the type of data (e.g., text from a collection of articles, survey responses, social media posts, etc.), the general subject matter and any specific aspects you are interested in.
4 **Objective:** Clearly state what you are looking to achieve with the thematic analysis. Are you looking for common themes, trends, patterns of sentiment or something else?
5 **Specific areas of interest:** If there are particular themes or aspects you are especially interested in, mention them. For example, if you are analysing customer feedback data, you might be interested in themes like product quality, customer service experience or pricing.
6 **Constraints and considerations:** Include any constraints or special considerations I should keep in mind, such as focusing on a specific time period, demographic group or geographical area.
7 **Explanation:** To mitigate against hallucinations, ask the LLM to explain each step it undertakes.
8 **Chunk the data:** If you require a long piece of work, get the LLM to produce the output in smaller chunks, say 250 words. Just say 'continue' to get the next batch of data.

7

DONATING VIA THE DIGITAL DOMAIN

A 360° of the Online Charitable Giving Landscape

David J. Hart

Introduction

Data consistently demonstrates that the UK is home to a hugely generous population, financially supporting over 168,000 active charities (Statista, 2023a). Despite numerous high-profile scandals that have placed the entire sector under increased scrutiny (£2.7m was diverted from charities by fraudsters in 2023 resulting in over 500 charity fraud crime reports: Action Fraud, 2023), public trust in charitable institutions remains high. Charity Commission (2023) data show a marginal increase in trust for the sector, scoring notably higher than banks, police, newspapers and politicians. Such public confidence is pivotal in an environment where the 'cost of giving' crisis (Enthuse, 2022) has simultaneously compromised the public's ability to support charities and increased their dependence on them.

Whilst charities are widely reported to be struggling to survive in the turbulent economic landscape (Charities Aid Foundation, 2023a), they must also adapt to a fundamental change in how donors wish to support their cause; the rapid transition towards online giving. The number of digital donation channels open to charities is vast, and in many cases represent a more cost-efficient means of fundraising. These channels range from standard websites, SMS and email through to social media, mobile applications and third-party operators such as JustGiving. Pre-pandemic evidence suggests that many developed nations with substantial levels of e-commerce had not seen such progress replicated by their nonprofit organisations, who remained reliant on cash giving or non-digital bank transactions (Nageswarakurukkal, 2020).

More recent data paint a far more progressive picture. The pandemic and subsequent lockdowns have positively influenced donor comfort in donating

DOI: 10.4324/9781003396802-7

via online channels, particularly for lower value donations (Giving USA, 2023). In the UK, it is estimated that at least 30% of donors use online channels (National Philanthropic Trust, 2022), a figure likely to increase as smartphone penetration rates approach 90% (Statista, 2023b) and the use of cash fails to return to pre-pandemic levels, suggesting a permanent shift towards digital payment methods (Bank of England, 2022). Charities are observing donation growth via debit card, website and mobile applications, and a sustained reduction in cash donations (Charities Aid Foundation, 2023b). This has partly been enabled by the rapid increase in the use of digital wallets such as ApplePay and GooglePay that facilitate swift online transactions (Charity Digital, 2021).

This move towards digital donations is particularly challenging for the 130,000 small and micro charities who have annual incomes under £100,000 and subsequently account for a tiny percentage of the sector's fundraising spending (National Council for Voluntary Organisations, 2022). Indeed, the Charities Aid Foundation (2022) Landscape Report uncovered that whilst 89% of charity leaders felt that technological change was central to their work, and over 70% were experimenting with new digital giving channels, only a quarter reported confidence in their own ability to do this effectively. The benefits of successfully pivoting towards digital are clear:

- Wood for Trees (2022) reports that digital tools, alongside direct mail, are a core driver of recent increases in donor recruitment.
- Email has been acknowledged as the most critical tool used to promote engagement with charitable events (CCS Fundraising, 2023).
- The average nonprofit online crowdfunding campaign generates over £7000 (Non-profit Source, 2023).
- Around 80% of charities have received donations both directly to their website and via third-party donation platforms (Barclays, 2022).
- Charities raised £590m using the platform JustGiving in 2022 (which like other online platforms makes it easier to secure GiftAid from the UK Government: Civil Society, 2023). Promoting such tools via social media can increase viewer empathy and subsequently donation intention (Park & Rhee, 2019).

Collectively, such findings suggest that charities should utilise digital channels to communicate not only the beneficiaries and outcomes of their work but also the convenience and security offered by donating online. It is therefore surprising to see a dearth of academic work which attempts to understand the wider landscape of digital giving. Research to date typically investigates a single digital donation channel such as crowdfunding platforms or social media. The aim of this chapter therefore is to adopt a more panoramic viewpoint, leading to the development of a working taxonomy of digital donation channels which addresses four central questions from the perspective of the donor:

1 Which digital communications channels are used to promote charitable causes and appeals?
2 What types of financial contribution can donors make online?
3 Will their donation be made directly to a charity or elsewhere?
4 What specific digital channels may they use when making a donation?

In doing so, we must of course acknowledge the relationship between online and offline fundraising. The two are inherently linked and can be combined to great commercial effect (advocated by marketing theorists the world over as Integrated Marketing Communications: see the work of Philip Kitchen and Don Schultz). For example, many fundraising activities exist in the physical world but utilise the virtual world to generate donations, and donations via SMS can be triggered by all manner of traditional communication channels. This taxonomy does not wish to downplay the value offered by non-digital donation channels, more to explore the range of digital options open to nonprofit marketers. The resultant taxonomy has the potential to act as a catalyst for future academic work surrounding online giving and provide something of a 'menu' of options for nonprofit marketers still finding their feet in the virtual fundraising arena.

Tier One: Communication Channels

Considering the early stages of the donor journey, a useful starting point is to consider which digital channels are utilised to make prospective donors aware of a particular cause, and thus kickstart a thought process which may eventually convert to a donation. The donor behaviour literature clearly demonstrates that the majority of donations are a consequence of solicitation (Bekkers & Wiepking, 2011), and the digital revolution has served to equip fundraisers with a wider range of means through which to execute the perfect 'ask'. Whilst some donors may already know which cause(s) they wish to support, others may find their eventual decisions influenced by the communication channels used by charities and the modes of giving available.

Digital solicitation channels may remove the perceived social unease that can arise from being approached for a donation in-person. Denying a request for help can be awkward and embarrassing because it violates a social norm to assist those in need (Flynn & Kale, 2008), and potentially result in donations being made purely to alleviate said discomfort (Zhou et al., 2020). Conversely, the lack of personal contact combined with an increasingly tech-savvy society may mean that digital solicitations are easier to ignore (Hossain, 2018). For example, a recent report from the Data Marketing

Association (2023) indicated that charitable emails enjoy a click-through rate of just 1.5%, and the average Google Ads click-through rate around 4% (WordStream, 2023). Despite these challenges, the cost efficiencies and data collection opportunities offered online make such tools an increasingly attractive option for fundraisers. The core digital marketing channels open to fundraisers include:

- **Website:** A charity-owned site is a core tool that allows charities to tell their story, demonstrate their effectiveness and generate donations. Indeed, over 30% of visitors to a donation-focused landing page will provide a donation, higher than other platforms such as peer-to-peer fundraising pages (Classy, 2020). The same report also underlined the importance of website stickiness: conversion rates were highest for visitors who spend 4–5 min on the website. A key challenge facing charities is ensuring their websites are designed to be mobile-friendly, given that 58% of all website visits globally are via a mobile device (Statista, 2023c)
- **Search Engine Optimisation (SEO)/Pay-Per-Click (PPC) Advertising:** Both techniques serve the overarching goal of driving traffic to a specific website or landing page. The (slightly) erroneous distinction often made between the two is that whilst SEO is free, PPC is not. In reality, both require different forms of investment. SEO requires the development of carefully curated content designed to elevate a charity's organic search rankings, although achieving this is seemingly more important to charity leaders than it is to donors (Bennett, 2017). For PPC, 'Google for Non-profits' is a global program of particular value to small and micro-charities. It provides fundraisers with access to up to $10,000/month of text-based ads across their display network (PPC advertising without the 'pay'), as well as resources to better utilise YouTube (as a key means of storytelling via video) and Google Maps. Of course, there are multiple large-scale advertising platforms (including Amazon, Facebook and Microsoft) which offer similar functionality in terms of budget flexibility, measurability and targeting (Forbes, 2022).
- **Social Media:** It is estimated that 87% of all charities globally use some form of social media in their fundraising activity (Charity Digital, 2023), with over 95% of US charities using Facebook, X (formerly Twitter) and Instagram. Such platforms have the potential to create viral charitable campaign content such as the infamous ALS Ice Bucket challenge and the Great Ormond Street #Whamageddon contest, both relying heavily on the gamification aspect to drive engagement (Conlin & Santana, 2022). Indeed, involving users in creative activities that may not even be linked to the cause in question improves affective state and thus donation likelihood (Xu, Mehta & Dahl, 2022). It is therefore unsurprising that social media represents the facet of digital donations that has been most explored in

academic study. Bilgin and Kethüda (2022) explored how social media can facilitate outcomes such as awareness, user interaction, currency of content and customisation that can in turn drive trust and improved brand image.

Of course, there exists huge variance in the extent to which charities deploy social media: whilst those with fewer resources may simply set up a page designed to keep key stakeholders updated on their activity, others may invest significant sums into content creation that is shared across social platforms using both organic and paid means. Across both extremes, the hope is that users will engage with charitable content, make a donation and subsequently share this with their network. The desired outcome is a form of peer pressure amongst social neighbours (Jiao et al., 2021) which convinces others to donate, something that can be effective with younger audiences who prefer to be solicited online and have a genuine personal connection to the cause (Konstantinou & Jones, 2022).

- **Email Marketing:** This tool has the potential to contribute across both donor acquisition (provided email addresses are secured in a GDPR compliant manner) and also donor retention, as it allows relationships to be nurtured and communications to be tailored to the donor. Email requires fundraisers to adapt the direct marketing planning process advocated by Sargeant & Ewing (2001) characterised by targeting and personalisation of messages. Such communications are most effective when personalised to the prospective donor (Sanders, 2017) and have the ability to soften the impact of scandals in the sector that have the potential to reduce donations (Minguez & Sese, 2023). Whilst most other channels cannot compete with the return on investment generated by email marketing campaigns, fundraisers ought to note that younger donors are typically less receptive (Statista, 2022a; 2022b).

- **Mobile:** As well as representing a huge channel in its own right given high global smartphone penetration rates, mobile is often the means through which an individual will be exposed to many of the tools named above (for example, an individual may use their phone to check emails or see charitable content on social media). Here, though we are focusing on activity that is specific to smartphones: text messaging (SMS) and mobile applications. SMS facilitates 'Text-to-give' (Linos, Jakli & Carlson, 2021) campaigns that allow charities to collect donations directly and for the donor to make payment via their next phone bill. Once a donation is made, this offers similar relationship building opportunities to email, although the effectiveness of such an approach is threatened by the declining popularity of telethon events and wider economic uncertainty (ThirdSector, 2023). In some cases, the availability of apps might dictate whether a donation is made directly to the charity or via an intermediary (see tier three). Investing in a bespoke app to generate donations is unfeasible for the vast majority of charities and would likely require a strong gamification theme to drive downloads and engagement. However, giving platforms such as Just Giving and GoFundMe can host individual charities on their apps which have millions of downloads to mobile devices.

Whilst people may be attached to their smartphone for significant periods, this does not necessarily transfer to increased donations: Chung and Hair (2021) found that donors report lower mood when seeing charitable solicitations on their phone (and as such report lower levels of donation). Elsewhere, it has been reported that mobile payment capability does not predict donation intentions as much as the charity's reputation and level of donor engagement (Maleki & Hosseini, 2020). The solution to this may lie in segmenting donors based on their awareness of an intention to engage with mobile donation channels (Zheng, 2020).

Of course, the channels utilised by fundraisers will naturally vary when communicating with prospective versus existing donors. The core distinction is that existing donors are identifiable, have previously indicated some empathy with our cause and are likely to have consented to some form of marketing communications, which lends itself to the sorts of personalised communications that have long-since been deployed in direct mail (Feld et al., 2013). The above digital tools can of course be employed alongside traditional marketing communications to influence all stages of the donor journey (Polivy, 2013).

Tier Two: Donation Type

Once a potential donor has been engaged via digital communications, the second issue to navigate is the form of financial contribution they may wish to make. Much like for-profit marketers, charities with suitable expertise and resource will assess the potential lifetime value of a donor and adapt strategies to maximise their donations over time (Bennett, 2006). In many cases, the desired 'upsell' is to convert a one-off donor to a frequent one, and a frequent donor to someone who engages in legacy giving. Such a positive trajectory is, however, not a foregone conclusion; the majority of cash donors are lost by charities before they make a further donation (Sargeant & Woodliffe, 2007). Indeed, Thomas, Feng and Krishnan (2015) observed that direct solicitations asking donors to increase their contribution actually reduced their propensity to do so.

Historically, the two forms of giving most relied upon by fundraisers were one-off and regular donations. These aligned themselves naturally with certain non-digital channels; whilst one-off giving was aligned with street collections, offline sponsorship and raffles/competitions, regular giving was normally facilitated via direct debits or workplace giving programs (the latter being especially popular in the United States where they provide certain tax benefits: Adena, 2021). However, it is now common to see charities offering both options on the same webpage, and in an increasingly number of cases offering the additional option of legacy giving.

One-off donations are often driven by impulsivity and the very act of being asked to give – prosocial decisions are typically made quicker than selfish ones and may also be subject to time pressures (for example, being approached on the street for a cash donation: Rand, Greene & Nowak, 2012). In the digital realm, the most common form of one-off donations would appear to be text message giving (Erlandsson et al., 2022) and online sponsorship, where there is no explicit expectation of future donations. One-off donations may also be a consequence of an immediate need, for example, a response to a natural disaster, for example, the American Red Cross text-to-give campaign after the 2010 Haiti Earthquake generated over $22m in donations within a week (Heath, 2010). Despite the huge growth of mobile donations since, this channel does offer people the opportunity to respond to a solicitation by promising to do so later via their phone (a promise they will often not fulfil: Fosgaard & Soetevent, 2022).

In contrast, frequent giving (primarily when donations are made on a monthly basis) represents a larger financial and emotional commitment to a given cause which the donor may feel a closer connection to (Prendergast & Hak Wai Maggie, 2013). As one might expect, the longer an individual supports a given cause, the greater their sense of belonging to that organisation and likelihood of increasing their support (Ki & Oh, 2018). Email marketing offers a logical and low-cost digital channel through which to show appreciation to frequent givers (Merchant, Ford & Sargeant, 2013).

Legacy giving has seen a rapid increase in popularity over the last decade, with one in five people over 40 having already included a charity in their will (UK Fundraising, 2023). The typical model adopted starts with a charitable cause promoting leaving a legacy to prospective donors (often via their website or email for existing donors). In many cases, legacy fundraising solicitations ask the donor to 'leave a gift in their will', which reflects the findings of Wang, Wang and Jiang (2023) that framing the contribution as a gift rather than a donation increases donation intention and amount. This will drive donors to a partnered will-writing service, with the cost of this (often totally online) process covered by the charity in exchange for the legacy gift. This appeals to legacy donors who are far more concerned with the impact their gift will have on a cause close to their heart than the technicalities of managing their estate (Johnson, 2010). The obvious limitation of this model is that charities may have to wait many years for the desired return (Wishart & James III, 2021), but at least the ability to conduct such a process largely online limits the upfront cost.

Tier Three: Donation Destination

Any framework of online giving must acknowledge that not all donations will go directly to a specific charity. For simplicity, we can surmise that when a donation is made, it goes either to a charity (who convert the donation into products/services for identified recipients), to an intermediary (who we hope add value to the process) or directly to the beneficiary (who then convert the donation into the desired products/services). The range of intermediary giving vehicles involved, such as Donor Advised Funds, foundations and trusts (Phillips, Dalziel & Sjogren, 2021) further complicate a digital giving arena the majority of charitable leaders are already struggling to navigate (Charities Aid Foundation, 2022).

A charity which possesses means of accepting digital donations directly represents a more efficient transactional process for the donor. However, charities may often benefit from intermediaries who provide not only financial support but also guidance on building infrastructure and funding applications (Williamson & Leat, 2021). That said, in some cases giving to an intermediary may result in the donor being unclear exactly which charity will benefit from their donation. Coffman (2017) concluded that this can cause charities perceived as less attractive receiving more support than they otherwise would have. Elsewhere, Chlaß, Gangadharan and Jones (2023) recently concluded that the use of intermediation decreases donations on average, perhaps owing to concern as to how much of the money will reach the end recipient.

It is therefore unsurprising that attention has turned to charitable disintermediation, which involves the removal of charities and other intermediary organisations from the donation value chain (MacQuillan et al., 2023). They propose a taxonomy which outlines the various means by which intermediaries (including traditional charities themselves) may be removed from the process. In a digital context, the breakthrough and continuing growth of donation crowdfunding platforms such as GoFundMe and JustGiving, who combined have tens of millions of app downloads, make it easier for individuals to fundraise without utilising a registered charity, often for supporting personal medical circumstances (Mayer, 2022). Of course, even in these cases, it could be argued that disintermediation is never truly achieved: the fundraiser after all utilises both a crowdfunding platform and social network sites to publicise their cause.

Tier Four: Donation Channel

Our final question is how the donation transaction is actually completed, which we refer to here as the donation channel. This will be a consequence of other decisions made by the donor such as the charity they are seeking to support, whether the donation goes direct to the beneficiary, a charity or other intermediary and the type of donation they wish to provide.

The core channels available include going through the charity's website to make either a single payment by card or setting up a direct debit for frequent donation, using a mobile app to perform the same task (in most cases, this will likely be one-off donations in response to request for sponsorship) or making a donation via SMS messaging (with payment deferred until the donor's next phone bill). As personal devices have the functionality to store card details, such processes can be incredibly straightforward to complete. In the case of ongoing direct debit payments, charities need be wary of inertia; a donor forgetting about their monthly payment might sound appealing if the money keeps rolling in, but in reality, this represents a barrier to relationship expansion (Henderson et al., 2021).

All digital transactions offer charities the opportunity to identify the donor, request gift aid from the UK government, demonstrate their gratitude to enhance positive donor emotions (Merchant, Ford & Sargeant, 2013) and attempt to develop longer-term supporters by encouraging them to provide support in multiple ways (Khodakarami, Petersen & Venkatesan, 2015).

Towards a Taxonomy of Digital Donation Channels

Figure 7.1 attempts to assemble these four underlying questions into a single framework that captures the sheer breadth of options available to prospective donors, providing a starting point for nonprofit marketers seeking to allocate limited resources towards a more focused digital fundraising strategy.

The application of customer journey mapping principles to donors has the potential to identify their preferred digital touchpoints (Kumar & Chakrabarti, 2023). Figures 7.2 and 7.3 demonstrate how we can use this framework to appreciate how digital donor journeys may differ.

Of course, any such taxonomy has to be malleable to changes in the digital environment. As new technologies emerge, payment methods evolve and lifestyles shift, charities must remain vigilant to how this may impact their digital fundraising model. Some interesting digital developments include:

- **Cryptocurrency:** Charities may wish to consider a future where donations are made with decentralised virtual currencies such as Bitcoin and Ethereum. Such crypto-giving empowers donors with greater control and transparency as to how their donation is subsequently utilised which may stifle a charity's ability to react flexible to recipient needs (surveillance philanthropy: Howson, 2021). Charities could also consider how adopting intermediary crypto platforms such as BitGive or GivingBlock could provide access both younger donors (Pew Research, 2023) and the increasing number of corporates utilising such currencies (Deloitte, 2023).

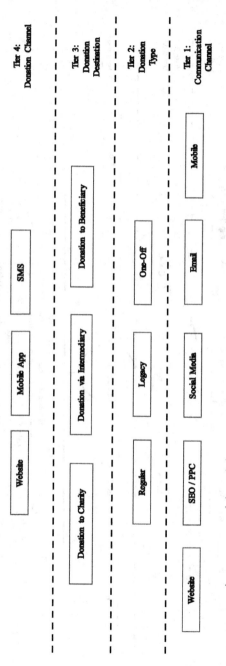

FIGURE 7.1 A taxonomy of digital donation channels.

Source: Authors own.

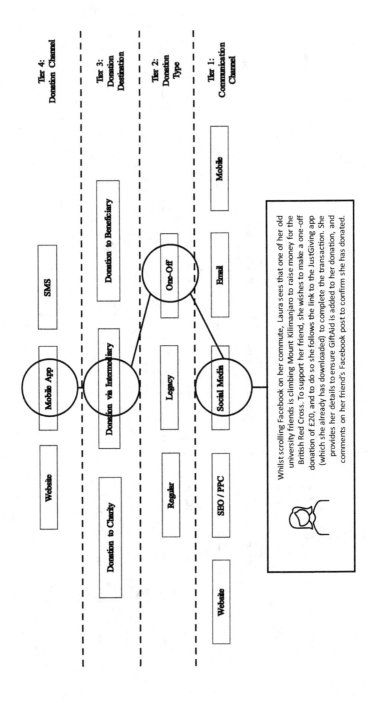

FIGURE 7.2 One-off digital donation journey.

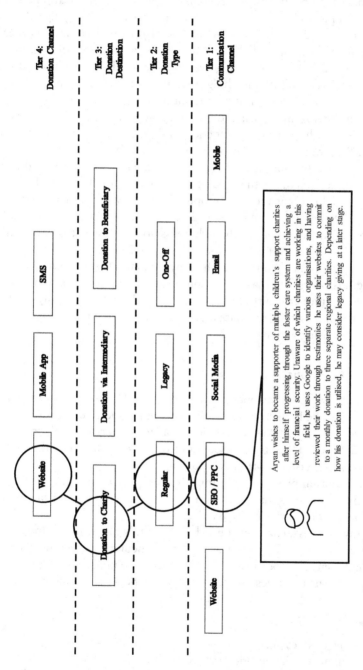

FIGURE 7.3   Regular donation journey.

- **Digital wallets:** Systems offered by Apple, Google and Paypal enable users to manage their payments, travel plans and personal identification digitally. In 2023, almost 40% of one-off donations were made using digital wallets (GoDonate, 2023). This efficient means of donating digitally is a cause for optimism amongst charities who are in close physical proximity to potential donors. The increasing overlay between digital wallets and social media, such as TikTok launching a wallet to expedite in-app commerce, presents further opportunities for fundraisers.
- **Artificial intelligence (AI):** Much is already written on how AI can revolutionise the marketing function and enhance its capability (Manis & Madhavaram, 2023). There is no reason why such potential is not transferable to the nonprofit sector where it can be used across fundraising, grant applications and the trading side of the organisation. That said, AI-generated content must be adopted cautiously in a charitable context (Arango, Singaraju & Niininen, 2023), as it is crucial that charities employing AI technology such as chatbots do so in a way that still conveys human-like emotions (Lee, Park & Chung, 2023).
- These trends alone demonstrate that any framework attempting to capture the digital donation arena is by definition a work-in-progress. Whilst under half of charities currently have a clear digital strategy (Catalyst, 2023), those that successfully navigate digital transformation to can expect to see their fundraising activity optimised.

Discussion Questions

1 How can charities that operate digitally (and therefore have no physical presence on the high street) gain the trust of prospective donors?
2 Imagine a donor makes a first donation to a charity via their website. What data could the charity ascertain from this and how could they use it to build a longer-term donor relationship?
3 A charity has approached you for advice on potentially diversifying into accepting donations via cryptocurrency. What are the main factors they should consider before making a decision?
4 Like any business, charities must think carefully about their tone of voice when communicating via social media, particularly if they deal with an especially sensitive social issue. What are the potential dangers of trying to convey serious messages about a charity's work on social media?

References

Action Fraud (2023). *Charity Donation Fraud*. Available at: www.actionfraud.police.uk/a-z-of-fraud/charity-donation-fraud (Accessed: 11 December 2023).
Adena, M. (2021) 'How can we improve tax incentives for charitable giving? Lessons from field experiments in fundraising', In Peter, H. and Lideikyte Huiber, G. (eds.)

The Routledge Handbook of Taxation and Philanthropy. London: Routledge, pp. 354–353. https://doi.org/10.4324/9781003139201-22.

Arango, L., Singaraju, S. P., and Niininen, O. (2023) Consumer Responses to AI-Generated Charitable Giving Ads, *Journal of Advertising*, pp. 1–18. https://doi.org/10.1080/00913367.2023.2183285.

Bank of England (2022). *Knocked Down During Lockdown: The Return of Cash.* Available at: www.bankofengland.co.uk/quarterly-bulletin/2022/2022-q3/knocked-down-during-lockdown-the-return-of-cash (Accessed: 10 November 2023).

Barclays (2022). *Giving: A New Landscape.* Available at: www.barclayscorporate.com/content/dam/barclayscorporate-com/documents/insights/Industry-expertise-22/Barclays-Giving-a-new-landscape-charity-report.pdf (Accessed: 10 November 2023).

Bekkers, R. and Wiepking, P. (2011) A literature review of empirical studies of philanthropy: Eight mechanisms that drive charitable giving, *Nonprofit and Voluntary Sector Quarterly*, 40(5), pp. 924–973. https://doi.org/10.1177/0899764010380927.

Bennett, R. (2006) Predicting the lifetime durations of donors to charities, *Journal of Nonprofit & Public Sector Marketing*, 15(1–2), pp. 45–67. https://doi.org/10.1300/j054v15n01_03.

Bennett, R., (2017) Relevance of fundraising charities' content-marketing objectives: Perceptions of donors, fundraisers, and their consultants, *Journal of Nonprofit & Public Sector Marketing*, 29(1), pp. 39–63. https://doi.org/10.1080/10495142.2017.1293584.

Bilgin, Y., and Kethüda, Ö. (2022) Charity social media marketing and its influence on charity brand image, Brand Trust, and donation intention, *VOLUNTAS: International Journal of Voluntary and Nonprofit Organizations*, 33(5), pp. 1091–1102. https://doi.org/10.1007/s11266-021-00426-7,

Catalyst (2023). *Charity Digital Skills Report.* Available at: https://charitydigitalskills.co.uk/wp-content/uploads/2023/07/Charity-Digital-Skills-Report-2023.pdf (Accessed: 11 December 2023).

CCS Fundraising (2023). *Philanthropy Pulse.* Available at: https://go2.ccsfundraising.com/rs/559-ALP-184/images/CCS2023PhilanthropyPulseReport.pdf?aliId=eyJpIjoiOUZ6MzVSSzM5NzIrYmRZViIsInQiOiIwRkc5K0NPVWo3ckR3ZmFwdVN1WlZnPT0ifQ%253D%253D (Accessed: 11 December 2023).

Charities Aid Foundation (2022). *Charity Landscape Report.* Available at: www.cafonline.org/docs/default-source/about-us-research/charity_landscape_report_2022.pdf (Accessed: 10 November 2023).

Charities Aid Foundation (2023a). *Cost of Living: Charities Still Struggling to Meet Demand and Cover Costs.* Available at: www.cafonline.org/about-us/press-office/cost-of-living-charities-still-struggling-to-meet-demand-and-cover-costs#:~:text=Seven%20in%2010%20(70%25),Charities%20are%20still%20feeling%20stretched (Accessed: 13 December 2023).

Charities Aid Foundation (2023b). *UK Giving Report.* Available at: www.cafonline.org/docs/default-source/about-us-research/uk_giving_2023.pdf (Accessed: 10 November 2023).

Charity Commission (2023). *Charities and Their Relationship with the Public.* Available at: https://assets.publishing.service.gov.uk/government/uploads/system/uploads/attachment_data/file/1165655/Public_trust_in_charities_2022-23.pdf (Accessed: 13 December 2023).

Charity Digital (2021) *Extent of Online Giving Boom Revealed*. Available at: https://
charitydigital.org.uk/topics/topics/extent-of-online-giving-boom-revealed-8841
(Accessed: 10 November 2023).

Charity Digital (2023) *Social Media Facts You Need to Know*. Available at: https://
charitydigital.org.uk/topics/topics/social-media-facts-you-need-to-know-in-2024-
10992 (Accessed: 12 December 2023).

Chlaß, N., Gangadharan, L., and Jones, K. (2023) Charitable giving and
intermediation: a principal agent problem with hidden prices, *Oxford Economic
Papers*, 75(4), pp. 941–961. https://doi.org/10.1093/oep/gpad023

Chung, S., and Hair, N. (2021) The adverse effects of mobile devices on willingness
to donate and online fundraising outcomes, *International Journal of Advertising*,
40(8), pp. 1343–1365. https://doi.org/10.1080/02650487.2021.1985773.

Civil Society (2023). *Record £590m Raised Through JustGiving in 2022*. Available
at: www.civilsociety.co.uk/news/record-590m-raised-through-justgiving-in-
2022.html#:~:text=Some%20%C2%A3590m%20was%20raised,both%20figu
res%20including%20Gift%20Aid (Accessed: 8 January 2024).

Classy (2020). *The State of Modern Philanthropy: Deconstructing the Online Donor
Journey*. Available at: https://learn.classy.org/rs/673-DCU-558/images/classy_st
ate-of-modern-philanthropy-2020.pdf (Accessed: 13 December 2023).

Coffman, L. C. (2017) Fundraising intermediaries inhibit quality-driven charitable
donations, *Economic Inquiry*, 55(1), pp. 409–424. https://doi.org/10.1111/
ecin.12379.

Conlin, R. P., and Santana, S. (2022) Using gamification techniques to enable
generation Z's propensity to do good, *Journal of Nonprofit & Public Sector
Marketing*, 34(5), pp. 553–571. https://doi.org/10.1080/10495142.2021.1941
498.

Data Marketing Association (2023). *Email Benchmarking Report*. Available
at: https://dma.org.uk/uploads/misc/dma-email-benchmarking-report-2023.pdf
(Accessed: 12 December 2023).

Deloitte (2023). *The Use of Cryptocurrency in Business*. Available at: www2.deloi
tte.com/us/en/pages/audit/articles/corporates-using-crypto.html/ (Accessed: 22
January 2024).

Enthuse (2022). *Donor Pulse Report*. Available at: https://enthuse.com/wp-cont
ent/uploads/2022/03/Donor-Pulse-Spring-Report-2022.pdf (Accessed: 10
November 2023).

Erlandsson, A., Nilsson, A., Alì, P. A., & Västfjäll, D. (2022) Spontaneous charitable
donations in Sweden before and after COVID: A natural experiment, *Journal
of Philanthropy and Marketing*, 27(3), pp. 1–12. https://doi.org/10.1002/
nvsm.1755.

Feld, S., Frenzen, H., Krafft, M., Peters, K. & Verhoef, P.C. (2013) The effects of
mailing design characteristics on direct mail campaign performance, *International
Journal of Research in Marketing*, 30(2), pp. 143–159. https://doi.org/10.1016/
j.ijresmar.2012.07.003.

Flynn, F.J. and Lake, V.K. (2008) If you need help, just ask: Underestimating compliance
with direct requests for help, *Journal of Personality and Social Psychology*, 95(1),
pp. 128–145. https://doi.org/10.1037/0022-3514.95.1.128.

Forbes (2022). *Pay Per Click Advertising: The Ultimate Guide*. Available
at: www.forbes.com/advisor/business/ppc-marketing-guide/ (Accessed: 13
December 2023).

Fosgaard, T. R., and Soetevent, A. R. (2022) I will donate later! A field experiment on cell phone donations to charity, *Journal of Economic Behavior & Organization*, 202, pp. 549–565. https://doi.org/10.1016/j.jebo.2022.08.025.

Giving USA (2023). *The Annual Report of Philanthropy*. Available at: https://store.givingusa.org/collections/home-page-2023/products/2023-key-findings?variant=44055760896224 (Accessed: 12 November 2023).

GoDonate (2023). *Online Donation Insight Report*. Available at: https://go-donate.uk/reports2022/?utm_source=WPNC&utm_medium=WPNC+page+link&utm_campaign=Online+Donations+Report+2023+request&utm_id=Online+Donations+Report+2023+request/ (Accessed: 8 January 2024).

Heath, T. (2010) *U.S. Cellphone Users Donate $22 Million to Haiti Earthquake Relief via Text*. Available at: www.washingtonpost.com/wp dyn/content/article/2010/01/18/AR2010011803792.html (Accessed: 12 December 2023).

Henderson, C. M., Steinhoff, L., Harmeling, C. M., & Palmatier, R. W. (2021) Customer inertia marketing, *Journal of the Academy of Marketing Science*, 49, pp. 350–373. https://doi.org/10.1007/s11747-020-00744-0.

Hossain, M. (2018) Understanding the attitude of generation z consumers towards advertising avoidance on the internet, *European Journal of Business and Management*, 10(36), pp. 86–96.

Howson, P. (2021) Crypto-giving and surveillance philanthropy: Exploring the trade-offs in blockchain innovation for nonprofits, *Nonprofit Management and Leadership*, 31(4), pp. 805–820. https://doi.org/10.1002/nml.21452.

Jiao, H., Qian, L., Liu, T., & Ma, L. (2021) Why do people support online crowdfunding charities? A case study from China, *Frontiers in Psychology*, 12, 1–12. https://doi.org/10.3389/fpsyg.2021.582508.

Johnson, K. (2010) *The Power of Legacy and Planned Gifts: How Nonprofits and Donors Work Together to Change the World*. San Francisco, CA: John Wiley & Sons.

Khodakarami, F., Petersen, J. A., and Venkatesan, R. (2015) Developing donor relationships: The role of the breadth of giving, *Journal of Marketing*, 79(4), pp. 77–93. https://doi.org/10.1509/jm.14.0351.

Ki, E.J. and Oh, J. (2018) Determinants of donation amount in nonprofit membership associations, *International Journal of Nonprofit and Voluntary Sector Marketing*, Vol. 23(3), pp. 1–9. https://doi.org/10.1002/nvsm.1609.

Konstantinou, I., and Jones, K. (2022) Investigating Gen Z attitudes to charitable giving and donation behaviour: Social media, peers and authenticity, *Journal of Philanthropy and Marketing*, 27(3), e1764. https://doi.org/10.1002/nvsm.1764.

Kumar, A., & Chakrabarti, S. (2023) Charity donor behavior: A systematic literature review and research agenda. *Journal of Nonprofit & Public Sector Marketing*, 35(1), 1–46.

Lee, S., Park, G., and Chung, J. (2023) Artificial emotions for charity collection: A serial mediation through perceived anthropomorphism and social presence, *Telematics and Informatics*, pp. 1–13. https://doi.org/10.1016/j.tele.2023.102009.

Linos, K., Jakli, L., and Carlson, M. (2021) Fundraising for stigmatized groups: A text message donation experiment, *American Political Science Review*, 115(1), pp. 14–30. https://doi.org/10.1017/s0003055420000787.

MacQuillin, I., Kottasz, R., Locilento, J., & Gallaiford, N. (2023) A typology of disintermediated giving and asking in the non-profit sector, *Journal of Philanthropy and Marketing*, e1820. https://doi.org/10.1002/nvsm.1820.

Maleki, F., and Hosseini, S. M. (2020) Charity donation intention via m-payment apps: donor-related, m-payment system-related, or charity brand-related factors, which one is overkill? *International Review on Public and Nonprofit Marketing*, *17*, pp. 409–443. https://doi.org/10.1007/s12208-020-00254-3.

Manis, K. T., and Madhavaram, S. (2023) AI-Enabled marketing capabilities and the hierarchy of capabilities: Conceptualization, proposition development, and research avenues, *Journal of Business Research*, *157*, pp. 1–20. https://doi.org/10.1016/j.jbusres.2022.113485.

Mayer, L. H. (2022) Regulating charitable crowdfunding, *Ind. LJ*, *97*(4), pp. 1375–1437.

Merchant, A., Ford, J. B., and Sargeant, A. (2013) 'Don't forget to say thank you: The effect of an acknowledgement on donor relationships', In Bennett, R., Kerrigan, F. and O'Reilly, D. (eds.) *New Horizons in Arts, Heritage, Nonprofit and Social Marketing*. London: Routledge, pp. 5–22. https://doi.org/10.1080/0267257100 3780064.

Minguez, A., and Sese, F. J. (2023) Philanthropy scandals and regular donations: the role of email marketing communications, *Journal of Marketing Management*, *39*(15–16), pp. 1592–1619. https://doi.org/10.1080/0267257x.2023.2268087,

Nageswarakurukkal, K., Gonçalves, P. and Moshtari, M. (2020) Improving fundraising efficiency in small and medium sized non-profit organizations using online solutions, *Journal of Nonprofit & Public Sector Marketing*, *32*(3), pp. 286–311. https://doi.org/10.1080/10495142.2019.1589627.

National Council for Voluntary Organisations (2022). *UK Civil Society Almanac*. Available at: www.ncvo.org.uk/news-and-insights/news-index/uk-civil-soci ety-almanac-2022/?gclid=Cj0KCQjwhL6pBhDjARIsAGx8D59abufnjUROf l3Sz7YDQEFLo2ikOSPsbPsp-pSYSc4UaniUiXiP91waAtXrEALw_wcB#/ (Accessed: 12 November 2023).

National Philanthropic Trust (2022). *Charitable Giving Statistics in the United Kingdom*. Available at: www.nptuk.org/philanthropic-resources/uk-charitable-giv ing-statistics/ (Accessed: 12 November 2023).

Non-profit Source (2023). *The Ultimate List Of Charitable Giving Statistics for 2023*. Available at: https://nonprofitssource.com/online-giving-statistics/ (Accessed: 14 November 2023).

Park, E.Y. and Rhee, J.H. (2019) Who clicks on online donation? Understanding the characteristics of SNS users during participation in online campaigns, *Sustainability*, *11*(13), pp. 3674. https://doi.org/10.3390/su11133674.

Pew Research (2023). *75% of Americans Who Have Heard of Cryptocurrencies Are Not Confident in Their Safety and Reliability*. Available at: www.pewresearch.org/ short-reads/2023/04/10/majority-of-americans-arent-confident-in-the-safety-and-reliability-of-cryptocurrency/ (Accessed: 22 January 2024).

Phillips, D. S., Dalziel, K., and Sjogren, K. (2021) Donor advised funds in Canada, Australia and the US: Differing regulatory regimes, differing streams of policy drift, *Nonprofit Policy Forum*, *12*(3), pp. 409–441. https://doi.org/10.1515/ npf-2020-0061.

Polivy, D. K. (2013) *Donor Cultivation and the Donor Lifecycle Map + Website: A New Framework for Fundraising*. New Jersey, NJ: John Wiley & Sons.

Prendergast, G. P., and Hak Wai Maggie, C. (2013) Donors' experience of sustained charitable giving: A phenomenological study, *Journal of Consumer Marketing*, *30*(2), pp. 130–139. https://doi.org/10.1108/07363761311304942.

Rand, D. G., Greene, J. D., and Nowak, M. A. (2012) Spontaneous giving and calculated greed, *Nature*, *489*(7416), pp. 427–430. https://doi.org/10.1038/natu re11467.

Sanders, M. (2017) Social influences on charitable giving in the workplace, *Journal of Behavioral and Experimental Economics*, 66, pp. 129–136. https://doi.org/ 10.1016/j.socec.2015.12.004.

Sargeant, A., and Ewing, M. (2001) Fundraising direct: A communications planning guide for charity marketing, *Journal of Nonprofit & Public Sector Marketing*, *9*(1–2), pp. 185–204. https://doi.org/10.1300/j054v09n01_12.

Sargeant, A., and Woodliffe, L. (2007) Building donor loyalty: The antecedents and role of commitment in the context of charity giving. *Journal of Nonprofit & Public Sector Marketing*, *18*(2), 47–68.

Statista (2022a) *Share of Nonprofit Organizations Using Social Media in the United States in 2022, by Platform.* Available at: www.statista.com/statistics/ 1371096/social-media-usage-nonprofit-organizations-platform-us/ (Accessed: 14 December 2023).

Statista (2022b). *Email Marketing Worldwide.* Available at: www.statista.com/topics/ 1446/e-mail-marketing/#topicOverview. (Accessed: 12 December 2023).

Statista (2023a). *Number of Charities in England and Wales from 2000 to 2023.* Available at: www.statista.com/statistics/283464/number-of-uk-charities-in-engl and-and-wales/#:~:text=There%20are%20168%2C850%20charities%20operat ing,seen%20in%202007%20by%202017 (Accessed: 8 January 2024).

Statista (2023b). *Smartphone Penetration rate in the UK 2019–2028.* Available at: www.statista.com/statistics/553707/predicted-smartphone-user-penetration-rate-in-the-united-kingdom-uk/ (Accessed: 17 January 2024).

Statista (2023c). *Percentage of Mobile Device Website Traffic Worldwide.* Available at: www.statista.com/statistics/277125/share-of-website-traffic-coming-from-mob ile-devices/ (Accessed: 17 January 2024).

ThirdSector (2023). *Text Donations to Charity Fell by More than a Quarter Last Year, Figures Show.* Available at: www.thirdsector.co.uk/text-donations-charity-fell-quarter-last-year-figures-show/fundraising/article/1833324 (Accessed: 8 January 2024).

Thomas, S. A., Feng, S., and Krishnan, T. V. (2015) To retain? To upgrade? The effects of direct mail on regular donation Dinsdale, *International Journal of Research in Marketing*, *32*(1), pp. 48–63. https://doi.org/10.1016/j.ijresmar.2014.09.001.

UK Fundraising (2023). *Legacy Giving Up 43% in a Decade.* Available at: https://fund raising.co.uk/2023/04/03/legacy-giving-up-43-in-a-decade/#:~:text=Legacy%20 giving%20has%20risen%20by,compared%20with%2014%25%20in%202013 (Accessed: 12 December 2023).

Wang, P. X., Wang, Y., and Jiang, Y. (2023) Gift or donation? Increase the effectiveness of charitable solicitation through framing charitable giving as a gift, *Journal of Marketing*, *87*(1), pp. 133–147. https://doi.org/10.1177/0022242922 1081506.

Williamson, A. K., and Leat, D. (2021) Playing piggy (bank) in the middle: Philanthropic foundations' roles as intermediaries, *Australian Journal of Public Administration*, *80*(4), pp. 965–976. https://doi.org/10.1111/1467-8500.12461.

Wishart, R., and James III, R. N. (2021) The final outcome of charitable bequest gift intentions: Findings and implications for legacy fundraising, *Journal of Philanthropy and Marketing*, *26*(4), e1703. https://doi.org/10.1002/nvsm.1703,

Wood for Trees (2022). *State of the Sector Report*. Available at: https://woodfortrees. net/state-of-the-sector-report-2022-request/. (Accessed: 14 November 2023).

WordStream (2023). *Google Ads Benchmarks by Industry*. Available at: www. wordstream.com/blog/ws/2016/02/29/google-adwords-industry-benchmarks (Accessed: 14 December 2023).

Xu, L., Mehta, R., and Dahl, D. W. (2022) Leveraging creativity in charity marketing: The impact of engaging in creative activities on subsequent donation behavior, *Journal of Marketing*, 86(5), pp. 79–94. https://doi.org/10.1177/002224 29211037587.

Zheng, Y. (2020) Using mobile donation to promote international fundraising: A situational technology acceptance model, *International Journal of Strategic Communication*, 14(2), pp. 73–88. https://doi.org/10.1080/1553118x.2020. 1720026.

Zhou, G., Xue, K., Yu, M. & Zhou, N. (2020) The effects of perceived deceptiveness and pressure on consumer donation: a mixed-methods study, *Social Responsibility Journal*, 16(1), pp. 91–108. https://doi.org/10.1108/srj-05-2018-0114.

8

RECRUITMENT MARKETING IN CHARITIES

Challenges and Opportunities

Emma Reid and Kerry Martin

> Now more than ever we need to equip individuals to be able to practice marketing appropriately and successfully within this unique sector.
>
> (Hyde & Mitchell, 2022, p. 1)

Challenges in Recruiting for Charities

Being passionate about an organisation's mission can be a great motivator to attract employees; however, salary remains a significant motivational factor for a large section of the working population (Bandono et al., 2022). Charities and not-for-profit organisations traditionally offer lower salaries than private companies due to funding limitations (including the cost of fundraising) and a focus on prioritising the charity's mission over staff costs. This can cause a shortfall in attracting skilled and diverse talent to an organisation. Charities note that the recruitment and retention of staff is a key issue (Civil Society, 2024). Wang & Seifert (2021) also highlight concerns around the purpose behind the charity potentially being neglected with a greater focus on operating more like a business than a charity, noting.

> Charitable NPOs, in general, have become more business-like and market-facing; as a result, there has been increasing concern of mission-drift, namely a move away from its mission in pursuing financial success
>
> *(p. 1178)*

Thus, there are concerns around the initial recruitment of staff who may not share the beliefs and mission of the charity that employs them. A recent study by Nottingham Trent University (Third Sector, 2023) highlights a

DOI: 10.4324/9781003396802-8

'recruitment crisis', citing reasons including poor pay (average of 7% less per/hour compared to private sector), terms and conditions, lack of skilled applications, reduced application numbers overall and private sectors offering more attractive opportunities. This in turn has led to increased pressure on existing workforces and evidence of burnout. The care sector notes a staff turnover of 34%, with many employees changing job or moving sector due to the low wages.

Recruitment Marketing

Recruitment marketing is the practice of using marketing strategies and tactics to attract, engage and retain skilled employees in organisations and businesses. It centres on promoting a company as a great workplace and creating a positive employer brand that resonates with potential candidates through traditional and digital marketing channels. Instead of focussing on the organisation or businesses products and services, it promotes company culture, values and career opportunities with the goal of building relationships with potential candidate before they start applying for roles to build employer brand recognition and create a talent pool of employees who want to work for the organisation/business.

Recruitment marketing is a more recent concept in marketing, gaining prominence in the mid-2000s and has begun to establish itself as an essential output of an organisation's marketing mix (Kandoth & Shekhar, 2022). Successfully executed recruitment marketing strategies can help an organisation stand out and showcase the unique qualities of the staff and what it is like to work there.

Benefits of successful recruitment marketing include attracting more qualified candidates who are a good culture-fit for the organisation, which can provide financial benefits in the prevention of recruitment costs of rehiring. It can reduce the time to hire new candidates, by providing engaged audience of candidates who are excited about the prospect of working for the organisation.

Recruitment Marketing for Charities

Charities marketing efforts are more commonly focused on targeting various donor types or recruiting volunteers. Charity brands have moved towards focusing on purpose and values (Dufour, 2021) as a way of increasing satisfaction with employees. Wang and Seifert (2021) argue for a need to "move away from management-consultancy-led formulaic employee relations practices and develop a sector-specific approach rooted in charities' own mission and values" (p. 1179).

There has been a lack of research into recruiting paid staff to charity organisations. Since its introduction to HR and marketing in 1996, employer branding has enjoyed a resurgence in the digital era (Gilch & Sieweke, 2021) and is seen as necessary to build relationships with potential candidates (Alashmawy & Yazdanifard, 2019) through the distribution of content.

Traditional recruitment techniques, for example, online job advertisements, should be carefully written to attract the highest quality of applicants. For charities, this should focus on the skills required and developed, how the successful applicant would contribute to the charity's mission and values. Clarity about the role and any perks/rewards is also crucial, and finally ensuring that the more appropriate keywords are incorporated in the job advert to ensure it can be found by potential applicants (Charity Jobs, 2021).

Recruitment marketing using a charity's social media platforms can be more cost-effective than using traditional advertising or online recruitment sites, where a posted job advert could cost hundreds of pounds. It can also help organisations attract employees with specific skillsets often required for roles in charities by allowing the targeting of specific demographics and tailored messages, helping to build trust and transparency by addressing the misconceptions that individuals share about working in the nonprofit sector.

Charities can leverage recruitment marketing and talent brand building more than most organisations through the telling of compelling stories of the people who work there and the people they help through their work. They can also use this space to promote some of the softer benefits of working at a charity including dedicated learning and development opportunities and progression opportunities. Charities can also benefit from people's positive perceptions of their brand and the specific type of work that they carry out.

Using Social Media to Promote Charities as a Positive Place to Work

Social media has become a recognised tool to raise awareness of charities and more recently to encourage donations. There is significant growth in the use of the platform TikTok globally with the platform reaching 1.92 billion users in 2023 (Hootsuite, 2024) and with 29% of all users opening the app at least once a day. The short videos focus on storytelling in an engaging way, often using filters or lens to present their content in an innovative way. The design of the app, with the 'For You' page using an algorithm to display user-generated content like the type of content they have engaged with previously. Furthermore, the use of hashtags and sharing of content by users can also drive organic traffic to the charity's TikTok content. The ability to tap into current trends, memes and user-generated content by influential users all encourage interaction and engagement with the platform.

Using TikTok is an excellent way to showcase the charity brand's personality, through delivering content which is designed to engage audiences and encourage interaction on the platform. This also helps to give more of a human side to the charity, by showing the people who work for the charity and the activities carried out on behalf of the charity. It also can encourage transparency by showing, for example, how donations and support from the public has led to change (Platypus Digital, 2023).

Charity Digital (2023) reported that British Red Cross successfully implemented a TikTok strategy aimed at young people during COVID as a way of "sharing vital information about the virus". Furthermore, there is increased evidence in the use of social media as a tool to encourage recruitment and staff retention in the charity sector (Charity Digital, 2023). Again, the British Red Cross used its established engaged audience to share the work carried out by the organisation with educational and fun videos.

Care for All: Recruitment Marketing in Action

'Care for All', the charity that was used with the first-year students in-class activity currently has around 3000 employees and 20,000 volunteers. The charity is well known for its work internationally, but less known for its UK-based work. The charity employs around 25% of its staff in its Health directorate which aids vulnerable people who can end up in hospital A&E wards due to several factors including loneliness, poor mental health, addiction issues and age. The charity struggles to attract employees in this directorate due the low salary offered which is less than competitors, and perceptions of the work carried out around personal care and hours worked.

To gain a greater understanding of how the role of recruitment marketing was performed by the charity, the Talent Acquisition Manager was interviewed by the first author. The aim of this interview was to inform the teaching materials for this class and highlighted several benefits and challenges in working in recruitment for a charity. She first outlined her motivations for working for a charity compared with a private organisation.

It was a goal of mine to work for a charity after I worked at a private company for four years and organised fundraising activities for employees including a team zipline, a skydive and regular office events (bake sales etc.) Through these activities, I met with representatives from several charities including visiting a hospice. I began to realise that my career path was my own to define and would like my contribution as an employee to mean something, rather than help business owners make profits. It was around a year later that I applied for the recruitment marketing job with the charity. It seemed that an amazing opportunity had landed in my lap;

to tell the stories of the people who work at the charity to attract new people to the organisation. The mission of the charity didn't resonate with me personally but that didn't make a difference as to how passionate I felt about the job that I was recruited to do.

The manager highlighted a few benefits in working for the charity, drawing on her experience as an employee:

As with any workplace, there are various positives and negatives that come with working there. Knowing that my work was making even a small impact on the charity was a great feeling. Working alongside a diverse group of people who were very passionate about their work and making a difference was also fantastic and helped motivate me on a regular basis. The size and scale of the charity meant that there were more resources for training, and professional development was strongly encouraged, including being provided with a study loan. They also supported my studies with a significant number of days that I could take to complete coursework, and reduced my workload whilst I completed my qualification. The charity also made sustained efforts to ensure our wellbeing was a priority, and as such offered healthcare resources and flexible working arrangements to ensure we achieved a work/life balance.

She identified the challenges working with a charity, focusing on the bureaucracy and budget constraints.

A charity of this size made decision making slow due to the structure of the organisation, layers of approval and policies and procedures in place. This could make the achievement of objectives and goals a slow, often delayed process. Financial constraints and last-minute budgetary changes meant that work could be paused or cancelled completely, making for a frustrating loss of work and hours.

Specific challenges were discussed around recruitment marketing, specifically a lack of management buy-in and lack of financial support.

The biggest setback in the role came from the nature of the role itself. Recruitment marketing and building an employer brand were often a forgotten or ignored priority. Asking for support from main marketing teams resulted in lack of support and a focus on fundraising priorities. There appeared to be a lack of understanding in what recruitment marketing within the organisation was trying to achieve both internally and externally, or how it was important to the overall financial and mission objectives of the organisation. However, these negatives were often eclipsed by the pride that I felt working for an internationally known humanitarian charity. During a hospital stay, I was chatting with a lady in the next bed who lived alone and had no support. She told me that its due to the charity that she gets taken home from regular hospital stays, and that the staff from our Health service help her settle in back home. I felt particularly emotional at hearing her story and how the charity's work helped her personally, and often referred to this story when marketing our Health service and its roles. It is emotive storytelling like this which ties audiences to any charities mission and can help tremendously in attracting an engaged and talented workforce.

Developing the Teaching Materials

The authors met on several occasions to collaborate on developing teaching materials and activities. As this lecture and workshop participation would also inform the main findings for this book chapter, the authors sought university ethics approval to collect data from students. The session, entitled 'Marketing for Charities' was the first taught topic within a core module for first-year undergraduate marketing students. The module explores marketing activities that tackle social issues, improve communities and livelihoods, support charities, protect the environment and contribute to creating a better future for all. It was delivered in term 1 and was the first interactive session for the new students. It took place in the campus and students have been enrolled for around 2 weeks prior to attending the session. Thus, these students were at the very beginning of their academic journey in marketing, and perhaps have not yet considered the different opportunities and careers possible with a degree in marketing.

The lecturer began the session by delivering a short presentation which provided an overview of marketing for charities highlighting the distinction between charities and for-profit organisations. She highlighted several challenges facing charities around funding, skillsets required and took a particular focus on how charities use digital marketing, drawing on her previous work (Reid, 2022) in an earlier edition of this book.

The Talent Acquisition Manager's lecture discussed some of the issues facing the charity, as highlighted in the interview exerts above. She then focused specifically on some of the marketing techniques she had used within her role.

Using Traditional Marketing Techniques to Attract Potential Applicants

The manager explained that there is still a place for traditional marketing techniques to attract potential applicants and to help convert volunteers into staff members. However, she highlighted the additional resource that this requires, plus the cost of designing and producing the physical posters.

Posters are crucial in our shop's windows; it alerts passersby to vacancies for paid roles and volunteer roles. It helps promote paid roles to volunteers (turning volunteers into staff members was always a great thing) ...the only thing issue with posters is the distribution if they were to go into the wider community, as that takes resource to plan and put them up. But I believe that audiences seeing posters in addition to say scrolling on social media and seeing something related to the charity will reinforce the message.

Discussing the Use of Social Media to Promote Working at the Charity

The manager recognised that there was a need to offer an integrated approach to recruitment marketing for the charity, blending traditional and digital marketing approaches to attract a wide range of applications and encourage diversity within the workforce.

I think charities can utilise TikTok and other social media platforms extensively to show the range of people that work for an organisation and talk about issues that matter to a younger demographic, including neurodiverse staff and how they are supported, transgender staff and support, variety of races, backgrounds and sexuality etc. For example, at the charity I worked at, there was a neurodiversity network that I was a part of that offered peer advice and support. Showing potential employees that these support groups exist could make a huge difference in their perceptions of an organisation. Things that make an organisation unique but that also reflect what people want, e.g. flexibility, can be easily promoted on social media.

Utilising New Social Media to Engage the Audience and Measuring Success

The manager had worked in a digital marketing role prior to taking her position at 'Care for All'. She also completed an MSc in Digital Marketing and a professional Digital Marketing qualification while in the role (supported by the charity). This, along with her own passion for social media, ensured she stayed ahead of digital marketing trends and was trained in innovative uses of social media.

I used TikTok to create content to promote internship vacancies as I believed it was a good channel to communicate with the target audience (young people, although anyone could apply for the internship if they had an interest in the area i.e. career returners, people who want to change career. History told us from the first set of internships that applications were 99.9% were from young people) ... I didn't have much time so recorded a straight to camera piece talking about the benefits of the internship roles (paid, real experience, not just an 'internship' where you make the tea etc.). The post got good engagement and clicks but no direct applications – I believe this is probably down to someone seeing the ad but not been ready to apply at that point and returning to the website at a later date. This is sometimes the difficulty of tracking job applications.

Challenges in Using Social Media

In the lecture, the manager discussed one experience in using social media which was not well received within the charity.

From my own experience, I failed completely when I posted pictures of the new Paisley office on Twitter and was told to take them down from the marketing team. I was obviously only thinking about the potential audience of people who might want to work with us, and not the fact that we have a critical audience who will question (probably rightly) how decisions are made and what money is spent on. Charities are under extra scrutiny with regards to transparency and spending which affected the content I could put out. Going forward I then always considered how content would be perceived from this point of view.

Encouraging People to Work for a Charity

The manager concluded her lecture reflecting on how charities could attract young people, in particular ensuring messages could resonate with the right audience.

I have interviewed many young people who have shown so much passion for the various humanitarian causes that the charity helps people with. They have tonnes of energy and great ideas and should be nurtured. With the internship programme, we wanted them to leave their internship with the goal of one day returning to the charity as a permanent member of staff.

I believe we can see the power of social media to start to attract people who resonate with the charities message. Show people who work there in a variety of roles who have gained something from their work, be it helping someone home from hospital who expressed their genuine thank you, to the mum who is most productive working flexibly to achieve her work/life balance, to the person like me who was able to complete their master's due to support from the charity.

The students then took a short break and moved into the in-class activity:

You have been asked to do a piece of consultancy work for 'Care for All'. Around 20% of the chosen charity employees in the UK are made up of workers in their Health directorate. The charity struggle to recruit to these roles due to lack of awareness and as they are a charity, salaries are lower than those offered by other companies advertising the same roles. The charity wants you to devise a communications plan to raise awareness of these roles and ultimately, increase applications.

Students were set the following task:

1. *Work in a team, start by researching the charity. What kind of work do they do in the UK? Check their social media, what do they post about? How often? What about engagement (likes, shares, comments). Which platforms are the most popular? Are there any gaps in the type of content they post?*
2. *Think about who the target audience might be for the kind of roles that the charity wants you to promote? What social media do you think they use? How else do you think they could be targeted offline?*
3. *Start to think of some of the key messages you'd like to promote and how/where you could do this.*

Students could select their own groups made up of four members and were given an hour to create a 5 minute group presentation which addressed the above task. The teaching team spent time with each group to ensure full comprehension of the task and to give the students the opportunity to ask questions. Three groups participated in the presentations.

The first group suggested the following ideas.

- 'Care for All' could take part in university and college open days to highlight careers and internships.
- They could have advertisements in their charity shops.
- Post on YouTube Shorts and TikTok as the shortform content has the most impact.
- Post on LinkedIn (entry level roles), also post about internships and part time roles as you study.
- Advertise to new graduates as they also get experience from the role.

The group suggested that the content should communicate the following key messages:

- Improved work/life balance.
- The rewarding feeling of working with charities and helping others.
- Ability to see a direct impact in the local community.

The second group focused on the ageing workforce and suggested focusing on the human aspect of the role in the charity, for example, building on current TikTok trends with office and support staff. They suggested collaborating with influencers who align with the mission and values of the charity. Furthermore, increased presence and activity on Instagram would help gain more followers, improve engagement and help to make the sector a more attractive employment prospect.

The final group also focused on the ageing workforce and suggested utilising social media to promote job adverts. This group also suggested more traditional methods of issuing leaflets and posters advertising job opportunities to local colleges and universities.

Following the presentations, the lecturer used Mentimeter, an anonymous polling tool, to ask questions to the class: (1) what have you learned today and (2) based on today, would you work for a charity?

The responses for question 1 focused on now understanding the benefits of a charity, the value in helping others, the recruitment challenges facing the sector and that there was more to charities than they had imagined.

When asked if the students would work for a charity, the responses were mixed, with comments including "maybe", "in my early career" and "not at the moment". We discussed this in more depth in class and it appeared that some students already had a fixed idea for career prospects, while others were already employed in the private sector. However, as we note and through later informal discussion with the students, we reflect that students were at a very early point in their academic journey. As academics, we should ensure that examples from the third sector are included in teaching materials and activities, this will maintain interest in this sector as a viable career option.

Conclusions: What Can We Learn from This?

The case discussed in this chapter outlines a several challenges facing the charity sector around staff recruitment and retention especially in the care sector. Our interviews with a former charity representative highlight the growing use of social media platforms, in particular TikTok as a new and innovative way to attract young people to work in this sector. Surprisingly, our activity found that undergraduate students still perceive traditional marketing as effective (posters/Freshers' events) as well as using social media and tapping into current trends.

Charities could utilise the opportunity to engage with college and university marketing students by offering mentoring programmes, internships and guest lectures as a recruitment marketing tool to promote roles to the future workforce.

In developing teaching marketing, we recognise that undergraduate students might not be aware of the different sectors that they can work in, and offering interactive sessions such as this can broaden their mindset when considering roles and sectors. Offering a session like this early in a student's academic journey encourages students to consider the difference between the private and not-for-profit sector. It would be of interest to offer a project or module later in the degree journey which delves into the charity sector in more depth. This would also encourage collaboration between Higher Education Institutes and local charities.

Discussion Questions

1 How can educational establishments and charities work together to encourage new graduates to consider working in the third sector?
2 How can emerging social media be used to attract young people into charity sector?
3 Long term – how can the charity sector ensure it retains engaged staff, despite challenges with resources?

References

Alashmawy, A., & Yazdanifard, R., (2019). "A review of the role of marketing in recruitment and talent acquisition". *International Journal of Management, Accounting and Economics*. 6. 2383–2126.

Bandono, A., Nugroho, S.H., Suharyo, O.S. and Susilo, A.K., (2022). "The influence of salary, work facilities, and leadership factors on employee performance". *Journal of Theoretical and Applied Information Technology*, 100(21), pp. 6311–6321.

Charity Digital (2023) "*A Charity Guide to TikTok*" available at https://charitydigi tal.org.uk/topics/topics/a-charity-guide-to-tiktok-8245 (Last accessed 21/2/24).

Charity Job (2021) "*Recruitment Guide for Charities 2021*" available at www.cha rityjob.co.uk/recruiterinsights/tools-and-resources/ (Last accessed 21/2/24).

Civil Society (2024) "*Staff Costs Increase by £9m at Major Care Charity to Keep Up with Wage Inflation*" available at www.civilsociety.co.uk/news/staff-costs-increase-by-9m-at-major-care-charity-to-keep-up-with-wage-inflation. html#:~:text=with%20wage%20inflation-,Staff%20costs%20increase%20 by%20%C2%A39m%20at%20major%20care,keep%20up%20with%20w age%20inflation&text=Palliative%20care%20charity%20Sue%20Ryder,fall ing%20by%20114%20to%202%2C811 (Last accessed 21/2/24).

Dufour, D. (2021) *"The Changing Face of Charity Branding"* available at www.chari tycomms.org.uk/the-changing-face-of-charity-branding (Last accessed 16/9/23).

Gilch, P. M., & Sieweke, J. (2021) "Recruiting digital talent: The strategic role of recruitment in organisations' digital transformation". *German Journal of Human Resource Management*, 35(1), 53–82. https://doi.org/10.1177/239700222 0952734

Hootsuite (2024) *"The 2024 Guide to TikTok"* available at https://blog.hootsuite. com/tiktok-marketing/ (Last accessed 21/2/24).

Hyde, F. and Mitchell, S.L. eds., (2022) *Charity Marketing: Contemporary Issues, Research and Practice*. Abingdon, Oxon: Routledge.

Kandoth, S. and Shekhar, S.K. (2022) "Recruitment marketing-a bibliometric analysis". *International Journal of Professional Business Review*, 7(2), p. 0431.

Playtpus Digital (2023) *TikTok for Good – A Beginners Guide for Charities"* available at www.platypusdigital.com/tiktok-for-good-a-beginners-guide-for-charities/ #:~:text=Use%20donation%20stickers&text=Content%20creators%20can%20 choose%20a,available%20to%20US%2Dbased%20charities (Last accessed 19/ 2/24).

Reid (2022) "Digital marketing for charities, reflections from a collaborative project" cited in Hyde, F. and Mitchell, S.L. eds., 2021. *Charity Marketing: Contemporary Issues, Research and Practice*. Abingdon, Oxon: Routledge.

Third Sector (2023) *"Staff Shouldering the Burden as Charity Recruitment Crisis Deepens"* available at www.thirdsector.co.uk/staff-shouldering-burden-char ity-recruitment-crisis-deepens-%E2%80%93-report/management/article/1818 147#:~:text=Researchers%20discovered%20that%20more%20than,sector%20c ontributing%20to%20the%20challenge (Last accessed 21/2/24).

Wang, W. and Seifert, R. (2021) "The end of meaningful work in the not-for-profit sector? A case study of ethics in employee relations under the new business-like operation regime". *Journal of business ethics*, 181(1), pp. 1–14.

9

PATHWAYS TO PROGRESS

The Social Impact Chain in Charitable Sector Evaluation

*Julia Carins, Sebastian Isbanner and
Sharyn Rundle-Thiele*

Introduction

The Australian charitable sector employs 10.5% of all Australian employees (circa 1.38 million people), is valued at A$176 billion and tackles Australia's most wicked challenges (Australian Charities and Not-for-profits Commission, 2022). Over 168,000 charities were registered in the UK in March 2023 receiving 88 billion pounds in income (Policy Bee UK, 2024). Charities tackle complex issues such as equity, violence prevention, homelessness, legal or advocacy advice, child sexual exploitation, health, well-being and social care. However, the continuous growth of socio-economic gaps, increasing crime rates and declining mental health and well-being suggest there is a need for focused investment to achieve more outcomes capable of delivering the greatest social impact.

Those seeking to create change and others funding those efforts urgently need to understand which charity activities produce outputs that lead to outcomes capable of delivering social impact. Consultation, thinking and planning provide the illusion of industrious activity; however, they often end in outputs such as reports and plans, which alone cannot translate into outcomes and impact. A greater understanding of activities and outputs ensures more productive activities are supported, allowing adjustments to enhance success further. Reporting of outcomes or impact is not common practice. However, there is a growing understanding of the need to report outcomes and impact.

Asthma Australia published their first impact report in 2023. To understand the pathway to impact, Asthma Australia developed their Theory of Change which details an outcome framework (see Asthma Australia,

DOI: 10.4324/9781003396802-9

2023). Their report extends organisational reporting beyond reach statistics (e.g., 620,000 people visited asthma.org.au) to considerations of outcomes achieved following interactions with Asthma Australia. For example, the impact report states 72% of adults with asthma who have interacted with Asthma Australia report they have seen a health professional for an asthma review in the last 12 months. This rate is higher than the general population of Australian adults with Asthma, where only 60% had seen a professional for an asthma review (Asthma Australia, 2023).

The lack of understanding of how to achieve impact is severely limiting progress. Australian charities must effectively showcase how their activities deliver a return on investment benefitting the community. Impact measurement offers an effective mechanism to demonstrate what works (and what does not). A further benefit of impact measurement is that the cost savings experienced by the community can be calculated, through social return on investment approaches. Demonstration of social return on investment communicates how the work delivered by a charity is benefitting the community supporting that work. The reporting of positive return on investments for communities creates compelling cases leading to continued, or increased funding. Social return on investment delivers a clear understanding of the long-term cost savings achieved from investments in the programs, products and services offered by charities.

What is impact measurement? Intuitively, examining and documenting the change that occurs, or the 'social impact', is impact measurement. Charities may seek to create several changes for individuals that relate to broader impact goals. Asthma Australia (2023) defines impact for their organisation in a few ways (see Figure 9.1). Their theory of change posits that people who interact with services offered by their organisation improve their knowledge and confidence to manage asthma and are supported to take steps to improve their asthma management. When people maintain asthma self-management strategies, they experience fewer flare-ups, helping them to achieve their life goals. Impact for Asthma Australia is people being free to live robust healthy lives. Impact is people being active and engaged in employment, school or fulfilling caring responsibilities.

Defining Social Impact

To allow charities to see, measure and communicate the impact they have within or across the social issues they are tackling, there needs to be a common understanding of what social impact means. Impact has been described as the "portion of the total outcome that happened as a result of the activity of the venture, above and beyond what would have happened anyway" (Clark & Rosenzweig, 2004, p. 7). Clark and Rosenzweig's (2004) definition identifies the role of the charity (as a 'venture') in creating change.

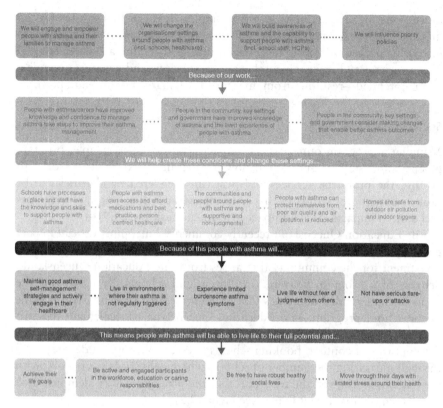

FIGURE 9.1 Asthma Australia's Theory of Change.
Source: Asthma Australia (2023).

Other scholars have provided definitions that elaborate on what Clark and Rosenzweig refer to as the 'total outcome'. These definitions focus attention on both positive and negative, unintended and intended and short- and long-term effects (Blankenberg, 1995; Wainwright, 2002). Scholars go further to indicate dimensions of breadth (across numerous outcomes), repetition (outcomes occurring more than once), interconnectedness (outcomes effecting other outcomes), manifesting (outcomes compounding over time) and spillover (outcomes occurring in those who were not the initial target group) (Blankenberg, 1995; Hadad & Gauca, 2014; Latané, 1981; Rawhouser et al., 2019; Vanclay, 2003).

Taken together, definitions indicate that impact is complex and there are challenges identifying a start and endpoint. But, much like the wicked problems that charities tackle, to be worthy of funds invested the impact that charities seek to create must also be broad, sustained and manifesting over time. Much like a ripple effect that expands, maintaining momentum as it moves, meeting several things, so is the complex and perpetual nature of social impact. Therefore, extending the definition of Epstein and Yuthas (2017) to include its perpetual nature, this chapter defines social impact as referring to "both societal and environmental changes—positive and negative, intended, and unintended—resulting from investments" (Isbanner et al., n.d., p. 8).

Social Impact Mapping

Mapping a program onto a social impact pathway helps people, program planners and staff to understand how a program is expected to work. To do this, the products, services and programs delivered by charities can be broken down into pathways that map inputs, activities, outputs, outcomes and desired impacts (Social Impact Investment Taskforce, 2014).

Life Education Queensland recently commenced mapping a social impact pathway for one of its programs. This work aims to quantify the return on investment for the community that arises from Life Education Queensland's delivery of a program delivered in Queensland schools. By narrowing the focus to the intended outcomes that are expected for students who partake in the school program, Life Education Queensland can calculate the cost of all activities needed to deliver the program in schools (e.g., planning, development of content, booking schools and school program delivery) and through measuring the number of schools where deliveries occur, along with the outcomes achieved the true 'effect' of the program can be demonstrated as a return on investment figure (see Figure 9.2).

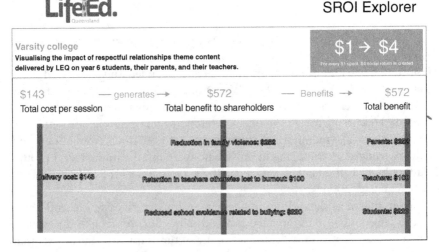

FIGURE 9.2 An example of an impact dashboard.

Note: Mock-up, any outcomes or figures in the diagram are for illustration purposes only.

For example, a data dashboard could demonstrate SROI for any program, product or service. Using the illustrative dashboard data, we can see that if the school program cost $143 to plan, implement and deliver in one school and the outcomes were a reduction in family violence, increased retention of teachers otherwise lost to burn out and reduced school avoidance due to bullying which is currently estimated to cost the community $572, the return on investment would be a cost savings to community of $4 for every $1 invested into the Life Education Queensland school program.

Social impact pathways align activities and outputs with outcomes allowing contributions to any resulting social impact to be examined and learnings from one program to be shared with other programs. This ensures that everyone can clearly understand the links between actions, outputs, outcomes and the contribution each makes to impact. The Life Education Queensland mock-up in Figure 9.2 demonstrates how social return on investment can be reported. Input costs (e.g., cost per session) could be linked to the impact arising from programs (e.g., reduction in family violence).

Within the charity sector, the social impact agenda is advancing. The Asthma Australia (2023) Impact Report provides an example of narrative approaches to communicate impact. While case studies and narratives can provide detailed examples of impact, they may run the risk of overclaiming. A more standardised approach is needed to avoid overclaiming and to build an understanding of the true investments needed to overcome complex social problems. Approaches are needed to make it easier for the broader research and practitioner community to understand outcomes and impact. The social impact mapping process aims to reduce the effort required to conduct social impact evaluations and, in doing so, help increase the uptake of this evaluative approach.

Description of the Steps Involved in Mapping the Social Impact Value Chain

Measuring or assessing social impact can demonstrate that a charity offers a real and tangible benefit to the community or the environment. This is typically conducted using an impact value chain, which comprises the following elements: (1) inputs, (2) activities, (3) outputs, (4) outcomes and (5) impact (Social Impact Investment Taskforce, 2014).

1 **Inputs** encompass the resources dedicated to or consumed by a social project or initiative. These resources include financial capital, physical assets (e.g., equipment or infrastructure), human resources (e.g., staff and volunteers), time and expertise. The adequacy and strategic allocation of these resources play a critical role in the success of a social initiative. For

instance, having sufficient funding and skilled personnel can enhance the project's effectiveness.

2 **Activities** are the specific actions and interventions to transform inputs into tangible outputs. These actions are purposefully designed to address a particular social issue or achieve a specific goal. Examples of activities might include conducting workshops, organising community events, providing training sessions or developing, designing and distributing educational materials. Activities are the 'how' behind a project's mission, representing the practical steps to create change.

3 **Outputs** are the immediate and measurable results of the activities. They provide a quantitative summary of what has been accomplished within a community or project. Outputs can be counted, observed or documented and include metrics like the number of workshops held, the quantity of educational materials distributed or the frequency of service delivery. Outputs serve as progress indicators and are essential for tracking and evaluating the project's performance.

4 **Outcomes** are the broader and often qualitative changes experienced by participants or beneficiaries due to the activities and outputs. They represent the effects, benefits or transformations that occur. Outcomes can encompass changes in knowledge, behaviour, attitudes or living conditions. For example, if an activity involves providing nutrition education, an outcome might be an increase in the percentage of individuals who improve their dietary habits based on that education.

5 **Impact** is the ultimate and long-term consequence of a social intervention. It describes the enduring changes or effects on individuals and society that result from the outcomes. Impact is often the most challenging aspect to measure because numerous factors influence social issues and may take time to materialise fully. Impact can involve systemic changes, improved quality of life, increased equity or a reduction in the prevalence of a particular issue. For instance, the impact of a nutrition education program might be a noticeable decrease in obesity rates within a community over several years.

In summary, the social impact chain begins with the allocation of resources (inputs), progresses through the implementation of purposeful actions (activities) to produce measurable results (outputs), leads to meaningful changes in participants' lives (outcomes) and ultimately culminates in the long-term, transformative effects on society (impact). This framework helps charities and other organisations understand the pathway to achieving their social goals, assess their effectiveness and make informed decisions to maximise their positive influence on communities and society. The Social Impact Pathway is shown in Figure 9.3.

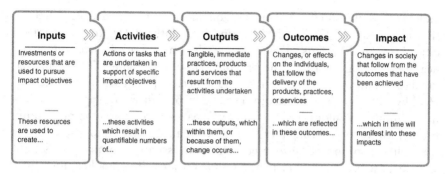

Inputs ≫	Activities ≫	Outputs ≫	Outcomes ≫	Impact
Investments or resources that are used to pursue impact objectives	Actions or tasks that are undertaken in support of specific impact objectives	Tangible, immediate practices, products and services that result from the activities undertaken	Changes, or effects on the individuals, that follow the delivery of the products, practices, or services	Changes in society that follow from the outcomes that have been achieved
These resources are used to create...	...these activities which result in quantifiable numbers of...	...these outputs, which within them, or because of them, change occurs...	...which are reflected in these outcomes...	...which in time will manifest into these impacts

FIGURE 9.3   Social impact value chain pathway.

Source: Adapted from Social Impact Investment Taskforce (2014).

Case Studies

To demonstrate how social impact value chains are created, this chapter uses case studies from three charities, namely Life Education Queensland, Asthma Australia and City Impact. The three cases provide an outline to explain how any program, product or service offered by a charity can be mapped onto a social impact pathway. The examples include programs that aim to increase children's health and wellbeing through school-based activities, another committed to ensuring no one in Australia lives a life restricted by asthma and a third that collaborates with communities aiming to reduce the incidence of domestic violence.

The first charity, Life Education Queensland, delivers the 'Healthy Eats' program in primary schools, in Queensland, Australia. Heathy Eating programs are an important means of improving the dietary behaviours of children. In Queensland, very few children (5%) consume the recommended daily serves of fruit and vegetables (Department of Health, 2018). An unhealthy diet has consequences for children's educational achievements (Burrows et al., 2017), and also for their health. In Australia, 28% of children are either overweight or obese (Australian Bureau of Statistics, 2022). These children are at increased risk of experiencing adverse physical and mental health outcomes in adulthood (Dalwood et al., 2020). The school environment is a key setting offering the opportunity to take socio-ecological approach to addressing diet-related health problems (Frerichs et al., 2015; Story et al., 2009).

The key objectives of Healthy Eats include: (1) improving the healthy eating environment and culture at each school, including providing children with greater access to healthier food options at school; (2) improve children's knowledge of the importance of healthy food choices; (3) increase children's intention to make healthier food choices;

and (4) increase children's consumption of vegetables and fruit at school (Isbanner et al., 2022; Social Marketing @ Griffith, 2021). To achieve these objectives, Healthy Eats takes a socioecological approach that extends its health education efforts to the broader school community. This approach involves tailoring responses to the unique needs of each school community. Healthy Eats assigns Community Development Officers to support schools in maintaining momentum, fostering partnerships and implementing program initiatives throughout the school year. The program also includes the delivery of nutrition-focused education sessions to primary school students, the provision of print and online resources to school communities, incentivisation of children to consume more fruits and vegetables, assistance to schools in implementing changes to their food environment and facilitation of partnerships between schools and external organisations to sustain improvements in school food environments (Isbanner et al., 2022; Social Marketing @ Griffith, 2021).

The second charity, Asthma Australia, is working towards their vision of ensuring no one experiences a life restricted by asthma. In Australia, around 39,000 people are hospitalised each year because of asthma (Asthma Australia, 2023), and in 2022, 455 people died due to asthma (Australian Bureau of Statistics, 2023a). Of the 2.7 million people in Australia who live with asthma, for 45% of them, their asthma is poorly controlled (Asthma Australia, 2023). Asthma Australia's services include helplines, the provision of training, advocacy and more. Asthma Australia is undertaking multiple approaches aimed towards different audiences, including individuals, communities, schools and healthcare organisations. Their activities include awareness raising, providing assistance to individuals, community engagement, school and healthcare staff engagements and training and political advocacy (Asthma Australia, 2023).

The third charity builds government–church–business–charity coalitions to alleviate social problems in the city of Gold Coast, Queensland, Australia. One of the issues they tackle is domestic and family violence. One program has been delivered through a partnership with the Motivating Action Through Empowerment (MATE) bystander program. Gender-based violence is a global issue, with estimates indicating one in three women worldwide have experienced either physical and/or sexual intimate partner violence, or non-partner sexual violence in their lifetime (World Health Organization, 2021). In 2022, the number of victims of sexual assault increased to 32,146 in Australia, and 84% were female – almost a quarter of these sexual assaults occurred in Queensland (Australian Bureau of Statistics, 2023b).

The MATE bystander program seeks to generate cultural change by making people aware of the roots domestic violence has in gender inequality and providing participants with a framework for taking prosocial bystander action (Mazerolle et al., 2019; Pearce et al., 2022). A train-the-trainer course has been created to expand the reach of the program. The charity facilitated coordination and collaboration between Christian churches to recruit faith leaders or members of their congregation to become MATE program trainers (Pearce et al., 2022). The program consists of a three-day MATE train-the-trainer workshop, delivered by MATE facilitators and covering leadership, bystander intervention, the nature of violence against women, and gender inequality. Trainers receive a MATE trainer manual and PowerPoint slide deck to use in their subsequent deliveries, and support materials including a refresher workshop after 12 months. After completing the train-the-trainer workshops, participants are accredited and encouraged to deliver the MATE program thorough their church ministries (Pearce et al., 2022).

For each charity, a social impact chain can be described. Calculations of social impact can then be created by understanding the costs of resources (inputs). A detailed account of activities and outputs is needed for clear cost estimates to be calculated. Outcome evaluations are needed to understand what has changed because of a person's interaction with a program, product, or service that has been delivered by a charity. Once outcomes are known, the costs of their cumulative effect can be calculated delivering an estimate of the cost savings for community that arise because of the organisations work. Figure 9.4 provides an overview of the impact pathway for programs delivered by three Australian charities. Figure 9.4 illustrates how resources invested progress through the implementation of purposeful actions (activities) to produce measurable results (outputs), capable of leading to meaningful changes in participants' lives (outcomes) and ultimately culminate in the long-term, transformative effects on society (impact).

Discussion

Social impact pathways align activities and outputs with outcomes, which allows contributions to any resulting social impact to be examined. This allows an organisation to understand how their program is working (or not), to use this understanding to adapt and refine their program, products or services, to achieve greater impact. It also allows learnings from one program to be shared with other programs. The provision of social impact pathways ensures that everyone can clearly understand the links between activities, outputs, outcomes and the contribution each line of effort has towards the delivery of outcomes that, with time, accumulate to achieve impact.

Activities describes the actions that organisations do capturing all the things that happen inside organisations. Many activities such as meetings, analysing and planning are tasks that other people may not see or experience, and therefore these tasks alone are not capable of delivering changes. Outputs describes the visible and tangible things that organisations produce for the individuals and communities they serve. Outputs are something that

	Inputs	Activities	Outputs	Outcomes	Impact
Life Education Queensland / Healthy Eats Program	Government funds; Charity/Donor funds; Charity staff hours; School Staff hours	Design and development of school modules (children and teachers); Design and development of canteen resources; Engagements with schools; Scheduling for school deliveries; Post delivery follow up support services	Module deliveries in schools; Teacher resources; Parent resources; Canteen resources; Follow up support resources	Increased knowledge of healthy eating in school children; Increased healthier choices by school children; Increase knowledge of healthy eating in parents; More supportive food environment in schools	Improved health and wellbeing for children
Asthma Australia	Government funds; Donor funds; Investment funds; Staff hours; Volunteer hours	Information sourcing; Communication planning and design (e.g. newsletters, social media); Website creation and updating; Training planning (school, community and healthcare organisation visits); Staffing recruitment, management and training; Volunteer recruitment, management and training	Hotline calls; One on one engagements; Community sessions; School sessions/training; Healthcare organisation sessions/training; Reports/Government submissions; Politician meetings	Good practice of asthma self-management; Regular medical check ins; Less hospitalisations; Environments do not trigger asthma. People surrounding those with asthma can support them	People with asthma lead a full and unrestricted life
City Impact / MATE bystander program	Charity/Donor funds; Charity staff hours; Participating church trainer hours	Liaison with MATE program owners and execution of partnership arrangement; Recruitment of faith leaders or congregants for train-the-trainer MATE workshop; Post workshop communication plan and preparation	MATE trainer manual and PowerPoint slide deck; Three-day MATE train-the-trainer workshops; Online Community of Practice group; Online MATE Leadership group; Adhoc topic- and program-related communications by email	Increased number of accredited trainers to deliver MATE program thorough church ministries; Delivery of MATE workshops within faith communities; Workshop participants use MATE program framework to take prosocial bystander action	Reduced Domestic and Family violence

FIGURE 9.4 Social impact chain: three charities addressing social issues.

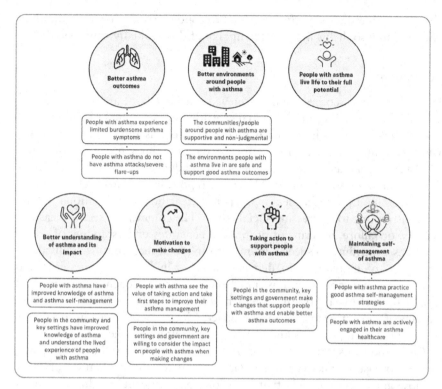

FIGURE 9.5 Asthma Australia's outcome framework.
Source: Asthma Australia (2023).

other people can interact with and experience. Outcomes are changes that occur in other people as a result of their interaction and experiences with an organisation's outputs. In the case of Asthma Australia, shown in Figure 9.5, the delivery of an outcome framework focuses attention on the changes that Asthma Australia's team are trying to achieve through delivery of programs containing outputs (e.g., hotline, training for school health staff, training for health professionals), advocacy (e.g., meetings with government), research (e.g., pilot programs).

Impact reporting moves the focus away from what charities say they do, and narrows focus onto what changes are occurring because of the charity's activities. Impact pathways offer a more standardised approach making it easier for the broader research and practitioner community to understand how intended outcomes are achieved. Impact pathways also support social return on investment calculations, which provide a deeper understanding of the levels of investment that are needed to deliver impact. The social impact chain aims to reduce the effort required to conduct social impact evaluations and, in doing so, helps increase the uptake of this evaluative approach.

Conclusion

Every day that outcomes are not achieved is a tragedy. A life is lost, another assault has occurred or an individual's health and wellbeing has continued to decline. This not only harms individuals, their friends and family, it costs the whole community. The charity sector is large, containing many organisations who seek to generate positive impact for individuals and communities across a wide range of social issues. However, reporting of outcomes or impact is not common practice, meaning it is not clear how organisational efforts are contributing to addressing social issues. The commercial sector measures success, or failure, in terms of profit, and generates understanding of which activities contribute to success by monitoring (and incentivising) individuals or groups of individuals to deliver outcomes in line with organisational goals. The charitable sector would benefit from approaches that produce a similar level of clarity about which activities lead to outcomes that are capable of generating lasting social impact, which would drive improvements to organisational practices and justify investment across the sector.

Clear and transparent reporting and governance approaches are urgently needed to ensure effective investment of resources, and utilisation of effort to close gaps in our society that have long been evident. Health and social inequities remain despite billions of dollars being invested, indicating a lack of understanding of how to effectively achieve the outcomes that are required. Evidence has accumulated across many social, health and environmental issues which clearly outlines what changes are needed to reverse the impact of social issues. While, in most cases, we already know what we need to do, it is clear not enough of the activities that we need to see are underway. Social impact measurement offers an approach to ensuring activities are focussed on the delivery of outputs capable of achieving intended outcomes. Social impact measurement will encourage organisations to focus activity on delivering outputs capable of achieving intended change. Measurement using social impact pathways will help to avoid overclaims and greenwashing. Outcomes can be saving a life, preventing an assault or improving a person's health or wellbeing so that people can lead full and unrestricted lives. Every intended outcome that is achieved by any organisation delivers change for the better.

Discussion Questions

1 When you think of particular charities, what are the impacts they seek, and how do those impacts manifest over time?

2 How could charities monitor data across their impact chain on a regular basis to improve their operations?
3 Long term – how can the charity sector better measure impact to understand how they jointly contribute to some of society's complex challenges?

References

Asthma Australia. (2023). *Impact Report 2022–2023 Influencing Change and Understanding Our Impact.* https://issuu.com/asthmaaustralia/docs/aa22-23_i mpact_report_v5_web?fr=sYmYzNjY3Nzk2OTk

Australian Bureau of Statistics. (2022). *Waist Circumference and BMI.* ABS. www.abs.gov.au/statistics/health/health-conditions-and-risks/waist-circumference-and-bmi/latest-release

Australian Bureau of Statistics. (2023a). *Causes of Death, Australia.* www.abs.gov.au/statistics/health/causes-death/causes-death-australia/2022#key-statistics

Australian Bureau of Statistics. (2023b). *Recorded Crime—Victims; 2021.* www.abs.gov.au/statistics/people/crime-and-justice/recorded-crime-victims/latest-release

Australian Charities and Not-for-profits Commission. (2022). *Major Rise in Australia's Charity Sector Revenue and Expenses.* www.acnc.gov.au/media/news/major-rise-australias-charity-sector-revenue-and-expenses

Blankenberg, F. (1995). *Methods of Impact Assessment Research Programme, Resource Pack and Discussion.* Oxfam UK/I and Novib, the Hague.

Burrows, T., Goldman, S., Olson, R. K., Byrne, B., & Coventry, W. L. (2017). Associations between selected dietary behaviours and academic achievement: A study of Australian school aged children. *Appetite, 116,* 372–380.

Clark, C., & Rosenzweig, W. (2004). *Double Bottom Line Project Report.* University of California, Berkeley.

Dalwood, P., Marshall, S., Burrows, T. L., McIntosh, A., & Collins, C. E. (2020). Diet quality indices and their associations with health-related outcomes in children and adolescents: An updated systematic review. *Nutrition Journal, 19*(1), 1–43.

Department of Health. (2018). *Are Queenslanders Meeting the Australian Dietary Guidelines? Daily Diets and Total Energy Intake.* www.health.qld.gov.au/__data/assets/pdf_file/0029/731198/diets-report-qld.pdf

Epstein, M. J., & Yuthas, K. (2017). *Measuring and Improving Social Impacts: A Guide for Nonprofits, Companies, and Impact Investors.* Routledge, Abingdon, UK.

Frerichs, L., Brittin, J., Sorensen, D., Trowbridge, M. J., Yaroch, A. L., Siahpush, M., Tibbits, M., & Huang, T. T. K. (2015). Influence of school architecture and design on healthy eating: A review of the evidence. *American Journal of Public Health (1971), 105*(4), e46–e57. https://doi.org/10.2105/AJPH.2014.302453

Hadad, S., & Gauca, O. (2014). Social impact measurement in social entrepreneurial organizations. *Management & Marketing, 9*(2), 119–136.

Isbanner, S., Carins, J., & Rundle-Thiele, S. (2022). Healthy eats—evaluation of a social marketing program delivered in primary school settings in Queensland. *International Journal of Environmental Research and Public Health, 19*(21), 14415.

Isbanner, S., Carins, J., & Rundle-Thiele, S. (under review, n.d.). Measuring what matters: An agenda to enhance the application of social impact in marketing.

Latané, B. (1981). The psychology of social impact. *American Psychologist*, 36(4), 343.

Mazerolle, P., Ross-Smith, S., & Dowling, A. (2019). Bringing in the bystander: Preventing violence and abuse. *Griffith Review*(65), 164–171.

Pearce, K., Borkoles, E., & Rundle-Thiele, S. (2022). Leveraging faith communities to prevent violence against women: lessons from the implementation and delivery of the Motivating Action through Empowerment (MATE) program. *International Journal of Environmental Research and Public Health*, 19(23), 15833.

Policy Bee UK. (2024). *UK Charity and Not-For-Profit Sector Statistics 2024*. www.policybee.co.uk/blog/uk-charity-statistics

Rawhouser, H., Cummings, M., & Newbert, S. L. (2019). Social impact measurement: Current approaches and future directions for social entrepreneurship research. *Entrepreneurship Theory and Practice*, 43(1), 82–115.

Social Impact Investment Taskforce. (2014). Measuring impact: Subject paper of the impact measurement working group. *Social Impact Investment Taskforce, UK Presidency of the G8*.

Social Marketing @ Griffith. (2021). Evaluation of Healthy Eats 2021. Griffith University. Retrieved 24 Jan from https://lifeeducationqld.org.au/wp-content/uploads/Life-Ed-Qld-Healthy-Eats-Evaluation-Report-March-2022.pdf

Story, M., Nanney, M., & Schwartz, M. (2009). Schools and obesity prevention: Creating school environments and policies to promote healthy eating and physical activity. *The Milbank Quarterly*, 87(1), 71–100. https://doi.org/https://doi.org/10.1111/j.1468-0009.2009.00548.x

Vanclay, F. (2003). International principles for social impact assessment. *Impact Assessment and Project Appraisal*, 21(1), 5–12.

Wainwright, S. (2002). *Measuring Impact: A Guide to Resources*. Harvard University Press, Harvard, MA.

World Health Organization. (2021). *Violence Against Women*. Retrieved 24 January 2024 from www.who.int/news-room/fact-sheets/detail/violence-against-women

10

LET'S GET SOCIAL

Why Charities Need to Consider the Social Enterprise Trading Model

Fran Hyde and Simon Pickering

Introduction

Charities need new income streams to secure their futures. Charities exist to focus on a cause or an issue requiring sustainable and predictable income so that they can continue to support their existing operations as well as innovate and grow. To generate the income needed to operate, charities in the United Kingdom (UK) have traditionally used a combination of donations, grants and commissioning, but the pressures on these traditional funding models is forcing charities to consider alternative ways to generate income to address need. Furthermore, charities need to consider that their next generation of supporters may be looking for different ways to show and give their support or to work with organisations that address causes, issues and need in society.

For charities to survive and thrive in the future, this chapter sets out why charities are well placed to consider social enterprise trading models to address social need <u>and</u> provide an income. Taking inspiration from the personal relationships and innovative methods which are often the hallmark of social enterprises, this chapter uses the approach of a 'professional conversation' recorded over a series of meetings with an experienced social entrepreneur, podcaster, trainer and consultant. Using a case study, we explore how the University of Suffolk has been part of work to educate and develop a deeper understanding of the opportunities for social enterprise within the area of Suffolk in the UK, showing the possibilities for university communities to play a key role in promoting social enterprise as a trading model within their regions.

DOI: 10.4324/9781003396802-10

Why Do Charities Need to Diversify from Traditional Income Streams?

Charitable organisations play a vital multifaceted role in society contributing to meeting need and addressing issues in areas ranging from healthcare and education to animal welfare and conservation, but to continue to operate charities need to look for new sources of income. In England and Wales, charities must be registered with the Charity Commission and among other requirements, evidence of their purpose of benefiting the public and the impact of their operations must be evident. The Charity Commission currently has 169,660 charities registered which employ 1,152,249 people (Charity Commission, 2024) and the National Council for Volunteer Organisations (NVCO) UK Civil Society Almanac reports an income for the charity sector of 56.9 billion pounds, with the public providing or donating 47% or 26.4 billion pounds in 2020/21 (NVCO, 2023). The activities, beneficiaries, volunteers, shops and fundraising efforts of charities have become an integral part of contemporary society, but charitable organisations are facing cuts to income just at a time when the demand for their services is increasing (Young, 2023).

UK charities have become dependent on income from a combination of donations, grants and commissioning of their services. At times, charities can become very reliant on just one of these three sources of income and with income levels varying each year this leaves charities vulnerable (McDonnell et al., n.d.). Diversifying funding sources so that charities can plan their existing operations and grow to meet future demand is not straightforward, as charities contend with challenging UK trading conditions described by economists as very complex and attributed to multiple interconnected issues (Millard et al., 2023). The impact on charities of some of these issues are outlined in a recent Charities Aid Foundation (CAF) Charity Resilience Index report. This report explains that in the UK, charities are now battling with higher demand for their services and requests of support, whilst simultaneously dealing with lower income and inflated operating costs. The report notes that whilst this began as result of the cost-of-living crisis in 2021, these conditions for charities have now become entrenched (CAF, 2023; Young, 2023).

Even before the current cost-of-living crisis, charity income had been severely impacted by the COVID-19 pandemic with the inevitable disruption negatively impacting on the sector. From the cancelation of large-scale fundraising and sponsorship events such as The London Marathon with the loss of 66 million pounds in income for charities (Cipriani, 2020) to the forced closure of charity retail shops in national lockdowns; however of even more concern to charities is that these resulting variations to income from donations during the pandemic appears to have become established (Smith, 2021). Significantly, the 2023 CAF UK Giving report, the UKs largest and longest running study on giving behaviour in the UK, reports that the proportion of people sponsoring someone for a charity and the number of individuals donating have not returned to pre-pandemic levels for UK charities (CAF, 2023). Worryingly for charities the CAF report states that "the value of the typical donation, in real terms has been eroding for some time" (CAF, 2023, p. 14) with the overall number of individuals donating falling and by far the largest group of donors aged over 65. Whilst fundraising activity will remain important to charities, and must be noted for other contributions in areas such as awareness, relationship building and outreach, charities urgently need to consider how to 'replace' this lost income as well as look for trading models to generate new and sustainable income.

Charities in the UK can receive commissioned funding from a variety of government organisations with funding linked to the charity for filling contracts to deliver specific services within a population or geographical area. For instance, in the hospice sector, services can be commissioned by local Integrated Care Boards (ICB) who may decide to commission a hospice to provide night care or home visits to people in an area of England with a terminal diagnosis. But this model of commissioned funding for charities is also under pressure. In 2019, a report by the social impact think tank and consultancy New Philanthropy Capital reported that two-thirds of charities were subsidising public sector contracts with other income (Collinge, 2019). *The Guardian* newspaper highlighted a worrying implication of current economic pressures for charities as charities heavily subsidise underfunded local authority and National Health Service contracts. *The Guardian* article outlined that it is donations to charities from the public which is providing the necessary additional income to ensure the fulfilment of commissioned services; therefore preventing insolvencies as a result of this underfunding of the commissioned work undertaken by the charity sector (Butler, 2023). This underfunding of commissioned services in the healthcare sector and its impact on hospices was highlighted in a recent All Party Parliamentary Group (APPG) for Hospice and End of Life Care (Hospice UK, 2024) which found that "despite a law passed in 2022, the way hospice services are commissioned in England is not fit for purpose" (p. 3) reporting that "hospices are not being commissioned on a level playing field with NHS services, as ICB funding often does not reflect the true cost of care.. leaving hospices to foot the rest of the bill through further fundraising efforts" (2024, p. 3). The challenge for hospices and other charities is how to reconcile this funding gap with their charitable purpose and objectives. In other words, simply withdrawing a service because the commissioned contract does not now cover the full costs of delivery is not a decision that charities make lightly knowing that in the current UK economic climate, those in need are unlikely to be offered any alternative provision.

Pressures outlined above on individual giving and government funded commissioned contracts are exacerbated by changes and new challenges emerging for grant making trusts and organisations who have long been an established income source for charities. Grant-making organisations are receiving unprecedented levels of applications which, coupled with the increasing base costs for charities due to the increasing cost of living, is putting pressure on the funds available. Effectively, the result is that the charity sector is 'more expensive to operate' with less grant-making capacity from grant-making organisations. In addition, a recent worrying development is that several grant-making organisations are ceasing their activities. Lankelly Chase who have provided grants for over 60 years recently cited their grant making model as "entangled with Colonial Capitalism that it inevitably continues the harms of the past into the present" (Lankelly Chase, 2024) and will now be redistributing and closing their fund. Such challenges associated with grant making threaten this source of funding for charities and what has historically been seen as a reliable income stream for maintaining charitable work.

Trading in Line with Charitable Objectives?

In the UK, some charities have already begun to explore new ways to trade which generate income to ensure financial resilience and adjust to changes in consumer behaviour. Whilst a good number of charities have operated more traditional trading models such as charity retail for a long time, many charities have begun to embrace digital technology to diversify into trading online, innovating to offer products such as ecards and securing retail income by incorporating e commerce into their existing retail model (St Christophers, 2024). Specialist charity retail shops can attract the interest of collectors or vintage enthusiasts and be considered desirable shopping locations (Cohen et al., 2022) and some charities have expanded their physical stores to incorporate cafes as well as expanding into catering services (Salvation Army, 2024). Developing trading in these and other ways will achieve some income diversification and relieve the pressure on the traditional funding models for charities, but will not necessarily be in line with a charities purpose or objectives. For instance, whilst charity lotteries have become an important revenue stream, there is some debate around whether this income is a gamified charity donation or income derived from encouraging gambling (Peloza et al., 2007). Trading which is not clearly linked to a charities charitable objectives may need to be accommodated through a separate trading subsidiary operating as a separate company, which may be owned by the charity with the subsidiary donating the bulk of its profits to the charitable organisation (NVCO, 2022b).

A social enterprise trading model will provide income as well as opportunities for charities to build on their core competences and continue to be purposeful in addressing social need. Using a series of professional conversations recorded with Simon Pickering founder of Dot-to-Dot Training and Consultancy between January and March 2024, we consider how the social enterprise trading model allows charities to continue to meet social need and address causes whilst delivering an income.

What Is a Social Enterprise?

A social enterprise is a business that incorporates three core elements; *'People, Profit and Planet'* and for Simon, a *'thoroughbred'* social enterprise trading model delivers all three, making a profit whilst creating social and environment impact. In the academic study of social enterprise, a widely agreed upon definition of social enterprise is hard to find, but from a recent extensive literature review the dual mission of social and economic value creation was established as an essential criterion for a social enterprise (Saebi et al., 2019). A social enterprise is a sustainable *'economic engine'* of trading that generates profit whilst achieving social and environmental impact. Simon explains that it is not very common for an organisation to cover all three core elements of people planet and profit, and that it is more usually profit and people or profit and planet. An example of a profit and planet social enterprise is environmentally focused social enterprises REMO who for almost 20 years have rescued, reused, repaired, refurbished and recycled materials to create sustainable, useful and creative products diverting material from landfill (REMO, 2024). Or, for a social enterprise which is a people focused social enterprise 'Half the Story' is a social enterprise biscuit company that employs individuals recovering from homelessness providing biscuits for the hospitality and conference sector (Half the Story, 2024). It is quite rare to find a social enterprise trading model delivering all three (people, profit and planet) in equal measure, but when you do in Simon's words *"that is a beautiful thing"*. For example, Simon worked with a social enterprise in East London called 'Bikeworks' who "believe everyone should have access to cycling to increase physical activity, wellbeing, and connectivity" (Bikeworks, 2024). The mission of Bikeworks is to encourage people to get into cycling through its trading activities of Team Building Challenges, Cycle Maintenance Courses and Cycle Instructor Training Courses. Bikeworks then use the surplus generated from these activities to provide free-to-access inclusive community cycling initiatives and have worked with over 3000 people with disabilities and carers attending regular club sessions for free.

The social enterprise trading model is an expression of intent and not a legal entity. For example, Simon explains that establishing a social enterprise is intentionally saying *"we are a company created to create social or environmental impact and by the way, we're going to make profit along the way too"*. According to Social Enterprise UK (SEUK), the UK's membership body for social enterprises, there are more than 131,000 social enterprises in the UK, contributing 60 billion pounds to the UK economy and employing around 2.3 million people (Social Enterprise UK, 2024). The trading model of a social enterprise can be formed under different legal structures, for example, as a limited company or under the structure of Community Interest Company (CIC). A CIC is a business model which recognises activities undertaken for the benefit of the community and not purely for a profit and was established in 2005 to encourage investment in the social enterprise sector with now over 30,000 companies registered in the UK (Edwards, 2023).

Just like pure for-profit organisations, successful social enterprises grow and expand through scaling their activities. For example, 'Invisible-Cities' trains people affected by homelessness empowering individuals to become walking tour guides of their own city offering alternative tours to tourists and locals (Invisible-Cities, 2024). Invisible-Cities is a social enterprise and not a walking tour company because through its activities, it raises awareness about homelessness and by working with people who have been impacted by homelessness, it is changing perceptions that exists around homelessness. So, Invisible-Cities addresses social need (people) encourages walking (planet) but also makes a profit. The ability of social enterprises such as Invisible-Cities to build successful businesses around diverse teams was noted by the Lord Victor Adebowde, Chair of SEUK. In a recent report, he noted that social enterprises are often operating in the most deprived areas of the country but through the social enterprise trading model have been able to retain staff at a time when for profit companies have had to shed staff to retain profits (Social Enterprise UK, 2023)

The role of social investment is a key element of the growth and scale of social enterprises. Social investment seeks to invest in organisations and projects which tackle social issues, generating positive social impact alongside financial returns. Social investment is not a new finance product for the charity sector and organisations such as Big Issue Invest (Big Issue, 2024), Social Investment Business (2024), CAF Bank (2024), and Big Society Capital (2024) are experienced organisations who are already supporting charities to access social investment. However, social investment is widely underutilised and misunderstood and for smaller charities, the concept of loan finance is not preferred by more risk adverse trustees, with understandable reasoning. However, it could be argued that whilst some trustees and boards of charities may wish to maintain the status quo and rely on traditional income streams, the considerable challenges surrounding these models is driving a need to explore and understand different financial models. Of course, charities could themselves act as investors, investing to scale their own trading entities to maintain growth.

The Opportunities for Charities

Successful Social Entrepreneur Matt Parfitt feels that a social enterprise needs to have *"the compassion and heart of a charity but the sustainability and creativity of a business"* (Parfitt, 2023). Drawing on these suggestions, Simon identifies the opportunity in social enterprise is for charities to leverage their expertise in areas such as identifying impact but also address a skills gap and build a more diverse workforce. Simon suggests that for charities there is a danger that innovation within the organisation can become stifled because of the overbearing governance structures of charities which are required by the Charity Commission, and the framework in which registered charities must operate. With its need for an entrepreneurial approach or the core requirement of social enterprise which Simon describes as the essential requirement of *"Entrepreneurial Flair"* social enterprise offers charities and their workforce a new opportunity.

The following section proposes the successful components of a social enterprise (see Figure 10.1) exploring these in more detail in relation to the skills and experience charities have in leadership and impact as well as identifying areas for development such as a requirement for innovation.

Leadership – Simon's experiences of working with social enterprises shows that the reality of running a social enterprise is far more complex and difficult than running a straight for-profit business but presents similar challenges to those regularly faced by leaders of charities. Citing *"more factors, more*

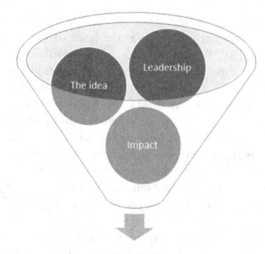

A successful Social Enterprise

FIGURE 10.1 A successful social enterprise.
Source: The authors.

stakeholders involved and so more accountability to other people", Simon sees that this expertise of dealing with multiple stakeholders as vital in the successful operation of a social enterprise. Drawing on recent work written on 'purposeful leadership' by social enterprise practitioner Liam Black (2023) Simon feels that whilst *"the individuals who can do this and make it work are a particular breed and species"*, the attributes of a charity leader such as their motivation by purpose make charity leaders well placed to lead a social enterprise.

A particular challenge for charity leaders looking into the social enterprise trading model would be how to address the *"Entrepreneurial Flair"* which Simon suggests sits at the heart of a successful social enterprise. It is interesting to note that whilst the CICs structure was introduced to encourage social entrepreneurship; establishing an organisation which can be socially or environmentally driven as well as making a profit. Simon feels that the charity structure can in some cases achieve the exact opposite. For example, the business model of a charity with the associated compliance and governance can stifle entrepreneurial people or as Simon suggests *"tie them up in all sorts of knots so they cannot move and create any social environment and impact"*. So, whilst charity leaders will be experienced at navigating complicated governance structures and dealing with a board of trustees, a social enterprise trading model will need a slightly different approach. Simon identifies this as an opportunity for charities to use the more exciting and dynamic social enterprise trading model to bring new skills and expertise into organisations and the charity sector.

The commercially viable idea – there are important questions Simon believes need to be asked about the product or service at the heart of the social enterprise trading model such as *"Is it a good idea, has it got mainstream appeal, is it marketable, is it a good product or service, do people need it?"* adding that for the social enterprise trading model to be successful, it is vital that the product or service does not need to be explained and must be of high quality. Simon views a challenge for charities is to understand that the product or service must *"stand alone and be competitive, high quality and reliable"*. So, many social enterprises flow back to needing the public sector as a core customer, but Simon explains that the ability to secure a product or service that is valuable to mainstream society, thus moving away from being fully reliant on the public sector, has a far greater potential for lasting success and scale. For example, Simon gives the example Recycling Lives as a standout example as the UK's largest TV recycling company working to support through employment those inside and on release from Prison (Recycling Lives, 2024).

An important area of expertise for charities to leverage according to Simon is that *"they are good at relationship building in a natural and authentic manner*" and a successful social enterprise requires the same approach. Simon gives the example of a social enterprise he worked with some time ago who secured a local council contract to cut the grass of elderly and disabled individuals. Staff were from a charity, so Simon saw that they understood the importance of the relationships and were aware of the issue of social isolation. Simon observed the staff behaviour with clients describing this as "*Let's stop and have a cup of tea with Elsie, who's 92 and hasn't seen anyone that week*". Staff at this social enterprise realised that this may contribute to 'Elsie' being less socially isolated. Simon suggests that this approach adds significant value offering charities operating in the social enterprise space some advantage over a traditional organisation. Charities have expertise and experience, and the established 'culture' which has embedded an understanding of the outcomes and social value in all the activities which they are undertaking.

Impact – as a key element which makes social enterprises distinct from what Simon sees as a "*a straight-line commercial organisation*" social impact must be embedded into the social enterprise model, not achieved when profits generated are then spent in a more 'traditional' approaches to achieve social impact, i.e., donating a percentage of profits to a charity.

Telling the impact story and communicating value proposition for all the stakeholder's involved in social enterprise is complicated, but Simon suggests this is a key area in which charities have relevant and valuable experience. Understanding the importance of tracking activities and collating outcomes to demonstrate impact is often the necessary work associated with receiving grants or funds for services commissioned by local Government authorities or in areas such as Health. The area of impact which may be new to charities Simon suggests is '*selling*' the social return of the services or products of a social enterprise business model. For example, for a construction company buying '*end of build*' cleaning services from a social enterprise and communicating the relationship they have with a social enterprise can lead to winning contracts through the procurement process. This is because employing a social enterprise is a far more genuine answer to questions often posed about social value and included in most public sector procurement processes. Thus, for a number of organisations, working with a social enterprise can become very commercially valuable.

Bridging the gap between charities and a social enterprise trading model, at the same time as introducing new communities to social enterprise, presents an opportunity for universities. And hosting activities fosters a deeper knowledge and understanding of the possibilities offered by a social enterprise trading model. Activities might include introducing start up programmes to student populations, engaging local stakeholders and initiatives such as the Civic Universities Network (2024). In the higher education sector such activities are frequently undertaken in Enterprise Education, Careers and Knowledge Exchange work to focus university activities on leading societal, economic and environmental advancements in their regions. Activities can be supported through Higher Education Innovation Funding (HEIF) from UK Research and Innovation awards to support knowledge exchange between higher education providers which benefits society and the economy (UKRI, 2024). The final section of this chapter details the case study of the University of Suffolk Business Engagement, Careers and Employability teams whose work with academics and the wider Suffolk community has begun to foster a deeper understanding of Social Enterprise within Suffolk.

Building Social Enterprise in Suffolk through Boot Camps

Over the last 2 years, the University of Suffolk 'Make a Difference Social Enterprise Boot Camps' (MAD Boot Camps) have been attended by over 40 individuals. The MAD Boot Camp is a start-up program but for individuals who are socially or environmentally motivated providing an opportunity for students to learn alongside members of the local community how to set up their own enterprise which creates impact as well as generates an income. Run over several days, these camps are promoted and open to the local community, current students as well as alumni. MAD Boot Camps aim to get young people familiar with the concept of social enterprise showing participants a business model which is a powerful way to tackle social problems.

Funded initially by a combination of HEIF government 'Levelling Up' funding (GOV, 2021) and Ipswich Borough Council, the programmes for the MAD Boot Camps was developed by members of the University of Suffolk Business, Careers, Employability and Entrepreneurship team (University of Suffolk, 2024). Taking participants through the social enterprise trading model step-by-step, the programme ends with an opportunity for participants to pitch for grant funding. The MAD Boot Camp includes sessions on a variety of areas such as Ideation, Business Canvass Modelling and Marketing with a range of University of Suffolk academics and local practitioners, including this chapter's authors, leading sessions. The camp includes a pitching masterclass to prepare participants for pitching in front of a panel of experts. The successful projects are awarded funding which can be up to as much as £2000 as well as being offered ongoing support and access to useful campus facilities such as the University of Suffolk Innovation Labs co-working facilities for startups and business. Three social enterprises from the MAD Boot Camps are now registered as CICs with several participants successfully attracting further funding from funds such as Innovate UK. The longer-term vision is to establish an incubation program to help these registered social enterprise startups to scale and grow.

Reflecting on the MAD program Simon concludes that it should be noted that participants may go through the MAD Boot Camps and get to the end and say *"actually I'm going to do a for-profit business"* but for Simon, this is still an important outcome because participants have had the opportunity to explore and develop a business model operating at the intersection of social motivation and entrepreneurship. As such, ensuring an understanding of social enterprise is introduced, developed and supported in a community is an important role for a university seeking to demonstrate its local impact.

Extending the reach of this programme students, as well as the University of Suffolk staff involved in MAD Boot Camps worked with Simon on the 'Let's Get Social Conference for Social Enterprises and Charities'. This day conference in Ipswich, Suffolk in November 2023 aimed to create connection, collaboration and creative social impact solutions for place-based issues that are pertinent to local communities in Suffolk. Held in Ipswich Town Hall with over 70 charities and social enterprise leaders attending the aims for the day were about demystifying the social enterprise trading model and showing the opportunities provided by social enterprise utilising a place-based approach in addressing social need.

The Future of Social Enterprise as Part of the Nonprofit Landscape

Uncertainties in all forms of income combined with rising demand mean charities need to focus not only on securing more income but considering new sources of income. This chapter has proposed that the social enterprise model offers a way for charities to leverage key competencies whilst developing income streams from trading aligned to their charitable objectives. Exploration of social enterprise by charities requires education of stakeholders in particular charity trustees. The opportunities for charities are that as well as securing much needed new income, they can offer work at the intersection of entrepreneurial and social motivation. Thus, social enterprise can reach beyond the activities and operations of the traditional charity model. Social enterprise offers charities a way with which to engage with individuals whose motivation is to build a profitable business, social need and have social impact embedded from the outset.

The University of Suffolk case study provides an example of a way forward for other universities showing how universities are well placed to operate at the core of the network needed to develop knowledge and expertise in social enterprise. 'Make a Difference Social Enterprise Boot Camps' run by the University of Suffolk offers stakeholder engagement as well as a chance to consider how to address place-based social need. The work at the University of Suffolk shows how universities can play a significant role in developing a workforce who understands the opportunities offered by the social enterprise model and reach out to bring charities into this network.

Discussion Questions

1 The chapter gave several different examples of social enterprises which have been established in the UK. Search locally to find an example in your local area and investigate the 'people, planet and profit' contribution of this social enterprise.
2 Communicating impact of a social enterprise trading model is a very important part of the success of a social enterprise organisation. Look for examples of how this is done well and not so well by charities and social enterprises.
3 Using the example given in the chapter of a building or construction company using a social enterprise to carry out an 'end of build' clean, consider how a building company buying an 'end of build' clean from a social enterprise can communicate this action to its own stakeholders?

Acknowledgements

The authors would like to acknowledge the valuable contributions of Amy Carpenter and Hannah Page as well as the wider work of the University of Suffolk Business, Careers, Employability and Entrepreneurship team in the development of this chapter.

References

Big Issue (2024) Big Issue Invest. Available at: www.bigissue.com/invest/ [accessed 20-Feb-2024].
Big Society Capital (2024) Investing for social capital. Available at https://bigsociety capital.com/ [accessed 20-Feb-2024].
Bikeworks (2024) There is a cycling experience for everyone. Available at: www.bikeworks.org.uk/
Black, L. (2023) *How to Lead with Purpose Publisher.* Northwich, UK: Practical Inspiration Publishing. ISBN: 9781788604079
Butler, P. (2023) www.theguardian.com/society/2023/nov/13/charities-near-insolvency-after-subsidising-public-sector-contracts
CAF (2023) World Index Giving. Available at: www.cafonline.org/insights/research/world-giving-index?gad_source=1&gclid=EAIaIQobChMI-rT409PihwMVrJNQ Bh0pCiKDEAAYASAAEgKAJfD_BwE [accessed 20-Jan-2024].
CAF Bank (2024) Helping charities to make a better society. Available at www.cafbank.org [accessed 20-Feb-2024].
Charity Commission (2024) Sector over view Jan 07 2024. Available at https://register-of-charities.charitycommission.gov.uk/sector-data/sector-overview [accessed 20-Jan-24].

Cipriani, V. (2020) London marathon postponed to October due to coronavirus. www.civilsociety.co.uk/news/london-marathon-postponed-to-october-over-coronavirus.html [accessed 7-Jan-2024]

Civic University Network (2024) A national network of universities committed to transforming lives and places. https://civicuniversitynetwork.co.uk/ [accessed 7-Jan-2024]

Cohen, S., Mackertich, J., & Lawrence, I. (2022) The best charity shops in London. www.timeout.com/london/shopping/best-charity-shops-in-london [accessed 7-Jan-2024].

Collinge (2019) Contracts. https://npproduction.wpenginepowered.com/wp-content/uploads/2019/03/Contracts-19-three-page.pdf [accessed 8-Jan-2024].

Edwards, L. (2023) An introduction to community interest companies. https://companieshouse.blog.gov.uk/2023/08/31/an-introduction-to-community-interest-companies/ [Accessed 8-Jan-2024]

GOV (2021) New levelling up and community investments. www.gov.uk/government/collections/new-levelling-up-and-community-investments [accessed 21-Feb-24].

Half the Story (2024) It's not about the biscuit. www.halfthestory.uk/ [accessed 21-Feb-24].

Hospice UK (2024) Government funding for hospices. https://hukstage-new-bucket.s3.eu-west-2.amazonaws.com/s3fs-public/2024-02/APPG%20Report%20-%20Government%20funding%20for%20Hospices%20HUK.pdf?VersionId=0l8T4jC5V2C0zRKQLFs9ClZ5QZ5xEiOs [accessed 20-Jan-2024].

Invisible – Cities (2024) Our Mission. https://in visible-cities.org/our-mission/

Lankelly Chase (2024) Lankelly Chase to wholly redistribute its assets over the next five years. https://lankellychase.org.uk/news/lankelly-chase-to-wholly-redistribute-its-assessts-over-the-next-five-years/ (accessed 20-Jan-2024]

McDonnell, D., Mohan, J., & Duggan, A. (n.d.) Income dependence and diversification of UK charities at the onset of Covid-19. www.birmingham.ac.uk/documents/college-social-sciences/social-policy/tsrc/incomedependencyanddiversification.pdf [accessed 16-Feb-2024]

Millard, S., Low, H., & Carbo. P B (2023) www.niesr.ac.uk/blog/what-are-main-issues-facing-uk-economy

NVCO (2022a) www.ncvo.org.uk/news-and-insights/news-index/uk-civil-society-almanac-2023/

NVCO (2022b) Trading and charities. www.ncvo.org.uk/help-and-guidance/running-a-charity/financial-management/tax-and-trading/trading-and-charities/ [accessed 20-Jan-2024].

NVCO (2023) UK civil society almanac. Available at: /www.ncvo.org.uk/news-and-insights/news-index/uk-civil-society-almanac-2023/?gad_source=1&gclid=EAIaIQobChMIz8D8rNzihwMVe5JQBh3ZeDkNEAAYASAAEgKmBvD_BwE [accessed 20-Jan-2024]

Parfitt, M. (2023) *The Story of Grace Enterprises. Let's Get Social Conference for Social Enterprises and Charities.* Ipswich November 2023

Peloza, J., & Hassay, D. (2007) Does vice make nice? The viability and virtuousness of charity lotteries, *Journal of Nonprofit & Public Sector Marketing*, 18:1, 57–80, DOI: 10.1300/J054v18n01_04

ReclingLives (2024) Recycling Lives Services. https://recyclinglives.com/

Remo (2024) Remo about. https://remo.org.uk/

150 Fran Hyde and Simon Pickering

Saebi, T., Foss, N. J., & Linder, S. (2019). Social entrepreneurship research: Past achievements and future promises. *Journal of Management, 45*(1), 70–95. https://doi.org/10.1177/0149206318793196

Salvation Army (2024) The Salvation Army Cafes - Serving the community. www.salvationarmy.org.uk/cafes

Smith (20 21) How has Covid-19 affected charitable giving? www.economicsobservatory.com/how-has-covid-19-affected-charitable-giving [accessed 21-Feb-24].

Social Enterprise UK (2023) *Mission critical. State of Social Enterprise Survey 2023.* UK: Social Enterprise UK

Social Enterprise UK (2024) Social enterprises are businesses with a social or environmental purpose. www.socialenterprise.org.uk/

Social Investment Business (2024) Finance and support for a more equal society. www.sibgroup.org.uk/

St Christopher's (2024) Our shops. www.stchristophers.org.uk/shops

UKRI (2024) Higher Education Innovation Funding. Available at: www.ukri.org/what-we-do/browse-our-areas-of-investment-and-support/higher-education-innovation-fund/#:~:text=We%20provide%20funding%20for%20knowledge,to%20the%20economy%20and%20society [accessed on 15-Feb-2024].

University of Suffolk (2024) Engagement careers and employability. www.uos.ac.uk/business/business-eng agement/

Young (2023) Spring budget 2023: funding and implications for charities. www.ncvo.org.uk/news-and-insights/news-index/spri.ng-budget-2023-funding-and-implications-for-charities/

11

CHANGING COURSE

American Arts Nonprofits, Inertia and Place-Based Marketing

Trevor Meagher

The landscape of the American arts sector is nearly as diverse as the nation itself. It swells with entertainment companies, boutique art dealers, privately owned studios and arts academies (Kim, 2017). Cultural nonprofits operating within this environment face an especially daunting array of challenges. Although nonprofit legal status provides significant benefits for these organizations – e.g., tax exemption, the ability to solicit charitable donations, and the implied legitimacy associated with recognition as mission-driven entities – they must also contend with structural and social hurdles that present additional difficulties (Kim, 2017). Compared with most other developed nations, centralized government spending on arts support is both miniscule and more controversial (Rius-Ulldemolins, 2023).[1] Further, the same nonprofit status that confers benefits to arts nonprofits also places them into competition with other mission-serving organizations, many of which are seen as more worthy of donors' limited philanthropic dollars (Kim & van Ryzin, 2014).

Arts administrators have historically attempted to navigate these difficulties, attract audiences and secure donor support by emphasizing the personal and economic value of arts engagement (Meagher, Bezboruah & Suh, 2024). In recent years, pro-arts voices have shifted towards emphasizing cultural nonprofits' place-linked qualities and potential in order to cultivate dense local support networks and insulate them from existential danger (Kim & Benenson, 2023). Now, advocates and marketers seek to depict these organizations as integral partners embedded within the fabric of their local communities. This marks a crucial shift in organizational promotion – from transactional to institutional (Rentschler & Radbourne, 2007).

DOI: 10.4324/9781003396802-11

This chapter explores the latter approach through both scholarly and journalistic[2] sources. It briefly traces its emergence as part of the larger cultural placemaking movement before providing examples of its use by arts organizations in three American communities. Following a brief discussion of the challenges and opportunities presented by this strategy, we conclude with a prediction: the future of cultural nonprofit marketing in America is locally focused, community driven and centered on attempts to transform arts organizations into local institutions.

Old Ways, and New: Utilitarianism and the Rise of Placemaking

Traditional arts marketing and advocacy

In American nonprofits, general arts advocacy – here understood as any attempt to garner social, political or financial support for the arts – is often closely intertwined with organization-specific marketing designed to increase event attendance or cultivate an organizational brand. Arts advocates and marketers frequently seek to connect the interests of their associated organizations with the health and wellbeing of the cultural sector as a whole (Scheff & Kotler, 1996). In an environment where governmental support is operationally insufficient, philanthropic dollars are scarce, and numerous organizations share overlapping missions, this approach makes sense (Bernstein, 2006; Boorsma & Chiaravalloti, 2010). By equating the good of the field with that of the organization, marketers and advocates hope to better attract the attention of sympathetic philanthropists, policymakers and audiences.

Traditionally, these arguments are utilitarian in nature. In a recent study examining publications across the six decades since the founding of the National Endowment for the Arts, Meagher, Bezboruah & Suh (2024) identified only five different approaches to arts advocacy in America. Four of these advocacy strategies shared a single central assumption: successful promotion of the arts requires demonstration that they _do_ something for individuals or contemporary society as a whole. Further, the relative proportional popularity of these arguments is shockingly static across different eras. Rentschler & Radbourne (2007) reveal similar trends at the organizational level, citing the consistency with which marketers traditionally focus on commodifying the arts to solicit audience attendance or philanthropic support.

Taken together, these studies reveal a conceptual inertia that has taken hold of the sector. There have been dramatic sociopolitical and economic shifts in American society, but advocates, researchers and marketers have remained remarkably consistent in promoting the arts with the same techniques. Despite these well-constructed assertions, arts organizations continue to struggle. They are still reeling from the combined pressures of the COVID-19 pandemic, the post-Great Recession economy and the existential attrition stemming from these existing promotional approaches' diminishing returns (Ostrower, 2021).

A place for placemaking

Recent developments in American arts advocacy indicate a shift away from this shared mentality. Following the intellectual traditions of seminal urbanist Jane Jacobs (1961), scholars, marketers and policymakers have developed a fascination with cultural placemaking. Rather than associating organizations with the cultural sector as a whole or focusing on prestige, commodification and value extraction, advocates are now beginning to emphasize arts organizations' potential for making meaningful civic contributions at the local level (Grodach & Loukaitu-Siders, 2007). This intellectual movement emphasizes the place-linked histories and characteristics that make communities unique, asserting that arts organizations can lead socioeconomic growth by simultaneously preserving and promoting shared cultural identities (Florida, 2014; Crisman, 2022). Ideally, this will result in tight-knit communities where arts nonprofits enjoy high levels of audience engagement as well as local political and financial support.

This argument is compelling – but not without its problems. Potential gentrification is a primary concern, as placemaking initiatives are often associated with aggressive construction and land development initiatives that may displace or disenfranchise local marginalized populations (Grodach, Foster & Murdoch, 2014). Additionally, placemaking initiatives remain largely untested. Their goals are often lofty but unspecific, meaning that 'success' is difficult to predict or evaluate (Markusen, 2013). Fortunately, recent scholarship highlights this gap, urging both general advocates and organizational marketers to carefully consider their goals and expectations while engaging in place-focused advocacy (Markusen & Gadwa, 2010).

Despite these challenges, place-focused arts marketing strategies have thus far demonstrated significant opportunities for nonprofit advocates. The central argument clearly resonates with audiences and stakeholders, as evidenced by arts investments and surging adoption of cultural policies at the state and municipal levels nationwide (Grodach & Loukaitu-Siders, 2007; Crisman, 2022).

The remainder of this chapter explores the use of place-focused arts marketing in three metropolitan contexts. Santa Fe, New Mexico offers a long-running historical example of placemaking done right. Dallas, Texas is a city transitioning between traditional and place-focused approaches to arts promotion. Finally, Detroit, Michigan represents a future filled with opportunities to implement these strategies.

Santa Fe, New Mexico: Crafting a History of Success

Context: A century of the arts

Santa Fe is home to a robust cultural ecosystem that consistently ranks among the most arts-vibrant communities nationwide (SMU DataArts, 2020). Scholars, artists and visitors flock to the city, contributing to a tourism-driven economy anchored by the region's cultural reputation (Hanifl, 2019; New Mexico Department of Cultural Affairs, 2023). Branded 'The City Different', Santa Fe possesses near-mythic status as a haven for arts-lovers. This image has been carefully and deliberately crafted over decades, with local cultural institutions playing a prominent role in its creation (Wilson, 1997; Hartley, 2005). The establishment of an artists' colony in the late 1910s and early 1920s represents the first recognizable beginning of this campaign, with several of the founding members and their associates noting that the area's character lent itself to compelling promotional storytelling (Gaither, 1957; Hartley, 2005).

Throughout the intervening century, arts advocates and marketers in Santa Fe have continuously emphasized the region's unique local culture, history and peoples in order to develop the city's reputation and economy (Wilson, 1997; Hartley, 2005; Hanifl, 2019). By almost any economic metric, the strategy has been remarkably successful. In 2023, Santa Fe ranked within the top 1% of US cities for the number of arts and culture nonprofits per capita (SMU DataArts, 2023). The year prior, the sector generated over $350 million in economic activity and directly supported over 1250 jobs – quite the feat for a town of approximately 155,000 residents (New Mexico Department of Cultural Affairs, 2023).

Rather than pinpoint a specific organization as the singular driver of this vitality, it is best to understand Santa Fe's cultural economy as a dense network of artists and nonprofits promoting a shared identity.

The Santa Fe approach: Begin with a sense of place

Although there is a healthy market for almost any type of art in Santa Fe, local artists and organizations have drawn most heavily from indigenous Pueblo and Zuni Indian cultural traditions and aesthetics – or have entered into direct partnerships with artisans from these tribes (Reeve, 1981). This influence is omnipresent in the city, easily identified by the variety of museums and artist co-operatives centering indigenous practices and artisans – and even the design of the city itself. Gleye (1994, p. 195) perhaps best captures the core of this approach in his description of local architecture, noting that "Santa Fe may be instructive regarding the identity of place...by having nurtured and codified significant traditional aesthetic elements...while other places were witnessing the diminishment of their own".

Rather than seek to erase this character, promoters have long sought to synthesize and integrate it into the city's development. In his brief article on the marketing strategies used to generate tourism in Santa Fe, Kimmel (1995, p. 30) asserts that it "has an undisputed authenticity due to its heritage as an artists' colony", and that indigenous arts play an integral role in such authenticity.

However effective, this approach is certainly far from perfect. Gentrification, stratification and an inequitable distribution of the economic growth stemming from this promotion are a perennial concern in the region (Rosenstein, 2000). Further, the very origin of the strategy, with nonnative artists deliberately leveraging the area's 'usable past', veritably reeks of appropriation (Hartley, 2005). Fortunately, local policies and practices involve safeguards to protect the artisans, organizations and people who have helped the region thrive[3] (Lechuza-Aquallo, 2013). Public policy contains statutes explicitly protecting indigenous artisans and their livelihoods, and local scholars and nonprofits consult with artists to simultaneously detect fraud and promote respectful engagement with authentic native works (Evans-Pritchard, 1987; Maruyama & Stronza, 2008).

Arts nonprofits and charitable organizations perform an integral function in this ecosystem, serving to provide access to cultural education while promoting community engagement with arts and artists. Many, like the Keshi Foundation, enter into direct partnerships with local artists in order to co-promote their works and provide them with access to an economic pipeline connecting them to potential customers (The Keshi Foundation, 2016). Likewise, these partnerships provide highly visible and compelling local stories ripe for promotional use. These organizations thus act as force-multipliers for local artists, amplifying their visibility and forming a network that supports the overall arts vitality of the community as well as the nonprofits and charities operating within it (New Mexico Department of Cultural Affairs, 2023).

Learning from Santa Fe

Santa Fe serves as an excellent historical example of place-driven nonprofit marketing 'done right' and provides an illustrative model for the future of charity marketing. The lessons this approach offers can be summarized in a few key points:

- Arts advocates and nonprofit marketers can craft compelling place-based reputations drawn from unique local history. When stories *integrate* the distinguishing characteristics of a place's identity – rather than *overwriting* them – the results may be powerful intersections of styles, media and voices.

- Marketing that emphasizes visible partnerships within local communities may be significantly more successful than those highlighting profit-making potential.
- When crafting stories, it is vital to protect constituents and beneficiaries along the way. In Kimmel's (1995, p. 30) words, a "primary factor in establishing an authentic art center is that the community must have working artists, not just galleries selling art. Thus, the community must make itself attractive to working artists".

Dallas, Texas: Marketing Arts in a Time of Change

Context: Even the best-laid plans

Describing the aspirations of the arts community in Dallas as ambitious would be an understatement. Dallas 'proper' features one of the world's largest contiguous urban arts districts, built up over four decades through the coordinated efforts of philanthropists, public administrators and nonprofit institutions like the Dallas Museum of Art, Dallas Symphony Orchestra and the AT&T Performing Arts Center. Organizations operating within the district have a long history of working with the city government – and each other – to pursue the ultimate goal of shaping the city into a prestigious destination for high-art lovers (Johnson, 2011)[4].

Guided for decades by the principles laid out in a master plan,[5] this complex network of shared management agreements, co-promotion and organizational interdependence perfectly represents traditional approaches to marketing arts and cultural organizations. Advocates have frequently emphasized the economic, sociodemographic and political value these organizations bring to the city, often focusing on the prestige associated with hosting them (Bonakdar & Audirac, 2021).

Results have been underwhelming. While the groups operating within the district have continued to attract respectable – albeit modest – audiences and operate with greater stability than many other comparable arts nonprofits, the lofty goals touted by advocates, planners and marketers as the project's inevitable destiny have largely failed to materialize (Johnson, 2011; Simek, 2019; Bonakdar & Audirac, 2020). Making matters worse, any operational shortcomings are entangled with – and exacerbated by – an image problem. Even cursory reviews of op-eds in local publications reveal frustrations with the organizations populating the Dallas Arts District. Articles frequently reference high-dollar taxpayer bailouts, make accusations of elitism and one critic even describes the project as "in Dallas but not of it" (Schutze, 2017; Wilonsky, 2019). Scholarly research on the district has likewise raised concerns about its historical roots, particularly the problematic nature of housing these organizations on land formerly comprising part of a post-slavery Black community (Prior & Kemper, 2005; Skipper, 2015). Although the displacement of Freedman's Town residents to make room for new developments occurred decades before the arts district was even conceived, such a blatant example of gentrification raises challenging ethical barriers to promoting the area's organizations as integral parts of the city's history or cultural landscape (Prior & Kemper, 2005).

Towards community-focused promotion: Early successes

While prestige-driven promotion may be attractive to donors and philanthropists, it is clearly inadequate when organizations are associated with a project that appears to alienate large segments of the local community. Fortunately, advocates, marketers and leaders from Dallas's arts organizations appear to be learning from the past. In partnership with each other and the city's Office of Cultural Affairs, these organizations have formed a committee to develop a place-based overhaul to the District's master plan (Dallas Arts District Connect, n.d.). The new iteration prominently emphasizes the connections between these organizations and existing neighborhoods and cultural communities throughout the city (Simek, 2018). Its boilerplate description explicitly centers the deliberate inclusion of as many local stakeholders as possible, casting audiences and community members as partners in developing the city's cultural environment – not customers purchasing experiences that feel commodified, manufactured or imported (Dallas Arts District Connect, n.d.).

This approach is similarly reflected at the organization level, with multiple nonprofits throughout the district developing new programming and campaigns that are simultaneously community-focused and marketing-friendly. Initiatives often involve offering and aggressively promoting free community engagement opportunities, such as the Dallas Museum of Art's move towards free general admission, the Nasher Sculpture Center's regular free "'til Midnight" social events, and regular district-wide 'block parties' featuring Dallas-based artists and performers (Dallas Arts District, n.d.; Nasher Sculpture Center, n.d.; Bentley, 2023). Other organizations have – quite literally – taken this approach on the road. During the COVID-19 pandemic, the Dallas Opera retrofitted a commercial freight truck to create a mobile stage, then sent performers throughout the city to produce free open-air concerts (Dallas Opera, 2021). The Dallas Symphony Orchestra has produced similar programming through a recurring partnership with external organizations like the Concert Truck, Inc. (Dallas Symphony Orchestra, 2023).

Collectively, these initiatives invert Dallas-based arts organizations' previous approaches to promoting the arts and cultivating new audiences. Rather than seek to compel audiences to trek to the arts district for high-art entertainment, these programs demonstrate a commitment to becoming members of a shared, place-based community. In this light, arts district-based nonprofits are not *imposing* elitist programming onto a disinterested populace; they are *inviting* audiences to be part of a unique and innovative local cultural network that embodies the city's self-styled spirit of innovation and connection (Rentschler & Radbourne, 2007). This strategy dovetails with research by Lee, Ha and Kim (2018), indicating that marketing expenses may counterintuitively increase donations to arts nonprofits by connecting them with receptive-but-unexposed new audiences who may become future patrons or donors. In Dallas, it seems to be working, as indicated by the fact that organizations within the arts district are experiencing a strong post-pandemic recovery (Americans for the Arts, 2023; Richard, 2023).

Lessons from Dallas

Dallas is a city in transition. The cultural nonprofits operating within the arts district are still working towards developing the right balance between marketing their prestige-driven values and their role in place-based community engagement. However, shifts towards the latter are promising. To that end, the story of the Dallas Arts District offers several valuable takeaways for nonprofit marketers:

- Marketing and advocacy strategies primarily based on arts nonprofits' prestige and economic utility may fail to connect with audiences if the organizations using them do not also make efforts to directly engage with local communities.
- Free promotional opportunities may spark connections with previously unreached audiences, thus attracting new stakeholders who may ultimately become regular event attendees or donors.
- Effective place-based marketing means not only forming and cultivating these relationships, but also actively promoting them as a part of the nonprofit's organizational identity.

Detroit, Michigan: Challenges – and Opportunities

Context: Dealing with a difficult reputation

If Santa Fe demonstrates the high potential of place-anchored marketing and Dallas highlights an artistic community shifting towards this approach, then Detroit represents abundant opportunity for its use in the future. 'Motor City's' decline is well-documented, frequently serving as *the* stereotypical example of a once-great American city now struggling against decay (Doucet, 2017). Formerly a densely packed metropolitan region with a robust manufacturing-based economy and a history of philanthropic support for public goods and the cultural sector, the city has more recently gained a reputation for abandoned urban ruins, high unemployment rates and a fragile economy (Marotta, 2011).

Despite this reputation and its veracity – or lack thereof, Detroit's post-pandemic recovery is seemingly outpacing that of many other American regions (Marotta, 2011; Bonner & Katz, 2023). Less than a decade ago, policymakers were advocating deliberate, controlled shrinkages in an attempt to stabilize the local economy and stave-off a downward spiral (Schindler, 2016). Now, the city is experiencing a cultural and economic renaissance, earning recognition as a model for post-crisis recovery and an aspirational 21st century city (Bonner & Katz, 2023).

Local, community-focused arts nonprofits are major players in this recovery, although they are still plagued by chronic accessibility issues (Doucet, 2017; Moldovanova, Meloche & Thompson, 2022; Bonner & Katz, 2023). These organizations are often credited with stabilizing the city during some of its most brutal economic downturns, and they now serve to lead the cultivation of the city's new identity (Bonner & Katz, 2023). Rather than attempting to manufacture this identity by emphasizing the prestige or philanthropic attractiveness of the arts, these organizations are instead centering the preservation and elevation of local histories, communities and stories (Doucet, 2017). By focusing on promoting these unique features of the city, pro-arts voices in Detroit are highlighting a future rich with opportunities for place-linked nonprofit marketing, arts advocacy and community engagement.

Telling the story, focusing on the place

Perhaps the most innovative new approach to promoting arts organizations in Detroit comes not from the organizations themselves, but their partners in City Hall. In 2018, the city appointed its first Chief Storytelling Officer – a public employee responsible for shaping the story of the city and its recovery (Bloomberg Cities, 2018). Though several individuals have held this position in the years since its creation, their charge has consistently been to shine a spotlight on local artists, small businesses and nonprofit organizations in order to steward the reputation of the city while simultaneously preserving its character and history (Michigan Chronicle, 2020).

Although not directly employed by any organization from the private nonprofit sector, this is the epitome of place-based advocacy and marketing. Further, this charge naturally brings the officer into collaborative contact with the arts organizations that define and steward the city's cultural heritage. Arts organizations can learn from the existence – and apparent success – of this role; focusing on the development of a culturally and historically sensitive place-associated story serves to highlight organizations' deep connections to their communities, which will naturally spark reputational benefits and strengthen community-based marketing efforts. Likewise, organizations may help to shape the overarching story and reputation of a place, which will in turn serve as a guidepost that marketers and advocates can use to frame their own promotional work within the context of their local ecosystem.

The Detroit Art Institute provides another example of the value that place-conscious organizational promotion can yield for arts nonprofits. The Institute serves as one of Detroit's premiere cultural institutions, and its past decade has been marked by visible attempts to bring the museum's public image in line with the values of the community it serves (Czajkowski, 2011; Sweeney & Daniel, 2018). Although not entirely representative of Detroit's population, its staff is much more diverse than comparable museums in other cities, and it frequently features exhibitions and programming focused directly on the interests and heritage of Detroit's citizenry, not prestige-based programming for its own sake (Czajkowski, 2011; Sweeney & Daniel, 2018). This approach has thus far appeared successful; the museum still faces challenges, but has adopted an organizational strategy designed to position it as a very public, highly engaged staple of the Detroit community that may help to equitably anchor the city's cultural future (Beehn, 2015; Sweeney & Daniel, 2018).

Lessons from Detroit

Detroit's future holds many opportunities for arts nonprofits looking to develop new approaches to organizational promotion that integrate the city's history and reflect the values and concerns of its populace (Doucet, 2017). The early success of place-focused marketing efforts in Detroit's artistic network offers several implications for nonprofit marketers looking to develop and implement these strategies:

- Although marketers may not necessarily choose an organization's programming, behavior or operational circumstances, they can contextualize them to highlight the nonprofit's story and its community relationships.
- Powerful and compelling place-based stories can deepen these connections, thus strengthening the organization's overall reputation.
- These stories will in turn attract audiences and cultivate local support owing to the perception that the organization serves as an important cultural anchor.

Common Themes and Looking Towards the Future

Throughout this chapter, we have examined traditional approaches to promoting the arts as a field and marketing specific cultural organizations.

These strategies typically entail heavily commodifying organizations' programming while promoting their potential utilitarian values. We have also explored the emergence of the cultural placemaking movement as a major influence on how arts nonprofits may reconceptualize their marketing strategies to reframe arts engagement as a deepening of the mutually beneficial relationship between the arts and their communities (Rentschler & Radbourne, 2007; Kim & Benenson, 2023; Meagher, Bezboruah & Suh, 2024). We have discussed scholarly literature – as well as opinion-editorials and journalistic publications – to examine how arts organizations in three distinct American communities are applying place-anchored marketing principles to strengthen their overall organizational reputations. These efforts seek to attract audiences and cultivate increased arts engagement based on a shared understanding of what it means to *be part of* the culture, history and community in Santa Fe, Dallas or Detroit.

But what does this mean for the future of charity marketing, especially as we approach the middle of the 21st century?

Looking ahead, we can likely expect more organizations to imitate this visible success and adopt place-driven marketing strategies that spotlight their roles within local communities, not just the services or experiences they provide. They will seek to draw attention to outreach efforts – and their partnerships with local governments, public organizations and each other – in order to emphasize their embeddedness within a community. Although this approach will almost certainly resonate with potential audiences, it may be less popular with some philanthropists who enjoy prestige-based imagery, or partner organizations that assess an initiative's success by its economic indicators and operational measures (Charles & Kim, 2016; Kim, 2017). As such, we can expect a synthesis of place-anchored and utilitarian marketing strategies. This eventual fusion will likely appeal to audiences and key stakeholders alike by simultaneously emphasizing arts organizations' potential for preserving community identities, contributing value to the local economy, and providing opportunities to engage with high-status events. Conscientious organizational advocates and marketing practitioners will – and crucially, *should* – also balance these messages with ethical considerations, especially concerning historically marginalized or exploited local populations (Kim & Mason, 2018; Crisman, 2022). Further, they will ensure that these stories center local community experiences, artists and identities, lest they appear opportunistic, cynical or insincere.

Ultimately, the future of arts nonprofit marketing in America features campaigns that integrate local identities, histories and cultural characteristics. Organizational advocates will use these campaigns to highlight community partnerships and project an image of the nonprofit as an institution – an indelible piece of local life worthy of support and protection. This approach is transferable to other types of charitable organizations, and by highlighting not just their services to a community, but *their place within it,* organizational advocates of any stripe may cultivate elevated reputations among their audiences and stakeholders.

Discussion Questions

1 What can marketers seeking to develop place-based initiatives do to promote ethics and avoid exploiting vulnerable populations?
2 How can charity marketers cultivate place-based marketing campaigns in regions where there is not a strong or cohesive sense of local identity?
3 Reflect on a well-known nonprofit from your hometown. How has this organization balanced long-term identity cultivation with short-term survival? Has the organization become more place-focused over time?
4 Place-based marketing often requires nonprofits to work alongside other local organizations, some of which may have different goals or priorities. How can charity marketers navigate these challenges to support their organizations and local networks overall?

Notes

1 While the National Endowment for the Arts stands as a symbolic representation of public support for the cultural sector, its resources and ability to mobilize them often pale in comparison to the needs of arts organizations throughout the country (Dorf, 1993; Rius-Ulldemolins, 2023).
2 This chapter's thematic material is primarily supported by scholarly literature and professional reports, but journalistic publications, organizational websites and opinion-editorials provide supplemental examples of public sentiment and specific organizational marketing initiatives not found in scholarly literature.
3 The contributions made to Santa Fe's cultural development by American Indian artists are immeasurable, and the interdependent relationships they share with the community are far more complex than could be covered in this chapter. For an excellent and culturally sensitive introductory exploration of these nuances, readers should refer to Reeve (1981): *Pueblos, Powers, and Painters: The Role of the Pueblo Indians in the Development of the Santa Fe-Taos Region as an American Cultural Center.*
4 It is important to note that the Arts District is not the only hub of cultural activity within the city limits. Nearby Deep Ellum has a rich history of arts-based activity and local nightlife. Bishop Arts, a neighborhood located in South Dallas, is similarly undergoing a years-long transformation that raises significant gentrification concerns. This chapter focuses exclusively on the formal Dallas Arts District, due both to its unique pre-planned heritage as well as the high concentration of formally classified arts nonprofits operating within it.
5 Colloquially known as the "Sasaki Plan" owing to the consulting firm commissioned to develop it. The plan emphasizes prestige-driven design, economic utility and market potential as the district's selling points. The archived plan may be found on the city's website at dallascityhall.com.

References

Americans for the Arts (2023) Welcome: Arts & economic prosperity 6 (AEP6), Welcome | Arts & Economic Prosperity 6 (AEP6). Available at: https://aep6.amer icansforthearts.org/.

Beehn, D.T. (2015). *Engaging Detroit: The Detroit Institute of Arts and the African American Community* (Doctoral dissertation, University of Illinois at Chicago).

Bentley, A. (2023) Dallas Museum of Art Launches New Program with Free Tickets on Sundays, CultureMap Dallas. Available at: https://dallas.culturemap.com/news/ arts/dallas-museum-art-free-sundays/.

Bernstein, J.S., (2006). *Arts Marketing Insights: The Dynamics of Building and Retaining Performing Arts Audiences*. San Franscisco, CA: John Wiley & Sons.

Bloomberg Cities (2018) How Detroit's Chief Storyteller is Crafting a New Narrative for His City, Bloomberg Cities. Available at: https://bloombergcities.medium. com/how-detroits-chief-storyteller-is-crafting-a-new-narrative-for-his-city-3c14d 0fa559c.

Bonakdar, A. and Audirac, I. (2021). City planning, urban imaginary, and the branded space: Untangling the role of city plans in shaping Dallas's urban imaginaries. *Cities*, 117, p.103315.

Bonner, K. and Katz, B. (2023) *Struggling Cities Should Take Notes on Detroit's Revival*, World Economic Forum. Available at: www.weforum.org/agenda/2023/ 06/struggling-cities-should-look-to-detroit-for-lessons-on-revival/.

Boorsma, M. and Chiaravalloti, F. (2010). Arts marketing performance: An artistic-mission-led approach to evaluation. *The Journal of Arts Management, Law, and Society*, 40(4), pp.297–317.

Charles, C. and Kim, M., 2016. Do donors care about results? An analysis of nonprofit arts and cultural organizations. *Public Performance & Management Review*, 39(4), pp.864–884.

Crisman, J.J.A. (2022). Evaluating values in creative placemaking: The arts as community development in the NEA's our town program. *Journal of Urban Affairs*, 44(4–5), pp.708–726.

Czajkowski, J. W. (2011). Changing the rules: Making space for interactive learning in the galleries of the Detroit Institute of Arts. *Journal of Museum Education*, 36(2), 171–178.

Dallas Arts District (no date) About, Dallas Arts District. Available at: www.dallasa rtsdistrict.org/about/.

Dallas Arts District Connect (no date) *Home: Dallas Arts District Connect*, Dallas Arts District Connect. Available at: www.dallasartsdistrictconnect.org/.

Dallas Opera, (2021). 'The Dallas opera's new OperaTruck brings family operas to community locations' *Dallas Opera* [Preprint]. Available at: https://dallasopera. org/wp-content/uploads/2021/04/TDO-OperaTruck-Press-Release-04-12-21.pdf.

Dallas Symphony Orchestra, (2023).'*Dallas Symphony Orchestra Returns to the Community with The Concert Truck*' [Preprint]. Available at: www.dallassymph ony.org/discover-connect/dso-vault/read/press-releases/dallas-symphony-orches tra-returns-to-the-community-with-the-concert-truck/.

Dorf, M.C. (1993). Artifactions: The battle over the National Endowment for the Arts. *The Brookings Review*, 11(1), pp.32–35.

Doucet, B. ed., (2017). *Why Detroit Matters: Decline, Renewal and Hope in a Divided City*. Bristol, UK: Policy Press.

Evans-Pritchard, D., (1987). The Portal case: Authenticity, tourism, traditions, and the law. *Journal of American Folklore*, pp.287–296.

Florida, R. (2014). *The Rise of the Creative Class--Revisited: Revised and Expanded.* New York: Basic Books (AZ).

Gaither, J.M. (1957). *A Return to the Village: A Study of Santa Fe and Taos, New Mexico, as Cultural Centers, 1900–1934.* Minneapolis, MN: University of Minnesota.

Gleye, P. (1994). Santa Fe without ADOBE: lessons for the identity of place. *Journal of Architectural and Planning Research*, pp.181–196.

Grodach, C., Foster, N. and Murdoch III, J., (2014). Gentrification and the artistic dividend: The role of the arts in neighborhood change. *Journal of the American Planning Association*, 80(1), pp.21–35.

Grodach, C. and Loukaitou-Sideris, A. (2007). Cultural development strategies and urban revitalization: A survey of US cities. *International Journal of Cultural Policy*, 13(4), pp.349–370.

Hanifl, B. (2019). Creative tourism in Santa Fe, New Mexico. *A Research Agenda for Creative Tourism*, p. 113.

Hartley, C.J. (2005). *Art in an Arid Climate: The Museum of New Mexico and the Cultivation of the Arts in Santa Fe.* University of California, Santa Barbara, CA.

Jacobs, J. (1961). *The Death and Life of Great American Cities.* New York: Random House.

Johnson, A.G. (2011). *Developing Urban Arts Districts: An Analysis of Mobilization in Dallas, Denver, Philadelphia, Pittsburgh, and Seattle.* Pennsylvania: University of Pennsylvania.

Kim, M. (2017). The relationship of nonprofits' financial health to program outcomes: Empirical evidence from nonprofit arts organizations. *Nonprofit and Voluntary Sector Quarterly*, 46(3), pp.525–548.

Kim, M. and Benenson, J. (2023). Arts and culture nonprofits as civic actors: Mapping audience, community, and civic engagement in nonprofit organizations. *The Journal of Arts Management, Law, and Society*, 53(4), pp.247–265.

Kim, M. and Mason, D.P. (2018). Representation and diversity, advocacy, and nonprofit arts organizations. *Nonprofit and Voluntary Sector Quarterly*, 47(1), pp.49–71.

Kim, M. and Van Ryzin, G.G. (2014). Impact of government funding on donations to arts organizations: A survey experiment. *Nonprofit and Voluntary Sector Quarterly*, 43(5), pp.910–925.

Kimmel, J.R., (1995). Art and tourism in Santa Fe, New Mexico. *Journal of Travel Research*, 33(3), pp.28–30.

Lechuza-Aquallo, A., (2013). Santa Fe Indian market: A history of native arts and the marketplace. By Bruce Bernstein. *American Indian Culture and Research Journal*, 37(4).

Lee, H., Ha, K.C. and Kim, Y., (2018). Marketing expense and financial performance in arts and cultural organizations. *International Journal of Nonprofit and Voluntary Sector Marketing*, 23(3), p.e1588.

Markusen, A. (2013). Fuzzy concepts, proxy data: why indicators would not track creative placemaking success. *International Journal of Urban Sciences*, 17(3), pp.291–303.

Markusen, A. and Gadwa, A., (2010). Arts and culture in urban or regional planning: A review and research agenda. *Journal of planning education and research*, 29(3), pp.379–391.

Marotta, S., (2011). *Creative Reconstruction in the City: An Analysis of Art, Shrinking, and the Story of the American Dream in Detroit, MI*. Tempe, AZ: Arizona State University.

Maruyama, N.U., Yen, T.H. and Stronza, A., (2008). Perception of authenticity of tourist art among Native American artists in Santa Fe, New Mexico. *International Journal of Tourism Research*, 10(5), pp.453–466.

Meagher, T., Bezboruah, K. and Suh, J., 2024. Fighting for survival: Analyzing strategic trends in arts advocacy. *Journal of Philanthropy and Marketing*, 29(1), p.e1822.

Michigan Chronicle (2020) Eric Thomas Joins the City of Detroit as Chief Storyteller, Michigan Chronicle. Available at: https://michiganchronicle.com/2020/01/29/eric-thomas-joins-the-city-of-detroit-as-chief-storyteller-city-of-detroit/.

Moldavanova, A.V., Meloche, L. and Thompson, T.L., (2022). Understanding the geography of access to cultural amenities: The case of Metropolitan Detroit. *Journal of Urban Affairs*, 44(4–5), pp.614–639.

Nasher Sculpture Center (no date) 'til Midnight at the Nasher, Nasher Sculpture Center. Available at: www.nashersculpturecenter.org/programs-events/programs-list/program/id/36.

New Mexico Department of Cultural Affairs (2023) *Arts and Economic Prosperity 6: The Economic & Social Impact Study of Nonprofit Arts & Culture Organizations & Their Audiences in City of Santa Fe*. Available at: www.nmculture.org/assets/files/reports/AEP6_CityOfSantaFe.pdf.

Ostrower, F., (2021). *Why Is It Important That We Continue?*. Some Nonprofit Arts Organizations. Prieiga per internetą: www. wallacefoundation.org/knowledgecenter/Documents/Why-Is-It-Important-That-We-Continue. Pdf (žiūrėta 2021 10 31).

Prior, M. and Kemper, R.V., (2005). From Freedman's town to Uptown: Community transformation and gentrification in Dallas, Texas. *Urban Anthropology and Studies of Cultural Systems and World Economic Development*, pp.177–216.

Reeve, K.A., (1981). Pueblos, poets, and painters: the role of the pueblo Indians in the development of the Santa Fe-Taos Region as an American Cultural Center. *American Indian Culture and Research Journal*, 5(4).

Rentschler, R. and Radbourne, J., (2007). Relationship marketing in the arts. *The Routledge Companion to Nonprofit Marketing*, p.254.

Richard, K. (2023) New Study Shows Dallas Arts Industry's Resilience through the Pandemic, NBC 5 Dallas-Fort Worth. Available at: www.nbcdfw.com/entertainment/the-scene/new-study-shows-dallas-arts-industrys-resilience-through-the-pandemic/3407395/.

Rius-Ulldemolins, J., (2023). The land of (almost) no central government arts spending? Cultural policy, protestant denominations, and the cultural policy singularity of Unites States of America. *The Journal of Arts Management, Law, and Society*, 53(4), pp.223–246.

Rosenstein, C.E., (2000). *Forms of Belonging, Forms of Difference: Art, Ethnicity and Stratifications of Culture in Contemporary Santa Fe*. Waltham, MA: Brandeis University.

Scheff, J. and Kotler, P., 1996. Crisis in the arts: The marketing response. *California Management Review*, 39(1), p.28.

Schindler, S., 2016. Detroit after bankruptcy: A case of degrowth machine politics. *Urban Studies*, 53(4), pp.818–836.

Schutze, J. (2017) Auditor *Warns* that *Arts Patrons May Need* a *Bailout Again After One Year*, Dallas Observer. Available at: www.dallasobserver.com/news/dallas-auditor-warns-that-atandt-performing-arts-center-may-need-another-taxpayer-bailout-9829818.

Simek, P. (2018) Dallas *Finally* has a *Strong Cultural* policy. *But Will It Be Implemented?*, D Magazine. Available at: www.dmagazine.com/frontburner/2018/12/dallas-finally-has-a-strong-cultural-policy-but-will-it-be-implemented/.

Simek, P. (2019) Assessing the *Dallas Arts District*, 10 *Years Later*, D Magazine. Available at: www.dmagazine.com/publications/d-magazine/2019/october/assessing-the-dallas-arts-district-10-years-later/.

Skipper, J., 2015. Saving St. Paul: Race, Development, and Heritage Politics in Dallas, Texas. *The Black Scholar*, 45(3), pp.24–38.

SMU DataArts. (2020). Key Findings, Arts Vibrancy Index Report VI. DataArts. Available at: https://culturaldata.org/arts-vibrancy-2020/key-findings/.

SMU DataArts. (2023). The Top 40 Arts-Vibrant Communities of 2023. DataArts. Available at: https://culturaldata.org/arts-vibrancy-2023/the-top-40-list/.

Sweeney, L. and Daniel, K., 2018. *Becoming a Public Square: Detroit Institute of Arts*. Ithaka S+ R.

The Keshi Foundation (2016) The Keshi Foundation, the Keshi Foundation. Available at: www.thekeshifoundation.org/.

Wilonsky, R. (2019) Thirty Years after Sasaki Plan created Dallas Arts District, a Call for a New Vision -- and Fast, Dallas NEWS. Available at: www.dallasnews.com/news/2015/06/19/thirty-years-after-sasaki-plan-created-dallas-arts-district-a-call-for-a-new-vision-and-fast/.

Wilson, C., (1997). *The Myth of Santa Fe: Creating a Modern Regional Tradition*. Albuquerque, NM: UNM Press.

12

CHURCHES IN THE UK AS HERITAGE CHARITIES AND PLACES OF COMMUNITY PARTNERSHIP

Sarah Rogers

Introduction

Churches have an uneasy relationship with commerce. This often means marketing alternative commercial models can be messy, with multiple stakeholders to consider – church governing bodies, congregation members, local authorities, heritage organisations, charity partners and funders to name a few. As a result, high mission-led initiatives such as food banks or warm shelters fit more comfortably within a church context, presenting a more straightforward model and marketing strategy. Equally, full commercial and cultural models present a welcome sense that church is something we can continue to discover. Culture shapes the way we understand our lives and the meaning we make of them, and it lies therefore at the basis of people-centred development. Furthermore, participation in the cultural life of one's own community, the safeguarding and renewal of heritage, creative expression and the celebration and discovery of diversity, among others, are integral to a healthy, inclusive society. We need to strengthen the narrative surrounding the contribution of churches and this is where charity-based marketing plays an important role. As a practitioner, the messiness of working with churches is both part of the challenge and the reward.

Churches are the original multi-use space in nature and function, historically acting as places of recreation, education and leisure rather than strictly for religious instruction and ritual (Olsen, 2003). In this case, formalising and celebrating a 'duality of place' highlights a transition for the role of the church, church charities and faith-based organisations in Britain. People's engagement with church spaces takes place in different settings and through different models of provision: the church as a place of worship, the

DOI: 10.4324/9781003396802-12

community cafe, the heritage funded destination, the Christmas carol service, the commercial venue, the concert hall, the community organisation, etc., with the boundaries of purpose becoming blurred. Consequently, we have to think beyond these cultural and heritage values, to try to better understand the future role of churches and their buildings as key assets in our communities (The Church Times, 2023). However, in the UK, churches are regulated differently by the Charity Commission: charities that are wholly or mainly for public religious worship are *excepted* if they generate less than £100,000 a year. This means they do not have to register or submit annual returns (gov. UK., 2014 This definition gives rise to questions on whether the excepted charity status is in fact a disincentive for churches to be a more commercially focused business enterprise, and therefore retain a viable future.

There are two areas that reflect these challenges and conversely, represent the marketing opportunity for churches and faith-based organisations. Firstly, maintaining the building and its contribution to national heritage; secondly, understanding its role as a cultural and social asset in the community. Churches play an important role in the nation's life: first as buildings, often of historic importance and, geographically, at the centre of every community – part of the nation's tangible heritage; and secondly, as a focus of cultural and social activity and assets – part of every community's intangible heritage. Where these two come together, the tangible asset of the building and the intangible asset of the activity, they have a relevance and importance which can be quite independent of their primary religious purpose. The following sections will look at the topic from the perspective of duality of place, the role of heritage and co-producing community partnerships. The three case studies are from three UK churches on how these concepts work in practice.

Duality of Place

> The end result of a touristification of religious sites is an overlapping of religious and tourist space, creating, in the words of Bremer (2001), a 'duality of place'
>
> *(Timothy & Olsen, 2006)*

Churches across the UK are confronted with the challenge of finding new uses for their buildings. Due to dwindling congregations and the lack of gifted income, the statistics are worrying for the ongoing maintenance of both the heritage and community asset churches provide, but also the economic and social impact churches have on the UK's economy. According to a survey conducted by Talking Jesus and the Evangelical Alliance (Paveley, 2022), just 6% of adults in the UK are practising Christians. A further study from the Church of England's Statistics for Mission found there were more mosque-going British Muslims, about 930,000, than regular worshippers in the Church of England. Average attendance for Church of England Sunday services in 2021 was 509,000 (Jenkins, 2023).

However, our nation's church buildings are a unique asset which the National Churches Trust calculate provides at least £50 billion in economic and social value to the UK each year (NCT, 2022). Provision of services ranging from drug and alcohol counselling to youth groups offers benefits to the volunteers who run them as well as to those who use them. Recent data from the Church of England gathered from 13,000 churches showed that the biggest area was in food banks, with 60% involved in either running or supporting food banks; whereas the Trussell Trust (The Trussell Trust, 2023) recently released figures indicating this figure is expected to rise as they forecast that food banks in their network will distribute more than a million emergency food parcels between December 2023 and February 2024. The Warm Welcome campaign developed first in response to COVID-19 and then soaring energy prices in 2022, brought together senior leaders across denominations and community groups to provide safe spaces offering warmth and company for people in need during winter months (Church Times, 2022). 7000 Warm Welcome Spaces are now registered across the UK. New research from the Joseph Rowntree Foundation has revealed that one in six people used a warm bank last year – and there are fears the situation is only getting worse with figures from National Energy Action predicting 6.3 million people will be trapped in fuel poverty and unable to afford their bills during winter 2024 (The Big Issue, 2023).

In addition to community action initiatives dealing with economic crises, nearly a third Church of England churches run or support parent and toddler groups; just over a quarter run lunch clubs; and one in five run community cafes. Holiday clubs and breakfast clubs, often providing meals to children from low-income families, are supported or run by nearly 17% of churches. Other projects supported or run by the Church of England's churches involved a range of activities from bereavement support, community gardens and community choirs to music events and English language tuition (Church Action On Poverty, 2024). Based on these statistics, it is clear that churches can and do bring people together for the common good and strengthen communities. In short, as the CEO of National Churches Trust explains "church buildings are in a prime position to help to level up every single day. It's what they do" (National Churches Trust, 2022).

However, especially in rural areas, and areas of social deprivation, local communities and congregations are experiencing difficulties in maintaining the considerable costs of architectural maintenance. Equally, whilst acknowledging the importance churches play in the economic landscape and in local community life, the lack of human resources poses significant challenges. The second biggest challenge is to maintain the level of volunteers needed in order to deliver the current volume of social and community 'work'. According to the National Churches Trust and the State of Life, a not-for-profit researching social value and wellbeing economics, the report *House of Good* (Gramatki et al., 2020) states that each church in the UK reported an average of 214 volunteer hours per month. Based on the average living wage calculation, that is around £850 million per year for all the UK's churches. This indicates a powerful community commitment and one most often generated by word of mouth – and highlights a paradox: while congregations are dwindling, the role of the church in meeting social needs is growing. The metrics are extraordinary.

Some communities, such as Wheatley village in Oxfordshire, thrive on the combination of energy and people sharing local news through the community Facebook and a bi-monthly newsletter through the letterbox. The United Reform Church, Catholic and Church of England churches send regular updates and news ranging from traditional services to the local food pantry supported by supermarket chain ASDA. These *informal* + *formal* + *local* initiatives defy the narrative of declining interest and engagement in the church. These local initiatives are clearly both church-led and community-led.

Hybrid partnerships led by local citizens or residents have a power base in the community and are fundamentally trusted if, and only if, they open up within the heart of a place. This becomes the main pipeline for volunteer support. Opportunities observed during the COVID-19 pandemic indicated untapped community energy and willingness to volunteer as a form of self-identity (Bowe, 2019). Moreover, a survey of community volunteers revealed that the more time participants committed to their volunteering, the more they identified with their communities, which in turn predicted higher levels of personal wellbeing (Bowe et al., 2020). This emphasises the overall positive impact volunteering has on the community's health and happiness.

Role of Heritage

> Those shared spaces and places that we hold in common and where we meet as equal citizens. The places that people instinctively recognize and value as not just being part of the landscape or townscape, but as actually being part of their own personal identity. That is the essential reason why people value heritage.
>
> Tessa Jowell, *Capturing the Public Value of Heritage* (Jowell, 2006)

All churches are heritage sites (Olsen & Timothy, 2006) complete with the additional layer of spiritual significance. Churches account for 45% of all Grade I listed buildings in England (English Heritage, 2024), a practice of designation listing and landmarking in the UK indicating a conception of heritage value. In practical terms, however, this represents operational and maintenance challenges in generating individual donations, raising sufficient funding from other sources, recruiting expertise and retaining volunteers.

There remains a strong case for the preservation of historic buildings, especially those linked to storytelling and an existing communal sense of belonging and ownership (Historic England, 2020). In addition, the cultural importance of the built environment has tended to focus on its tangible historic heritage. Heritage is one of the resources that is regularly transformed for tourism purposes, and from a tourism perspective religion is considered an component of heritage (Olsen, 2003; Oxford Economics, 2016).

Visit Britain's 2022 inbound visits and spend of tourists at visitor attractions in the UK, indicates visitor numbers, both domestic and international, to places of worship were up 7% compared with 2018 with revenue generated up 6% (Visit Britain, 2023). St Paul's Cathedral, Westminster Abbey and Canterbury Cathedral were all in the top 20 most 'paid for' visitor attractions in England, ranking fourth, seventh and eleventh, respectively. And, when looking at longer-term visits to places of worship in England, over time, the trend has increased 5% on average each year during the three years from 2017 to 2019.

Statistics from VisitBritain show that history and heritage are highly regarded attributes for overseas visitors in the UK. More than a fifth (21%) of all inbound trips include a visit to a religious building in the UK, equating to about seven million visits annually. Overseas travellers who visit a religious building as part of their trip usually spend £7 billion in the UK overall every year (Visit Britain, 2023). Visiting churches and places of worship are also a draw for travellers interested in finding out about their ancestors and with the UK's strong links to countries in the Commonwealth and North America, families from around the world pay their respects at war graves and in cemeteries to see the final resting place of loved ones. The rise in interest in ancestry or genealogy tourism has seen a rise in American tourists visiting the UK and UK churches (English Heritage, 2023; Oxford Economics, 2016).

The National Churches Trust has also been showcasing ways forward for churches to benefit directly from tourism spend. The 'Experiences by Explore Churches' project, which Visit England supported through the Discover England Fund, brings churches to life for today's visitors. By working with other organisations in their area, this project has supported churches in creating exciting itineraries that bring extra added value to a day-out and the wider visitor experience.

Not all church spaces can offer the same level of commercial activities as many other city centre locations; however, many churches across the UK attract tourists and as a result are key components of the cultural landscape. Owing to increased marketing, faith-linked tourism is differentiated as part of the visitor offer. Visit England listed faith attractions and accommodation as one of its key trends in 2023 (Visit England, 2023). The rise of coastal visits and walking links churches and walkers along the iconic National Trust Coastal Path, amenities, hospitality and accommodation or *champing* along routes (The Economist, 2022) The Cornish Celtic Way, a pilgrimage route covering 125 miles through Cornwall from St. German's to St. Michael's Mount, offers a Walk and Stay series staying in chapels along the Cornish north coast (Marns, 2023).

British Pilgrimage Trust (BPT) is a charity that promotes pilgrimage routes in Britain by

> publicising old and new paths as well as encouraging the practice of pilgrimage itself. Our mission is to advance British pilgrimage as a form of cultural heritage that promotes holistic wellbeing, for the public benefit.
>
> *(British Pilgrimage, 2024).*

The BPT publishes routes linking up churches, village pubs and accommodation.

Rural churches and rural communities receive less attention, have a harder time accessing expenditure and footfall, but share all of the same challenges as their urban counterparts. There are opportunities as suggested by pilgrimage tourism, and overnight church stays along walking routes, but there are also distinct cultural dimensions that smaller spaces provide including amateur arts, amateur theatre and local history. Touring theatre and music collectives use membership organisations such as the National Rural Touring Forum to perform in village halls, churches and small theatres. To capitalise on renewed footfall, churches can decide on the level of activity and involvement, but from a marketing perspective the network's website and corresponding social media reduces should do the marketing for the church, along with some kind of cash free donations mechanism to engage visitors en route.

Co-producing Partnerships in the Community

The 'Life on the Breadline' project is an extensive piece of research and analysis of the impact austerity has had on the Christian response to poverty (Shannahan & Denning, 2022) and highlights the extent to which the social capital the church brings has replaced former State provision. Shared social projects between churches and community organisations are becoming more common, perhaps because they offer a higher profile for funders, while enhancing social impact and marketing effectiveness (Russell & McKnight, 2022).

In terms of marketing, a shared aim and mission of the initiative is essential to sharing a compelling story, engaging volunteers and maintaining funding cycles. As a result, many community action partnerships and social enterprise initiatives will consider setting up a Community Interest Company (CIC) that can include multiple community stakeholders, or a secular charity separate from the church or a Charitable Incorporated Organisation (CIO).

Out of this research, Denning (2023) has focussed on the growth of Christian Faith-Based Organisations in the UK over the last two decades through social franchising in addition to CIC's and CIO's. Social franchising is a model that operates like commercial franchising, but in a not-for-profit context for social benefit (Naatu & Alon, 2019).

People and place have been key to the operational characteristics of successful faith-based social franchises (Denning, 2023) whether as an enterprise launched from within the church or as a partnership with a social franchise. Project funding, for commercial, capital project or social good purposes, requires ever-greater professional expertise to navigate the complex funding landscape. Furthermore, the combination of austerity and cost of living has led to an increase in the number of small local initiatives addressing social needs, causing market saturation and therefore increasing competition for diminishing resources. Social franchises offer a model for FBOs to work together, and at the same time professionalise their fundraising. As Denning concludes "It would be beneficial for more partnerships between faith-based organisations to further increase cooperation between organisations and to decrease unnecessary competition as social action providers seeking church and volunteer resources" (Denning, 2023, p. 20).

This chimes with the writing of Sam Wells, Vicar at St Martin's in the Fields who stresses that in partnerships, "we are more prepared to see how respective gifts can, when appropriately harnessed, together enable a team to reach a common goal". He encourages us to prioritise relationships, so that we are "being with" or "doing with" rather than "doing for" (Wells, 2016).

Partnerships can be full of tensions, but also a win–win for the charity, the development organisation, community business or the social franchise to share marketing, branding, segmentation/audience development and a wider access to volunteers with the church – as well as to share in a professional funding cycle. In addition, the metrics required for most funding cycles require data, mapping, KPI's and a level of strategic development that most small and large churches (and small charities) struggle to deliver. Therefore, a strategic alliance based on partnership provides benefits that go well beyond the management responsibility of the church building. Getting the right training and advice can be hard to find. The Plunkett Foundation works with the Benefact Trust to help churches explore options to kickstart businesses, with a range of online events and webinars hosted throughout the year giving access to free bespoke advice and grants for early feasibility studies (Benefact Trust, 2024).

In summary, forging partnerships are key and prioritising storytelling about those relationships are key. In marketing, strategic storytelling transports the audience into and through the story (Key et al., 2021). Smaller nonprofits can effectively use storytelling to inspire support and further their cause (Keel & Tran, 2023). One would imagine that the church, founded on the 'narrative', would have an innate capacity to market their partnerships, activities and relationships through strategic storytelling but this is more often not the case. There is an over-reliance on word-of-mouth, or 'what's on' posts rather than a proactive and compelling narrative supported by quality photographs and visuals. Either this stems from a reluctance to tell stories other than those that reflect the church itself or is due to lack of confidence. Either way, it is an affordable opportunity to build support and attract new resources, volunteers and funding.

Churches at the Heart of Place: Three Case Studies

A heritage disjoined from ongoing life cannot enlist popular support. To adore the past is not enough; good care taking involves continual creation.
David Lowenthal (Getty Conservation Institute, 2017)

Church buildings serve as a significant asset for communities due to their physical presence in every local neighbourhood, including rural, coastal, suburban and city centre areas. In spite of the many challenges, the primary asset is the actual building or buildings. Despite facing financial anxiety over maintenance and resistance to change, these buildings remain central to their respective areas, hosting various cultural events and social initiatives such as music programs, community choirs, food banks and social gatherings like community cafes. City centre churches and UK Cathedrals are at the forefront of front-facing commercial packages, a mix of in-house and outsourced delivery covering wedding and event venue hire, restaurants and cafes, music or comedy venues or as tourism attractions due to famous monuments or significant historic legacy. There is a demonstrated resilience and willingness to embrace innovative approaches within church communities to continue serving their neighbourhoods as seen in the following case studies.

Union Chapel, London: An Award-Winning London Music Venue and the Home of the Margins Project

The Union Chapel in London managed by Union Chapel Project Ltd with a remit to "care for the fabric of the building and open it up to as wide an audience as possible" (Union Chapel, 2024.) The limited charity runs both an award-winning London music venue and is the home of the Margins Project, running two weekly crisis drop-ins, offer of food, a hot shower and support covering housing and benefit issues. There are additional events and activities, including the Organ Programme and Sunday School, but the other important aspect to note is the charitable objective to maintain and manage the church (a separate legal entity) and its heritage assets. The ongoing maintenance of a heritage asset is a further responsibility for churches – or their commercial arm – and presents huge challenges.

As a brand, the Union Chapel is recognised in London as a well-respected arts venue, a collaborator in music partnerships and with this profile comes marketing opportunities to share the social purpose alongside ticket sales. Their annual report highlights the cultural and social benefits – as well as the financial challenges of their business model (Gov.UK, 2023).

The Union Chapel provides us with a snapshot of the challenges of sustaining a balanced scorecard: maintaining the congregation spiritually, sustaining community facing roles such as their response to poverty and homelessness; scheduling a delivery of music, culture and the arts to a wide audience and, lastly, maintaining a heritage asset.

Grand Junction at St Mary Magdalene, Paddington: Culture-Led Urban Regeneration

Partnership models in the commercial sector where a larger corporation partners with a start-up for both organisations to build and scale are growing (Brown et al., 2024). It is easy to see why this makes sense, both parties benefiting from access to new technology, data, access to funding and more resources. The same premise applies for a commercial partnership with the church with the added benefit of increasing funding opportunities.

A second case study from London, is the community and arts venue Grand Junction at St Mary Magdalene in Paddington managed by Paddington Development Trust on a 25-year lease with the Parochial Church Council (PCC). Paddington Development Trust is a community-based organisation and has worked in Paddington for over 25 years. Grand Junction is an iconic Grade 1 Listed building restored by Paddington Development Trust and the PCC and opened in 2019, six months before the pandemic completely closed things down. Since reopening in 2021 the Grand Junction@ St Mary Magdalene (GJ@SMM) Team has recovered cultural and community projects serving local residents and wider London audiences.

The Paddington Development Trust Impact Analysis 2023 shared by CEO, Neil Johnston, and shown in Table 12.1, highlights how the organisation continued to recover post pandemic and delivered:

Grand Junction's unique selling point is the inspirational beauty of the building, in what is referred to as a *cultural cold spot*, restricted and urban part of London, hemmed in by railway, canal and road. The success of the venue's community and commercial proposition rests in creating positive and intriguing stories that grow directly from these urban challenges while still remaining open for worship. Paddington Station, with the new Crossrail/ Elizabeth Line has already improved access to the Regent Canal and Grand

TABLE 12.1 Paddington Development Trust Impact Analysis 2023

Reach within the community:	• The adult community programme worked with 2992 adults • The Young People's programme worked with 2465 children and young people • Total community programme worked with 6100 people.
Reach outside the community:	• 23,599 visitors to GJ@SMM • 126 volunteers and placements worked with GJ@SMM over the year.
Reach through cultural engagement:	• The cultural programme was attended by 4575 people • Of 12 heritage tours surveyed in 2022/23, 32% of attendees come from ethnically diverse backgrounds • Out of the family shows, 58% of attendees come from ethnically diverse backgrounds.

Union Canal for pedestrians. Internal branding and interpretive signage champions the Living History of North Paddington with interactive elements greeting visitors on arrival with a Whispering Wall and heritage pages on their website. Branding identity celebrates the High Gothic features and Victorian colour palette in the stained-glass windows of the church and additional designs from interior floor tiles and architectural motifs. All elements of the visitor experience are congruent with the heritage of the building and its location in a modern, diverse community.

Early market research showed that there is both demand and a range of markets for GJ@SMM. In the early stages, it faced the challenge that, with the exception of the local North Paddington community, and heritage 'buffs', it was barely known to its target audiences and marketing focused on crucial profile-raising activities. This included collaboration with established heritage and cultural destination marketing and partnership with festivals representing the cultural diversity in West London; cultivation of tour companies and others to encourage group visits; and the development of a profile on social media, online and in the press.

Marketing continues to build a distinct reputation for GJ@SMM as a special place to be discovered, with clearly maintained links with its immediate community, with carefully selected event partners and promoters.

Grassmarket Community Project and Greyfriars Church, Edinburgh: Place-Based Social Enterprise

The Grassmarket Community Project (or GCP) is located in the centre of Edinburgh on Candlemaker Row and sees itself as both a charity and a social enterprise. Since its launch in 2010, GCP has established four main Social

Enterprises: Wood Workshop, which upcycles and makes new products out of old church pews; The Greyfriars Tartan, which weaves together the stories of Edinburgh's ancient Greyfriers Kirk; the legend of Greyfriers Bobby and the historic area of Grassmarket; Coffee Saints Cafe and their Events & Hospitality services.

In a podcast interview, Richard Frazer, Minister of Greyfriars Kirk told me and my fellow interviewer, "I had come with a bit of vision about what loosely might be described as a kind of 'hand up rather than a handout' culture. It was a recognition that if you just do things to people, it can be quite disempowering".[1]

They had to prove that Richard's philosophy of "a handup rather than a handout" could succeed commercially. "The Grassmarket had a bit of stigma still attached to it", Catering manager, Catherine Jones, remembers, "because the local community saw it as a homeless shelter, even though we didn't house anybody".[2] That image was at odds with the aim to provide quality services as a social enterprise.

The café's big moment came through partnership. The Grassmarket's central location in Edinburgh was an advantage they could exploit. Many of Edinburgh's walking tours were passing the Grassmarket daily, on their way to visit the famous Greyfriars Bobby grave in the kirkyard. Catherine followed some of the tour groups around, approaching them in person and emphasising the benefits for both partners. Sandemans New Europe agreed to a trial partnership with the Grassmarket Cafe and this, as well as nine other partners and clients, has further launched catering and events service in Edinburgh. Current figures from their Social Impact Report 2023 available on the GCP website (Grassmarket Community Project, 2024) highlight the work and commitment invested in their business model: 64,862 hot drinks served between our two Coffee Saints cafes, 500 PupCups sold to furry customers and 11,000 delegates hosted in events spaces and outside catering.

The Grassmarket's social enterprises have grown by taking opportunities that fit their identity, location and approach to volunteering. All their social enterprises are run by volunteers, who are called members, and everyone follows the same induction programme. The main four social enterprises create both paid and volunteer roles, offering opportunities, training and support to those furthest from employment and education. Some who join without skills do move on into employment – one even pursued a Master's degree in furniture design.

> Our social enterprises are core to our sustainability, generating vital income that is reinvested back into the charity, and providing valuable workplace opportunities for our members and volunteers. Overall £772k of sales has been generated through all social enterprises.
>
> *(Grassmarket Community Project, 2024).*

Conclusion

An increasingly mixed-use environment presents a significant marketing challenge for church organisations and for their futures. Yes, there are challenges, but there are also significant rewards as seen in the three case studies: current success stories with clear marketing messages on their websites and social media, where all three maximise their duality of place. Marketing messaging must remind that in addition to being charities as well as places of worship, churches can also run a successful music venue, launch social enterprises and celebrate heritage. In addition, each one strives to capitalise on developing partnership relationships, indicating that a challenging location, building and reputation can be turned into a valuable and positive USP. They show how cultural and commercial engagement shapes both operational practice and reflection about place and identity.

Co-production, partnership and power sharing with local people, community ownership, commercial clients and charities hold key opportunities for churches to continue to be relevant in a society that is largely secular. This presents innovative charity-based marketing opportunities to work with a range of social challenges, and therefore engage a wide range of potential partners, volunteers and funders. At the same time, celebrating a valuable asset, beautiful buildings located in the heart of our cities, towns and villages.

Discussion Questions

1 Why should we care about churches when Britain is a multi-faith society?
2 Why do churches often underutilise strategic storytelling in promoting their partnerships, activities and relationships?
3 What strategies can churches employ to move beyond word-of-mouth promotion and create proactive, compelling narratives?

Notes

1 HeartEdge *How* Podcast Interview with Richard Frazer, Minister of Greyfriars Kirk, Catherine Jones, Catering manager Grassmarket Community Project, Sarah Rogers and Bev Thomas, 2021.
2 HeartEdge Case Studies, 2020 researched by Dr Naomi Jacobs; script available for members at The Gregory Centre (ccx.org.uk).

References

Benefact Trust, (2024). *Plunkett Foundation: Helping Churches Get Down to Business*. Available at: https://benefacttrust.co.uk/who-we-help/community-owned-businesses-in-churches/ (Accessed: April 2024)

Bowe, M. *et al.* (2019). "Sometimes, it's not just about the food': the social identity dynamics of foodbank helping transactions', *European Journal of Social Psychology*, 49(6), pp. 1128–1143. doi: 10.1002/ejsp.2558.

Bowe, M., Gray, D., Stevenson, C., McNamara, N., Wakefield, J. R. H., Kellezi, B., Wilson, I., Cleveland, M., Mair, E., Halder, M., & Costa, S. (2020). A social cure in the community: A mixed-method exploration of the role of social identity in the experiences and well-being of community volunteers. *European Journal of Social Psychology*, 50(7), 1523–1539. https://doi.org/10.1002/ejsp.2706

Bremer, T., (2001). *Religion on Display: Tourists, Sacred Place, and Identity at the San Antonio Missions*. Princeton University ProQuest Dissertations Publishing. Princeton, NJ. Available at: www.proquest.com/openview/99eb1e059693a5581 df8f2bd6aa08a51/1?pq-origsite=gscholar&cbl=18750&diss=y)

British Pilgrimage (2023). About us. Available at: https://britishpilgrimage.org/the-bpt/ (Accessed: January 2024).

British Pilgrimage (2024). Discover a new direction. www.britishpilgrimage.org/ (Accessed: January 2024).

Brown, S., Henz, T. Sibanda, T., and Wang, M. (2024). *How to Raise the Odds of Lasting Mutual Benefits When Large and Small Companies Team Up*. Available at: www.mckinsey.com/capabilities/strategy-and-corporate-finance/our-insig hts/collaborations-between-corporates-and-start-ups (Accessed: January 2024).

Denning, S. (2023). *The Rise of Christian Social Franchises: Responding to UK Poverty*. Available at: https://breadlineresearch.coventry.ac.uk/wp-content/uplo ads/2023/10/Faith-based-social-franchises-report (Accessed: January 2024).

English Heritage (2024). About us. www.english-heritage.org.uk/ (Accessed January 2024).

Getty Conservation Institute (2017). "Assessing values in conservation planning: Methodological issues and choices." In *Assessing the Values of Cultural Heritage: Research Report*, edited by Marta de la Torre. Los Angeles, CA: Getty Conservation Institute, pp. 5–30. www.getty.edu/conservation/publications_re sources/ (Accessed: January 2024).

Gov.UK (2014). *Guidance Excepted Charities* www.gov.uk/government/ publications/excepted-charities/excepted-charities--2#church-charities (Accessed: January 2024).

Gov.UK (2023). *The Union Chapel Project*. Available at: https://find-and-update.comp any-information.service.gov.uk/company/02583801 (Accessed: January 2024).

Gramatki, I., Lawto, R., Trotter, L., Reed, H., Watt, W. (2020). *The House of Good Report*. State of Life, www.stateoflife.org/news-blog/2020/10/14/house-of-good-the-social-value-of-church-buildings

Grassmarket Community Project (2024). *GCP Social Impact Report 2023* Available at: https://grassmarket.org (Accessed: January 2024).

Historic England (2020). *Heritage and the Economy 2020*. Available at: https://hist oricengland.org.uk/content/heritage-counts/pub/2020/heritage-and-the-economy-2020/. (Accessed: January 2024).

Jenkins, S. (2023). *The decline of churchgoing doesn't have to mean the decline of churches – they can help us level up*. The Guardian. (Accessed: January, 2024).

Jowell, T., (2006). "From consultation to conversation: The challenge of better places to live." In *Capturing the Public Value of Heritage: The Proceedings of the London Conference 25–26 January 2006*, edited by Kate Clark, 7–14. Swindon, UK: English Heritage.

Keel, A. L. and Tran, A. T. K. (2023) 'Increasing small nonprofits' influence through strategic storytelling', *Business Horizons*, 66(3), pp. 359–370.

Key, T. M., Keel, A. L., Czaplewski, A. J., & Olson, E. M. (2021). Brand activism change agents: Strategic storytelling for impact and authenticity. *Journal of Strategic Marketing*, 31(7), 1339–1355.

Marns, N. (2023). *A Cornish Celtic Way*. 3rd edn.

Naatu, F. and Alon, I., (2019). Social franchising: a bibliometric and theoretical review. *Journal of Promotion Management*, 25(5), pp.738–764.

National Churches Trust (2022). *The Future of UK Churches*. Available at: The Future of the UK's Church Buildings. (Accessed: January 2024).

Olsen, D., (2003). Heritage, tourism and the commodification of religion, *Tourism Recreation Research*, 28:3, DOI:10.1080/02508281.2003.11081422.

Olsen, D. H., and Timothy, D. J. (2006). *Tourism, Religion and Spiritual Journeys*. Abingdon, UK: Routledge.

Oxford Economics (2016). *The Impact of Heritage Tourism on the UK*. Available at: www.heritagefund.org.uk/sites/default/files/media/research/201609 27_-_the_impact_of_heritage_tourism_on_the_uk_economy_-_final_repo.pdf. (Accessed: January 2024).

Paveley, R. (2022). *Christians are harder to spot in UK, survey finds*. The Church Times. (Accessed: January 2024).

Russell, C. and McKnight, J., (2022). The Connected Community. 1st edn. Oakland, CA: Berrett-Koehler Publishers. Available at: www.perlego.com/book/3392471/ the-connected-community-discovering-the-health-wealth-and-power-of-neighb orhoods-pdf (Accessed: 15 October 2022).

Shannahan, C. and Denning, S., (2022). Politics, poverty and the church in an 'age of austerity'. *Religions*, 14(1), p.59.

The Big Issue, (2023). *The Map Shows Where to Find a Warm Bank This Winter*. Available at www.bigissue.com/news/social-justice/map-shows-where-to-find-warm-bank-near-you/. (Accessed: January 2024).

The Church Times, (2022). *Churches Continue to Offer Warm Spaces as UK Temperatures Frop*. Available at www.churchtimes.co.uk/articles/2022/9-decem ber/news/uk/churches-continue-to-offer-warmth-as-uk-temperatures-drop. (Accessed: January 2024).

The Church Times, (2023). *Can Commerce and Worship Co-Exist? A Way Out of the Red for Churches*. Available at: www.churchtimes.co.uk/articles/2023/21-april/ features/features/can-commerce-and-worship-co-exist-a-way-out-of-the-red-for-churches. (Accessed: April 2024).

The Economist, (2022). *Britain's Empty Churches Are Turning Into Campsites*. Available at: www.economist.com/britain/2022/07/28/britains-empty-churches-are-turning-into-campsites. (Accessed: November, 2022).

The Trussell Trust, (2023). *1.5 Million Food Parcels Distributed As Need Continues to Soar*. Available at: www.trusselltrust.org/2023/11/08/1-5-million-food-parcels-distributed-as-need-continues-to-soar/ (Accessed: January 2024).

Timothy, D. J. and Olsen, D. H. (2006) *Tourism, Religion, and Spiritual Journeys*. London: Routledge (Routledge studies in contemporary geographies of leisure, tourism, and mobility, v. 4.).

Union Chapel (2023). *From 1799 to Today*. Available at: https://unionchapel.org.uk/ projects/about-us/from-1799-to-today (Accessed: January 2024).

Visit Britain (2023). *Report: International Passenger Survey Total UK Summary 2022 (Published 26 May 2023)*. Available at: www.visitbritain.org/research-insights/inbound-visits-and-spend-annual-uk (Accessed: January 2024).

Visit England (2024). History and heritage. www.visitengland.com/things-to-do/history-and-heritage (Accessed: January 2024).

Wells, S. (2016). *Being with Other Faiths – Diocesan Interfaith Advisers' Conference, Lambeth Palace*. Available at: www.churchofengland.org/sites/default/files/2019-05/sam-wells-on-being-with-other-faiths.pdf (Accessed: January 2024).

13

ENVISIONING THE ROLE OF 'PLACE' IN CHARITY MARKETING AND NONPROFIT BRAND IDENTITY

Shalini Bisani and Edward Cartwright

Introduction and Theory

The primary goal of nonprofit branding is related to fundraising and donations by building trust, effectively communicating the values and beliefs of an organisation, stimulating engagement and acting to reduce the perceived risk to a donor (Lee, 2023). Moreover, nonprofit branding is also about relationship building and fostering participatory processes and collaboration over competition. Thus, branding applied to nonprofit organisations is significant for realising these commitments through aligning organisational identity with the sector's mission, vision and values, creating internal coherence and building trust and relationships with stakeholders and partners (Kylander & Stone, 2012).

Place (in the socio-economic–cultural–political sense of the word) is integral in defining the engagement activities and impact of the voluntary and community sector (VCS). The rising pressure on the third sector to fill gaps in essential public and social services have been studied in the public administration and nonprofit literature (Emerson et al., 2012; Guo and Acar, 2005; Moore, 2000). In tourism development, nongovernmental organisations and charities are known to promote heritage and culture, environmental concerns, conservation and social justice (Yüksel et al., 2005; Cole et al., 2021). VCS plays a distinctive function in place leadership due to its sense of profound duty and rootedness in the community to assist those in need and to advocate for the local people (Rees et al., 2022). Their social impact can be transformative in deprived areas, where they can influence the sense of place and community by building social capital (NPC, 2020). This is seen in a range of services the voluntary sector provides, from tackling homelessness

DOI: 10.4324/9781003396802-13

to arts engagement to volunteer-run museums (Bisani, 2021). While the voluntary sector's role in place leadership, placemaking and physical and cultural regeneration is significant, how 'place' can be leveraged in nonprofit branding and marketing remains unexplored in academic research.

The voluntary sector operates on a local, regional, national and global level and represents a significant part of the economic system (Curran, 2017). However, similar to the evolution of branding in the commercial (for-profit) sector, the praxis of charity marketing tends to focus on international nonprofit and charity brands. The most obvious indicator of a place association in nonprofit brand identity is seen in the brand name. The *Red Cross* is a well-known international humanitarian nonprofit brand. Across its 191 societies worldwide, it adopts a 'glocal' identity (a combination of global and local) in each country in which it operates, such as the *British Red Cross, Red Cross of Cape Verde, Thai Red Cross Society*. Each national society comprises of community-based volunteers and staff and provides varied services in each country. While they share the same principles (vision, mission and values), their services differ in response to the varied needs of communities and the society's relationships with their respective public authorities. Commonly used in product branding, the glocal strategy enables global brands such as the Red Cross to adapt to local needs. Beyond the brand name, the centrality of 'place' is evident in the charities' service delivery, consideration for local context needs, community engagement for donations, recruitment of volunteers and building relationships and support networks with its various stakeholders. Thus, 'place' can also be seen as a locus for demonstrating the impact of global movements at the community level.

A glocal marketing strategy can effectively reach charitable ethnocentric and cosmopolitan donors. It can appeal to the former groups' preference for supporting national charities and domestic causes while also meeting the needs of the latter group by aligning with the ideals and principles of internationalism (Hart & Robson, 2019). However, there is a research gap in understanding the effects of promoting place identity and attachment in nonprofit branding, which may offer insights into preferences and stakeholder engagement for more local causes. This form of place association can be likened to the country or county-of-origin (COO) branding strategy, whereby emphasising the 'regional' or 'national' identity is favourable for building successful firms and industry networks (Brodie & Benson-Rea, 2016; Clifton, 2014).

Applying the COO strategy to nonprofit branding can enable place-based connections between the VCS and public authorities, successful private firms, donors, communities, volunteers, etc. Within the networked approach, small and large place-based organisations can benefit from working together to pool resources, apply for joint funding and create impact (Bisani, 2021). For local and regional charities that are commonly smaller and less resourced than state, national or international charities, they can increase and maintain donors, enable community engagement and demonstrate impact in their locale. Thus, this chapter aims to develop a more research-informed approach and recommendations for utilising 'place' in local and regional charity branding. In this chapter, the case studies of Leicester and Northamptonshire in the East Midlands region of the UK will illustrate the significant role of VCS in place-based partnerships and branding. It provides the way forward for how 'place' can be leveraged in building nonprofit brand identity and stakeholder relationships for local and regional charities.

Background on charities in the UK

Given that this chapter will primarily focus on England, we provide some background context relevant to the importance of place. The Charity Commission for England and Wales is a government department that registers and regulates charities (Gov.UK, 2023). Every charity must have a public governing document that sets out the charities aims and purposes, and the rules for how it must operate. A charity's trustees must make sure the charity operates towards its aims and purposes. Charities must also be run for the public benefit and be clear on who they plan to benefit and how. Every charity is also obliged to produce a publicly available annual report that sets out the public benefit of activities. Information about any registered charity in England is readily accessible on the Charity Commission's Register of Charities.

Place is often an important component of a charity's governing document and annual report. To illustrate, consider an example of mission statements from charities in Leicestershire and Northamptonshire:

> To promote any charitable purposes for the benefit of the community of Leicester, Leicestershire and Rutland and in particular the advancement of education and furtherance of health and relief of poverty, distress and sickness.
>
> The Foundation will be seen as a catalyst of social change, making community philanthropy compelling and engaging local people in making communities better places to live, work, play and do business.

We see that place and local community are core to these charities' objectives. Indeed, they can only operate outside of the prescribed area if they can show it will have an indirect benefit within the area. The legislative framework around charities, thus, obliges charities to define the place in which they operate. The majority of voluntary organisations are constituted to operate at a local level (NCVO, 2021). For instance, data from the current register (at the time of writing) show that 56% of registered charities in England and

Wales operate at the local authority level, indicating a very narrowly defined geographical focus. If a charity deviates from the governing document, trustees may need to repay spent funds.

Case Study of 'Super-diverse' Leicester Census (2021) and COVID-19 Pandemic

Our first case study concerns the focal role of VCS in shaping the image and reputation of Leicester city in the national media. Leicester is a city in the East Midlands of the UK with a population of around 370,000 (Nomis, 2023a). It is a city with high levels of poverty and deprivation, and a low wage economy (Cartwright et al., 2020). Indeed, according to the 2019 UK government Index of Multiple Deprivation, Leicester is the 32nd most deprived local authority in England (out of a total of 317) (Gov.UK, 2019). Leicester is also characterised by ethnic diversity, leading to the tag of a 'super-diverse' city. Specifically, the 2021 Census revealed that 45% of the population are White British, 37% are Asian/Asian British and 6.2% Black/African/Caribbean/ Black British (Nomis, 2023b).

Media reporting of Leicester often paints the city in a negative light. For instance, the city is home to a large textile industry that often attracts headlines for poor working practices, such as low pay (Butler, 2022). The city has seen violent clashes fuelled by disinformation and ethnic tension (Omer, 2022). The city was also badly impacted during the COVID-19 pandemic with the longest time in lockdown of any UK city (Cartwright, 2020). In 2023, the then UK Home Secretary, Braverman, even used Leicester in a flagship speech as an example of how multiculturalism has 'failed' (Quinn, 2023). Such negative headlines can give a warped view of a dynamic and diverse city. The VCS in Leicester plays a vital role in counteracting that narrative and showing the positive aspects of the city. In other words, the VCS helps shape the perceptions of place, both for local residents and the wider public. Two community engagement projects that one of the authors were involved with help illustrate the positive role of the VCS.

Both projects were built around a community reporter model in which enthusiastic and passionate members of the local community enabled an inclusive dialogue within their communities around issues of economic and social policy. One project was based around the England and Wales Census 2021, and the other around designing an inclusive smart city for Leicester. The census takes place every 10 years and requires every household in the country to complete a survey (either online or hard copy) with basic details on living conditions, work, ethnicity, etc. The data from the census is widely used to inform policy and research, and so it is essential that it is accurate. Unfortunately, certain sections of society, e.g., those who do not speak English, or have caring responsibilities, may be systematically less likely to complete the census, leading to 'missing data' and biased inference. This was a particular concern in Leicester, given residents' widespread disengagement from mainstream communication channels coupled with the rapid population change that we know took place in Leicester since the previous census in 2011.

Given the importance of the census in shaping our understanding of Leicester and the policy landscape, a concerted effort was put into engaging residents with the Census. While local and national governments led this effort, it is clear that the VCS in Leicester was critical to its success. In particular, public policy was based on a one-dimensional strategy of advertising on mainstream media followed by knocking on doors to encourage compliance. The VCS, by contrast, recognised the importance of spreading awareness through nonmainstream channels and also engendering a positive reason to complete the survey, one that viewed it as an opportunity to shape our understanding of Leicester.

As we will explain shortly, our community engagement model harnessed the power of community radio. Community radio stations in the UK are licensed, nonprofit organisations that operate within a small geographical area and provide voice for their community. In Leicester, there are several community radio stations serving different audiences, such as multilingual EAVA FM, and Leicester Community Radio. Such radio stations provide a means to reach diverse audiences disengaged from mainstream media. Crucially, however, engagement is driven by positive content and dialogue, rather than public messaging. In other words, it is about speaking with the community rather than to the community. In our project, we partnered with a range of organisations from the VCS to produce content, aired on community radio stations, designed to engage residents in the census.

The census completion rates in Leicester were well above those expected and the data are helping shape how Leicester is perceived as one of the first 'super-diverse' cities in the UK (Vynter, 2022). The 2021 census provides, therefore, a telling example of how the VCS came together to help shape a positive narrative around place. Our second project, still ongoing, was designed to embrace those principles in looking at how to design a smart city that is inclusive to all. Leicester, like many cities across the world, has ambitions to become a smart city. Smart technology can, however, alienate some and widen inequalities, particularly if it creates a dependence on digital devices, broadband etc. It is vital, therefore, that the VCS plays a role in shaping the design and implementation of a smart city. We adapted our community reporter model to create a cross-community debate on an inclusive smart city. Again, the VCS in Leicester were very interested in shaping how a smart Leicester should look.

A schematic of the community reporter model for our smart city project is provided in Figure 13.1. There are four aspects of the community reporter

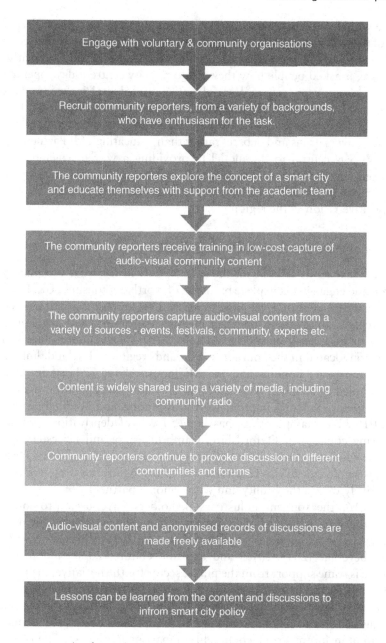

FIGURE 13.1   A schematic representation of the community reporter model.
Source: Author (E Cartwright).

model we would emphasise here: (a) The community reporters were selected because of their enthusiasm for community engagement; media and other skills were not needed. (b) Community engagement focused on lived experience. For instance, it asked people how they got to the city centre today, opening a conversation on economic and social policy, and digital inclusion. This approach enables anyone to engage in the conversation, irrespective of their expertise. (c) Dissemination, e.g., through community radio, is focused on provoking conversations and debate, rather than 'educating'. (d) Partnership with the VCS is central to the model in providing a way to engage with people from across different communities and backgrounds. This can be useful in amplifying the work that the VCS is doing in the region and provide a more positive vision of the region.

Case Study of Place Branding Northamptonshire

The second case study is built on the role of VCS in fostering community leadership and engagement in place branding of Northamptonshire, UK. Place branding is the practice of developing brands for geographical locations such as cities, regions and nations to trigger positive associations and distinguish a territory or location from others (Anholt, 2010). Northamptonshire is a county-region located in the South East Midlands region of England, linking Oxford, Cambridge, London and the Midlands. About 77% of its land area is occupied in farming, while 70% of the county's population lives in the urban towns of Northampton, Corby, Kettering and Wellingborough (NCC, 2019). Northamptonshire has higher levels of deprivation than its neighbouring counties of Oxfordshire, Cambridgeshire and Leicestershire, in terms of education, income and employment (Bisani et al., 2022). Place branding is significant to this county-region to distinguish itself by working collaboratively within the county and with regional partners.

Since 2016, the tourism industry stakeholders have been promoting Northamptonshire as 'Britain's Best Surprise', launching a themed campaign each year, starting with a focus on stately homes (in 2016), churches (2017), food and beverage (2018–2019) and arts and culture (2020) and so on. While there is some support from the public sector for the initiative, the main critique has been the lack of participation and representation from diverse communities and sub-cultures that are part of the fabric of the post-industrial towns. This has resulted in the promotion of 'mainstream' and 'dated' images of Northamptonshire as a rural county. In comparison, *Nenescape Landscape Partnership*, a voluntary- and public-sector-led scheme, exemplifies community engagement for river regeneration and tourism promotion in the county. In 2017, the partnership secured a five-year Heritage Funding to help protect and promote the natural and built heritage in the Nene Valley (Nenescape.org, 2017). Over and above the associations with ruralness and

nature, the project objective included the industrial Boot and Shoe heritage
of the towns:

> Promote the Nene Valley as a visitor destination and improve opportunities
> for local residents to learn about local heritage and traditions and identify
> with the River Nene as it progresses from an industrial landscape to a
> recreational space.
>
> *(Nenescape.org, 2023, p. 16)*

During the development of these place branding initiatives, one of the
authors led a qualitative research inquiry into voluntary and community
representations and participation in Northamptonshire place branding
from 2017 to 2021. The case study presented here is based primarily on the
accounts of the public, private, voluntary and community participants and
secondary documentation. The findings highlight how 'place' can provide
a locus and focus for nonprofit brand identity, public and private sector
partnerships, and community engagement to achieve the VCS's objectives
and impact.

The VCS is a prominent contributor to the county's economy, with 2600
organisations and groups registered on the database of Local Infrastructure
Organisations and attracting income close to £300m through external
funding and the procurement of grants and contracts (VIN, 2021).
Moreover, engagement in place-based schemes and partnerships is essential
to the VCS's work so they can continue to fund community activities, build
relationships with the public and private sectors, and demonstrate local and
regional impact. VCS participants in our study noted their role in place
branding as co-creating with communities to 'give them control' and foster
community pride.

> .. we try and encourage them to be proud of the village they live in. And
> things like community planning, neighbourhood planning, help us to do
> that, by giving them that control [..] And that often will bring out quite a
> lot pride in the people in the village they live in, their rural area.
>
> *(Voluntary sector participant)*

For engaging and empowering communities, the VCS provided grant funding
to community projects and included them in decision-making through
volunteer-led advisory panels. It supported these voluntary engagements
with skills training and workshops. The operationalisation of all three
engagement mechanisms was evidenced in the working of Nenescape. The
partnership awarded community grant funding to volunteer-led projects
that aligned with Nenescape's objectives. The grant supported various
initiatives that celebrated heritage in the Nene Valley and highlighted the

'hidden stories' that were not widely known before the scheme (Nenescape. org, 2023). Moreover, volunteers were invited to form an evaluation panel to select the grant awards. They were supported with guidance and tools, such as evaluation scorecards, and provided access to archival resources and training.

A commonality between the voluntary organisations we spoke to was their mission to serve the most vulnerable and 'hard to reach' groups in society. They were working in response to the complex environment and unique and granular details which underpin community needs and aspirations. They saw themselves as part of the 'bottom-up regeneration' of the area in response to local community needs. However, they faced immense 'pressure' to provide services and operate within already constrained resources and capacity. Under resource constraints, partnership working within the sector and with public and private actors was a key coping mechanism for the voluntary sector. For instance, to reach and engage a younger audience, Nenescape leveraged the community connections of one of its local partners (a film production company). This collaboration led to the co-production of a feature film about river Nene and an interactive map of the 'Northampton Boot trail' with young people from disadvantaged backgrounds – which was noted as a key achievement of the partnership:

> .. working with [the filming company], with its strong track record in engaging with diverse communities and disadvantaged people, was a key factor in its success reaching new audiences.
>
> *(Nenescape.org, 2023, p. 70)*

The voluntary and community organisations formed a regional consortium to consolidate the voices and interests of the sector, working collaboratively with parish, local and regional councils, community and charity groups, individual and ad-hoc volunteers, national funders and commercial partners. Further, the prominent voluntary organisations in the county were part of national networks and portfolio projects, which gave them access to participate in and represent local community needs in national policies and agenda setting. From the public sector perspective, VCS representatives played an important advocacy function for and in their communities. In doing so, they occupied a unique 'intermediary position' between regional institutions and local communities:

> .. we normally have a main representative to represent the organisation or the community group, and they would stand on a steering group or a panel and then it'd be their job to attend. They get the information, go back to, deliver it to their community.
>
> *(Public sector participant)*

TABLE 13.1 The role of voluntary and community sector in place branding

Roles	Codes from the data
Community engagement for bottom-up regeneration of places	• Knowledge and engagement with hard-to-reach, vulnerable groups • Funding community projects and activities through grants • Training and upskilling communities • Developing new mechanisms for participation
Community leadership	• Representation and advocacy on policy networks • Connections with public and private actors • Intermediary position between regional institutions and local communities • Linking local–regional–national and potentially international agendas

Source: Adapted from Bisani (2021).

Over and above leveraging the local–regional–national connections, one regional charity linked its community activities and impact with the international sustainable development goals set by the United Nations (UN SDGs). For contributing to *Goal 11: Sustainable cities and communities*, the charity reportedly collaborated with over a hundred organisations and community groups for its realisation. Consequent to its social mission, values and activities, VCS claimed the role of 'community leaders' and experts in 'community engagement for bottom-up regeneration' in place branding (see Table 13.1). They are able to do so by leveraging: (i) Local knowledge and connections with various deprived and hard-to-reach community groups, (ii) Collaboration within the third sector and partnerships with public authorities and private sector firms, (iii) Alignment of their mission, vision and values (brand identity) with place-based partnerships and coalitions and (iv) Links with universal social concerns and national networks, which can play to their advantage in fostering stakeholder relationships and influencing place-based policy.

Looking to the Future: How 'Place' Can Be Leveraged in Nonprofit Brand Identity and Relationship Building

Looking to the future, nonprofit organisations can strategically leverage the concept of 'place' to enhance their brand identity and cultivate stakeholder relationships. Three central recommendations emerge for local and regional charity branding from our case studies.

Linking local initiatives with global values: To broaden their appeal to wider audiences, local and regional charity brands should establish a clear

192 Shalini Bisani and Edward Cartwright

connection between their initiatives and national and international values and agendas. The introductory example of the Red Cross illustrates how 'place' can serve as a powerful focal point for demonstrating the impact of global movements at the grassroots level. The cases of Leicester and Northamptonshire demonstrate how local charities can position themselves as contributors to global agendas such as UN SDGs and smart city development. This strategic alignment bridges local community needs with broader global issues, amplifying the relevance and impact of their work.

Positioning themselves as an essential partner and voice for communities in place-based partnerships: Due to their intermediary role between the public sector and local communities, local and regional charities can position themselves as indispensable partners to the public sector and advocates for their communities in place-based partnerships and schemes (Bisani, 2021). The case studies of Leicester and Northamptonshire exemplify the unique role that community-based organisations play in enabling community representation and participation, while sharing resources and responsibilities with partners. By actively engaging in place-based collaborations, these organisations can not only achieve their fundraising and donation objectives but also become influential advocates for the communities they serve.

Positioning themselves as experts in community engagement for inclusive decision-making: To fulfil their social mission and secure a partnering role in place-based schemes, local and regional charities can leverage their expertise in community engagement. The case studies reveal VCS' innovative approaches, such as the use of film, community radio, interactive maps and the community reporter model, showcasing their proficiency in community engagement and co-creation strategies. By leveraging this expertise, particularly for engaging hard-to-reach and vulnerable groups, these organisations can actively contribute to inclusive decision-making processes within place-based partnerships. Furthermore, they can establish themselves as community leaders, playing a pivotal role in shaping local and regional policies (Rees et al., 2022). This leadership position not only aligns with their social mission but also positions them as agents of positive change in policy decisions, championing the interests and values of diverse and marginalised communities.

While our findings illustrate the significant contributions VCS make, a key challenge they must overcome is communicating the value-add from their services and activities that are often taken for granted by residents and local policymakers. Despite the impact of austerity on the reduced funding of VCS activities by the public sector, government support is vital for access to participation and influence in local and regional policy and securing private sector buy-in (Bowden & Liddle, 2018). Emphasising local knowledge and connections with the place in nonprofit branding can be favourable for building relationships with local authorities, communities, volunteers, etc. (Clifton, 2014). We argue that the key to the sector's future, especially smaller organisations, is that they are seen as an integral part of their community and local infrastructure. Leveraging place in nonprofit brand identity and engagement can help communicate their commitment to the equitable development of cities, towns and regions. This is significant for forging stronger relations with the institutional and community stakeholders and sustaining income from local and national government and place-based schemes.

In conclusion, the future of charity branding lies in strategically integrating 'place' into their organisational identity (mission, vision, values), operations (engagement activities) and demonstrating impact. By adopting these recommendations, local and regional charities can navigate the complexities of stakeholder engagement and contribute significantly to bottom-up regeneration, community engagement practices and community leadership. Thus, 'place' is not only integral to the brand image of these organisations but also ensures their sustained relevance and impact in the dynamic landscape of the nonprofit sector.

List of Abbreviations

VCS – Voluntary and Community Sector
UN SDG – United Nation's Sustainable Development Goal
COO – Country or County of Origin

Discussion Questions

1 Place identity: What are the pros and cons of using 'place identity' in charity marketing? What factors should local and regional charities consider when applying this concept?
2 Glocal marketing strategy: Besides referencing the UN SDGs, what other methods and frameworks can local and regional charities use to implement a glocal marketing strategy?
3 Community engagement: How do local charities engage with communities? How can they use community engagement to participate in government schemes focused on specific locations?
4 Long-term strategy: How can the charity sector maintain their role in place-based governmental schemes, despite challenges with resources?

References

Anholt, S. (2010) Definitions of place branding – working towards a resolution. *Place Branding and Public Diplomacy*. **6**(1), 1–10.

Bisani, S. (2021) *Exploring Stakeholder Participation and Representations in Region Branding: The Case of Northamptonshire, UK*. Northampton, UK: University of Northampton.

Bisani, S., Daye, M., Mortimer, K. (2022) Multi-stakeholder perspective on the role of universities in place branding. *Journal of Place Management and Development*. **15**(2), 112–129.

Bowden, A., Liddle, J. (2018) Evolving public sector roles in the leadership of place-based partnerships: from controlling to influencing policy? *Regional Studies*. **52**(1), 145–155.

Brodie, R.J., Benson-Rea, M. (2016) Country of origin branding: an integrative perspective. *Journal of Product and Brand Management*. **25**(4), 322–336.

Butler, S. (2022) Poor working conditions persist in Leicester garment factories, finds survey | Leicester | The Guardian. *The Guardian*. [online]. Available from: www.theguardian.com/uk-news/2022/jun/13/poor-working-conditions-persist-in-leicester-garment-factories-finds-survey [Accessed 25 January 2024].

Cartwright, E. (2020) Leicester economist: our city was vulnerable to a coronavirus outbreak. *The Conversation*. [online]. Available from: https://theconversation.com/leicester-economist-our-city-was-vulnerable-to-a-coronavirus-outbreak-141709 [Accessed 25 January 2024].

Cartwright, E., Luong, T.A., Payne, J., Virmani, S. (2020) *The Economic Impact of the Coronavirus Pandemic for Leicester*. SSRN. 3622981.

Clifton, N. (2014) Towards a holistic understanding of county of origin effects? Branding of the region, branding from the region. *Journal of Destination Marketing & Management*. **3**(2), 122–132.

Cole, S., Wardana, A., Dharmiasih, W. (2021) Making an impact on Bali's water crisis: Research to mobilize NGOs, the tourism industry and policy makers. *Annals of Tourism Research*. **87**, 103119.

Curran, R. (2017) *Unpacking Non-profit Brand Heritage: Creating More Satisfied and Committed Volunteers*. Edinburgh, UK: Heriot-Watt University.

Emerson, K., Nabatchi, T., Balogh, S. (2012) An integrative framework for collaborative governance. *Journal of Public Administration Research and Theory*. **22**(1), 1–29.

GOV.UK (2019) English indices of deprivation 2019. Ministry of Housing, Communities and Local Government. [online]. Available from: www.gov.uk/government/statistics/english-indices-of-deprivation-2019 [Accessed 14 April 2020].

GOV.UK (2023) *The Charity Commission – GOV.UK*. [online]. Available from: www.gov.uk/government/organisations/charity-commission [Accessed 25 January 2024].

Guo, C., Acar, M. (2005) Understanding collaboration among nonprofit organizations: combining resource dependency, institutional, and network perspectives. *Nonprofit and Voluntary Sector Quarterly*. **34**(3), 340–361.

Hart, D.J., Robson, A. (2019) Does charity begin at home? National identity and donating to domestic versus international charities. *Voluntas*. **30**(4), 865–880.

Kylander, N., Stone, C. (2012) The role of brand in the nonprofit sector. *Stanford Social Innovation Review*. **10**(2), 36–41.

Lee, Z. (2023) Building brands for nonprofit organisations: a review of current themes and future research directions. In *Era for Brand Management in a New Era of Consumerism*. Cheltenham, UK: Edward Elgar Publishing, pp. 257–272.

Moore, M.H. (2000) Managing for value: organizational strategy in for-profit, nonprofit, and governmental organizations. *Nonprofit and Voluntary Sector Quarterly*. **29**(1), 183–204.

NCC (2019) *Demography Update: Northamptonshire Joint Strategic Needs Assessment Insight Pack*, September 2019. Northamptonshire County Council, 28. [online]. Available from: www.northamptonshire.gov.uk/councilservices/health/health-and-wellbeing-board/northamptonshire-jsna/Documents/DemographyJSNA_2019.pdf [Accessed 1 January 2020].

NCVO (2021) Where are voluntary organisations based? – Profile I UK Civil Society Almanac 2021 I NCVO. UK Civil Society Almanac 2021 DATA. TRENDS. INSIGHTS. [online]. Available from: www.ncvo.org.uk/news-and-insights/news-index/uk-civil-society-almanac-2021/profile/where-are-voluntary-organisations-based/ [Accessed 25 January 2024].

Nenescape.org (2017) Nenescape project governance. *Nenescape Landscape Partnership Scheme*, 12. [online]. Available from: https://nenescape.org/partner-information/l3fb9dyerf8e5etb24m9c7hpj8jt8x?rq=governance [Accessed 1 January 2020].

Nenescape.org (2023) *Nenescape Landscape Partnership Scheme Final Evaluation Report*.

Nomis (2023a) Labour market profile – nomis – official census and labour market statistics. *Nomisweb.co.uk*. [online]. Available from: www.nomisweb.co.uk/reports/lmp/la/1946157130/report.aspx [Accessed 25 January 2024].

Nomis (2023b) Local area report for areas in England and Wales – Nomis. *Leicester Local Authority – Local Area Report*. [online]. Available from: www.nomisweb.co.uk/reports/localarea?compare=E06000016 [Accessed 25 January 2024].

NPC (2020) *Where Are England's Charities?*, 1–13.

Omer, N. (2022) Wednesday briefing: What's behind the violent clashes in Leicester I Leicester I The Guardian. *The Guardian*. [online]. Available from: www.theguardian.com/world/2022/sep/21/wednesday-briefing-whats-behind-violent-clashes-in-leicester [Accessed 25 January 2024].

Quinn, B. (2023) Rishi Sunak rejects Braverman claim multiculturalism has failed I Rishi Sunak I The Guardian. *The Guardian*. [online]. Available from: www.theguardian.com/politics/2023/sep/28/rishi-sunak-rejects-braverman-claim-multiculturalism-has-failed [Accessed 25 January 2024].

Rees, J., Sancino, A., Jacklin-Jarvis, C., Pagani, M. (2022) 'You can't Google everything': the voluntary sector and the leadership of communities of place. *Leadership*. **18**(1), 102–119.

VIN (2021) *Operational Strategy 2021–23. Connecting People to Places*. Northampton, UK: Voluntary Impact Northampton.

Vynter, R. (2022) 'Diversity is a beautiful thing': the view from Leicester and Birmingham. The Guardian. [online]. Available from: www.theguardian.com/uk-news/2022/nov/29/leicester-birmingham-first-super-diverse-uk-cities-census.

Yüksel, F., Bramwell, B., Yüksel, A. (2005) Centralized and decentralized tourism governance in Turkey. *Annals of Tourism Research*. **32**(4), 859–886.

14

WHAT A WASTE!

How Charities Can Help Use Food Wisely

M. Bilal Akbar, Alison Lawson and Barbara Tomasella

Introduction

Reducing waste is essential in a world where the number of people affected by hunger has been slowly rising since 2014, and tonnes of edible food is wasted daily (Butler, 2022). It was reported recently that in the UK, 9.5 million tonnes of food went to waste per year, which is alarming when 8.4 million people in the UK are in food poverty (Jeswani et al., 2021; Office for the National Statistics, 2021; Armstrong et al., 2021; Begho and Zhao, 2023). Even though the role of charities is commendable in reducing food waste through promoting awareness of the issues with various actors (Lohnes, 2021; Vlaholias et al., 2015), the issue of food waste is still growing in the UK (Jeswani et al., 2021). Food waste is a complex issue that involves many actors, including farms, food processing and packaging companies, restaurants, supermarkets, consumers and many more.

Charities, individual households and commercial businesses in the UK are making efforts to explore the idea of donating food to homeless shelters, food banks, local farms or food charities. This benefits the environment and reduces the damaging effects of landfills, incorporating the social responsibility to share needed food. However, more effort is needed to overcome the issue of food waste, considering 70% of all food produced and available to consumers is wasted (UN, 2021). Importantly, a huge amount of food waste is still edible when discarded. The National Resources Defence Council reports that the highest percentage of food waste is from consumers rather than food loss along the supply chain (NRDC, 2017). When consumers waste food, they also waste all the significant resources utilised to get it from the farm to plates (Jenkins et al., 2022). There are opportunities for charities

DOI: 10.4324/9781003396802-14

and nonprofit organisations to utilise social marketing techniques to achieve the transformative behavioural changes needed to tackle food waste. Such techniques are used by consumers and other actors involved in generating social change (Schmidtke et al., 2021).

This chapter aims to provide an overview of food waste issues in the UK and presents social marketing as a potential solution for the future. Social marketing goes beyond traditional marketing methods by utilising behavioural theories such as the nudge theory and, in some cases, even goes further and focuses on hugs, shoves and smacks using effective communication tools (French, 2011). Such approaches within social marketing propose ways to improve decisions related to social issues by encouraging positive behaviours that benefit individuals and society (Thaler & Sunstein, 2015; Lee & Kotler, 2022).

What Is Social Marketing?

Social marketing is defined by the International Social Marketing Association (ISMA) as an activity that integrates marketing concepts with other approaches to influence behaviour that benefit individuals and communities for the greater social good. Ethical principles guide social marketing practice by integrating research, practice, theory, audience and partnership to inform the delivery of competition-sensitive and segmented social change programmes that are effective, efficient, equitable and sustainable (ISMA et al., 2017).

Social marketing involves applying techniques to change or maintain people's behaviour to benefit individuals and society (Rodríguez-Sánchez, 2023). The growing political, economic and environmental challenges impacting the world have increased awareness of social marketing within the corporate environment and have convinced organisations to develop new ways to deliver value while also considering wider social issues (Manikam & Russell-Bennett, 2016; Aya Pastrana & Obregón, 2023). Whereas corporate social responsibility focuses on an organisation committing to responsible consumption and production processes (Gaski, 2022), social marketing is concerned with creating awareness and prompting socially responsible behaviour, assimilating the overall benefit for all involved parties (Gordon et al., 2016; Kamin et al., 2022).

Social marketing persuades individuals to adapt to the recommended behaviour; however, the critical insight for developing social marketing stems from social determinants. Lee and Kotler (2022) recommended that efforts to change citizens' behaviours are known as the downstream approach while making a case for policy change and influencing those with the power to make wider societal change for the good of society, which are widely acknowledged as an upstream approach in social marketing. Kennedy et al. (2018, p. 259) defined upstream social marketing as "a method for social marketers to influence policy and solution adoption, as it focuses on the macro/structural environment moving beyond the individual or community level of downstream and midstream social marketing." In contrast, downstream social marketing is mainly directed at individual consumers (Khajeh et al., 2015). Based on this definition, upstream social marketing tends to adapt the application of marketing to directly influence the decisions and attitudes of consumers by making changes in relevant policies, laws and regulations. Successful upstream social marketing helps practitioners develop interventions that help consumers cooperate with or adapt to the required change.

Social Marketing Fundamentals

Social marketing is inspired by commercial marketing, and its key principles are the same as commercial marketing; however, Andreasen (2002) provided specific benchmark criteria summarising key social marketing principles:

1 Behaviour change must be the benchmark used to design and evaluate interventions.
2 Interventions must use audience research to: (a) understand target audiences at the outset of interventions (i.e., formative research), (b) routinely pre-test intervention elements before they are implemented and (c) monitor interventions as they are rolled out.
3 Target audiences must be carefully segmented to ensure maximum efficiency and effectiveness when using scarce resources.
4 The central element of the intervention must be based on creating attractive and motivational exchanges with target audiences.
5 The strategy must use a traditional marketing mix; for example, it is not just advertising or communications. That is, it creates attractive benefits packages (products) while minimising costs (price) wherever possible, making the exchange convenient and easy (place) and communicating powerful messages through media relevant to – and preferred by – target audiences (promotion).
6 Careful attention must be paid to competing behaviours.

Social marketers consider the 4Ps of marketing to effectively bring change in people's behaviour; however, the significance of social marketing tends to come out through collaborating with social messages and actions (Dolan et al., 2019). The consideration of the 4Ps of marketing indicates the first major principle of social marketing implementation. Similarly, Hamid and Khan (2020) also stress the significance of segmentation in the target audience for social marketing practice. As mentioned in Andreasen's (2002) criteria, following the robust analysis of data collection from quantitative and qualitative research, the segmentation of the audience not only identifies the reachable group but also clarifies the messages for implementation to change behaviour. Thus, segmentation of the audience becomes the core principle in social marketing practice.

Using evidence-based approaches and consumer research that has identified 'mindsets' helps social marketers set clear goals for the desired behaviour. Understanding audience motivation brings systematic and targeted recognition of who will benefit and how they will benefit. Combining segmentation with the audience mindset makes the behaviour change focus more prominent in social marketing. Thus, identifying people's mindsets is an important step in implementing successful social marketing. Social marketing also recognises that citizens may face many barriers to adopting new behaviours. These barriers could be related to mindset but could also be related to cost, convenience, peer pressure and other factors. Careful consumer research should identify these barriers and potential solutions before implementing a behaviour change programme.

The contemporary social marketing practice uses Andreasen's (2002) criteria as a baseline to focus on value co-creation (Domegan et al., 2013), behavioural sustainability (Akbar & Barnes, 2023; Akbar et al., 2019), partnership approach (Bryant et al., 2014) and system thinking (Flaherty et al., 2020). As a multi-dynamic, interdisciplinary, cross-sector approach, social marketing tends to cut through the diverse ways of influencing behaviours to facilitate and encourage social change.

Social marketing interventions are based on step-by-step planning (Bhat et al., 2019). However, in developing and implementing social marketing, managers and marketers face real-time barriers that can pressure the circumstances and influence the outcome of social marketing interventions (Gbadamosi et al., 2013).

Co-creation – A Social Marketing Approach

Value for customers is an important aspect of marketing management, and how it benefits organisations and consumers, arguing the significance of value recognition and creation (Bhat et al., 2019). In marketing, value co-creation is "a complex blend of people, technology, organisations, and information through a complex interaction between service providers and customers" (Hamidi et al., 2020, p. 9). Similarly, social marketing encourages the target audience to engage in joint analysis, develop strategies and use collective learning to achieve behavioural change. Social marketing emphasises exchanges in value co-creation by consumers' active participation in planning (e.g., research, understanding consumers' needs, behaviours, ability to quit/adopt behaviours), designing (e.g., participation in designing messaging and material for the intervention) and delivering (e.g., feedback, lessons learning, celebrating successes, learning from failures) interventions (Domegan et al., 2013). More specifically, social marketing operationalises value co-creation by developing dialogue and encouraging audience interaction, communication and collaboration at various stages.

The value co-creation model, with its three dimensions of value-in-use, value-in-context and value-in-information (Akaka et al., 2012), is suggested to be highly effective in social marketing interventions (Hastings & Domegan, 2012). For example, the value co-creation model should be used in social marketing planning and implementation without any sequence and should be considered iterative with value-in-use, value-in-context and value-in-information occurring simultaneously within and across processes of co-discovery, co-design and co-delivery. The process of value co-discovery includes uncovering and exploring new types of value (Domegan et al., 2013). Value co-discovery theorises dialogue, interaction and mutual learning (value-in-information) to construct new value propositions (Ind & Coates, 2013). The aim is to build shared meanings and gain individual and collective insights (value-in-context) into what the involved actors can do to find solutions for social problems (value-in-use). Similarly, the process for value co-design takes co-created insights and knowledge (value-in-information) from the value co-discovery development and translates it into social offerings. As part of the value co-design process, the social marketers and target audiences collaborate to exemplify (value-in-context) and enable the desired behaviours. Value co-delivery takes ideas from value co-discovery and value co-design to scale through coordinated value-in-use, value-in-context and value-in-information strategies to facilitate interaction (Akaka et al., 2012), suggesting a collaborative approach. This involves joint knowledge production and integrating insights from all partners to develop resonant messaging and impactful programming (Akaka et al., 2012).

As co-creation is a social marketing approach to behaviour change that can be used by a range of organisations, such as governments, non-governmental organisations and charities, to tackle a range of societal issues, might it be useful to tackle the wicked problem of food waste?

Food Waste in the UK – A Wicked Problem

Unconsumed food results in food waste along the food supply chain, from the farm to distribution, production, processing and retail to the consumers. The reasons for food waste are losses from mould and pests, inadequate climate control, cooking waste and intentional food waste (Kennard, 2020). The main types of food waste are domestic and commercial. Domestic food waste refers to the waste generated by households through non-commercial activities, including meat, vegetables, grains, fruits and dairy wasted due to poor storage, preparation or during cooking, serving and after serving (Meah & Waston, 2011; Evans, 2012; Waston & Meah, 2013). Domestic food waste contributes to 6.6 million tonnes of waste, which accounts for 70% of the total waste generated annually in the UK (Jackman, 2023). Commercial food waste refers to unsellable food, leftovers from consumers and by-products from manufacturers.

The UK generates around 9.5 million tonnes of food waste annually, of which 1.1 million is from the hospitality and food sector. Restaurants in the UK throw away the equivalent of 320 million meals per year, whereas the retail industry is responsible for 0.3 million tonnes of food waste annually (WRAP, 2020). Every year, with most UK households celebrating Christmas, December alone accounts for an average of 30% of the annual food waste in the UK. One in every seven UK consumers purchases more food for Christmas than they need. More specifically, on average, more than 4.2 million Christmas dinners, 263,000 turkeys, 7.5 million mince pies, 740,000 Christmas pudding, 17.2 million Brussels sprouts, 11.9 million carrots and 11.3 million roast potatoes are wasted in the UK (Dobson, 2023). The major reasons for these statistics are consumers buying extra food, failing to store the leftovers, excessive cooking and letting food go off before eating.

Consumerism can also be seen as a major cause of Christmas food waste. Each product is carefully and strategically designed to affect the psychology of the buyers, increasing their desire to purchase. Accelerating consumerism means wanting more than needed, leading to overconsumption (excessive buying), overeating and food waste, resulting in an unhealthy population and environmental and societal issues (Jones-Garcia et al., 2022). Black Friday in the UK is another prime example of overconsumption, resulting in millions of tonnes of food waste (Kennard, 2020). The London Daily News (2023) claims that 80% of Black Friday products end up in landfills. In 2023, 429,000 metric tonnes of gas emissions from product deliveries were expected on Black Friday, equal to 435 return flights from London to New York (EveryDay Green, 2023).

Another notable example of food waste is in schools. With more than 32,000 schools in the UK, 90% of the children eat school meals. More specifically, only in England, schools contribute approximately 86,000 tonnes of food waste annually, with 68,000 tonnes from primary schools and 28,000 from secondary schools (Stein & Polychronakis, 2023). The reasons behind food waste at schools include extra food being prepared and not served, extra-large portions (e.g., portion size not appropriate to child age/appetite, food being thrown away uneaten because of portion sizes), poor eating environment (e.g., lack of time, poor dining experience), unappealing meal choices (e.g., taste) or a combination of all these factors (WRWA, 2023).

Role of the Charity Sector

In the hope of finding food waste solutions, in 2018, the UK launched the Food Waste Reduction Roadmap as an initiative comprising various milestones for food producers, manufacturers, retailers and hospitality and food service companies to consider and ensure the food waste problem is addressed. In 2020, 261 organisations reported their commitment to the roadmap, including 162 manufacturers, 16 retailers and 35 food and hospitality businesses. In mid-2020, 171 organisations reported implementing the 'Target, Measure, Act' strategy (WRAP, 2023). The main principles of the strategy are explained below:

Target – Targets set aims and ambitions, and ambitions motivate actions. The UK government and organisations must adopt food waste reduction targets following SDG target 12.3, which is to "halve per capita global food waste at the retail and consumer levels and reduce food losses along production and supply chains, including post-harvest losses" by 2030 (UN, 2021).

Measure – "What gets measured gets managed" is a claim describing food waste and is relevant to the overall food waste sector. Governments and organisations must have measurable food waste figures to identify the exact amount that needs action.

Act – Lastly, action is what matters the most. Based on the information from measurement, authorities must plan, develop and implement strategies for tackling the problem. National public and private partnerships, nonprofit organisations and food charities can take collaborative actions and establish practices and policies that engage everyone, from farmers to consumers, in a shared mission.

Various other initiatives and campaigns across the UK have been implemented, including:

- **Wasting Food** – *It's Out of Date,*[1] and *Love Food Hate Waste*[2] campaigns were launched to reduce household waste.
- **Grocery Code Action Network** calls for the Grocery Code Adjudicator in the UK.[3] Actions should be taken to prevent business and trading practices from producing large amounts of food waste.
- **Innovative Farmers** – A network of farmers researching and gathering data on food waste and its reduction practices.[4]
- **Guardians of Grubs** – Aimed at addressing food waste in the hospitality sector.[5]

Other food waste charities in the UK are *Feeding Britain,*[6] *FareShare,*[7] *UK Harvest,*[8] *The Felix Project,*[9] and *City Harvest.*[10] *Feeding Britain* is an award-winning charity with 80 regional and local anti-hunger partnerships with 700 organisations. *The Felix Project* promotes food waste reduction strategies via its social media channels. The project delivered 30,000,000 meals in 2021 to those in need. On the other hand, *UK Harvest* has incorporated visiting schools for food waste awareness and donations, conducting food drives in *The Regis School*,[11] and collecting 870 kg of food as donations on 5 December 2023. Similarly, *Fare Share* participated in *Tesco Winter Food Collection 2023*,[12] collecting food donations nationwide.

While large charitable non-governmental organisations such as WRAP are leading national initiatives to tackle food waste, there are ways that smaller charities can use co-creation to help local communities reduce waste. Food banks are, unfortunately, becoming more common and more necessary in the UK at the time of writing. While all the major supermarkets in the UK are partnered with charities to pass on surplus food, much of this goes to third parties for distribution to charities rather than food banks. Food banks require a specific range of foods to make up nutritionally balanced parcels for those who use the banks. Shoppers are encouraged to donate to food banks in supermarkets by providing collection points, often shopping trolleys or boxes in the stores. Even during hard times, such as the present cost of living crisis, many households could afford to donate one or two items a week. What could be done to increase the amount donated and encourage the donation of an appropriate range of food items?

It is clear from these examples that charities are already engaged in tackling the issue of food waste and that some efforts are being made at a national level to encourage this. But, how could charities use social marketing techniques to improve their effectiveness in combating waste?

Co-creation for Charities

We recommend a co-creation approach for charities to tackle food waste issues (See Figure 14.1).

Co-discovery: co-discovery is a forward-looking view that contains collaborative interaction and articulation. More specifically, co-discovery establishes key concepts, such as shared values among actors, initiating governance and leadership, justifying benefits, gaining trust and building engagement (Saragih et al., 2018). Establishing a co-discovery approach to tackle food waste requires a deeper understanding of the target audience and how and why people waste food, requiring rigorous consumer research (Morgan, 2015) and other actors who may contribute to food waste behaviour, for example, commercial businesses, promotional activities and discounts. Actors should be encouraged to contribute to the interactional process to create shared values and gain each other's trust (Zainuddin et al.,

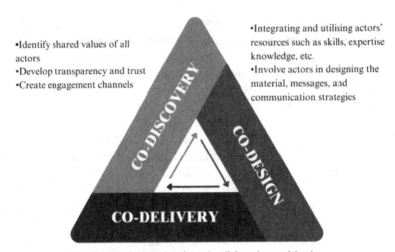

•Integrating and utilising actors' resources such as skills, expertise knowledge, etc.
•Involve actors in designing the material, messages, and communication strategies

•Identify shared values of all actors
•Develop transparency and trust
•Create engagement channels

Distribute the intervention through collaborative participation that creates value for all actors

FIGURE 14.1   Value co-creation approach for charities to tackle food waste framework.

2017). Such approaches integrate various stages to gain insight from the target audience to help analyse social problems, consumers' needs and their desired solutions for the food waste issue, reflection on consumers changing needs and feedback.

In the case of a food bank example, co-discovery would start with research about the issue – what stops citizens from donating? Is it a lack of awareness, inconvenience, worry about money, thinking that someone else should solve the problem, or just forgetting to put the extra items in the basket? And what is being done now to encourage donations? What would help citizens donate the range of items food banks need? What would help to motivate citizens to donate items or their time?

Such investigations would identify and define the shared values of various actors, resulting in developing transparency, trust and engagement with the intervention (Saragih et al., 2019). Co-delivery brings together expertise, knowledge and experience, including sharing or exchanging resources; it is not without challenges. For example, collaboration with various actors may result in communication issues, reputation risk through association, disproportionate contribution of resources, reaching agreements can take time and delay action, and maybe various partners are overly protective of their field or lifestyle. However, such challenges can be resolved through effective planning and are often outweighed by the potential advantages of campaigning in a network, coalition or alliance.

Co-design: Discussion with citizens in the co-discovery can help reveal the barriers and identify potential solutions, combining capabilities and sharing/exchanging resources (Saragih et al., 2019). It is important to understand that different actors may have different resources; for example, the target audiences must share their knowledge about food waste. The intervention planner may require operand and operant resources. For a food bank example, citizens could create ideas for programmes that would work for all parties and create value. Research at an early stage will help select appropriate marketing tools and techniques using the resources available for the intervention. Citizens might comment that they know that their regular supermarket collects for the local food bank and that there is a trolley or box for donations beyond the cashiers in the shop. They fully intend to buy some items for the collection but forget until they have paid and pass the donation point on the way out. A simple sign saying "Have you remembered something for the food bank?" near the cashiers might solve this problem but would need careful consideration for any potentially unintended consequences. Notices or shelf stickers saying 'food bank' on those items needed might prompt shoppers to pick them up as they shop.

Co-designing is a participatory approach to developing interventions that bring together all actors to find solutions for social issues. In the case of the food bank example, such solutions harness the collective creativity of the target audience, supermarkets, charities and other actors to ensure local ownership. Solutions designed this way are more likely acceptable to providers and end users and, therefore, adopted and sustained (Barber et al., 2011; Stewart & Liabo, 2012), ultimately reducing food waste. Although research has identified many advantages of co-designing the interventions, studies have also highlighted potential challenges (Fransman, 2018; Oliver et al., 2019). Challenges such as budget and time constraints are associated with the operational side, whereas diversity in participation, low literacy of the target audience or other actors, the false appearance of engagement (Osborne et al., 2016), power equalisation, power politics, poor governance and differences in values (Domecq et al., 2014) can damage the intervention. Most of these challenges are contextually dependent; however, clarity on the intervention's overall objectives can somewhat mitigate such challenges.

Co-delivery: Co-delivery is the distribution of the intervention through collaborative participations that add value for the target audience, requiring the integration of resources (operand and operant), co-creative labours (voluntary) and channel justifications (Saragih et al., 2019). It also includes the actions that occur in the co-delivery phase, where benefits are gained by the relevant actors (Saragih et al., 2019; Zainuddin et al., 2017). In a food bank example, working across sectors, charities, actors and target audiences must actively promote the messages and material (e.g., awareness about food waste) to maximise the outcomes within the target audience. Such messages to increase awareness of reducing food waste can be drawn from complementary knowledge to enhance contextual relevance, social value for the target audience and overall incentives for all actors. However, some potential challenges can occur during the co-delivery phase, such as balancing the conflicting expectations of different actors (Ramage et al., 2022). For example, meeting the demands of knowledge user informant groups, achieving shared power and collaborative decision-making, and optimising knowledge on food waste issues. Aligning ethos, recognition and opportunities for everyone to have an equal say and role in how food waste interventions should be delivered can overcome some of these challenges (NESTA, 2013).

Conclusion

Prioritising solutions for food waste is significant for all actors, including the target audience, charities, overall environments and more. In this study, we offered a co-creation approach for charities using the lens of social marketing to tackle food waste. It is suggested that charities must co-discover the deeply rooted causes among various actors that result in food waste. This would inform the message, material and mechanism of the food waste intervention that must be delivered in collaboration with all actors involved throughout the co-discovery, co-design and co-delivery phases. However, it must be noted that the co-discovery, co-design and co-delivery phases may pose various challenges. The charities must consider the context of the intervention and reflect on the following questions to mitigate such challenges:

Discussion Questions

1 How can charities involve various actors to identify shared values, especially when actors may have different expectations, values and knowledge about food waste?
2 How can charities manage various actors' power struggles and authority in the co-designing phase?
3 How can charities measure the activities in the co-delivery phase, especially when these activities are developed and delivered by various actors?
4 How can charities measure the value for all in the value co-creation process?

Notes

1 https://outofdate.org.uk/
2 www.lovefoodhatewaste.com/
3 www.gov.uk/government/organisations/groceries-code-adjudicator/about/our-gov
ernance
4 www.innovativefarmers.org/
5 https://guardiansofgrub.com/
6 https://feedingbritain.org/
7 https://fareshare.org.uk/
8 www.ukharvest.org.uk/
9 https://thefelixproject.org/
10 https://cityharvest.org.uk/
11 www.theregisschool.co.uk/
12 www.tescoplc.com/sustainability/communities/foodcollection

References

Akaka, M. A., Vargo, S. L., & Lusch, R. F. (2012). An exploration of networks in value co-creation: A service-ecosystems view. *Review of Marketing Research*, 9, https://doi.org/10.1108/S1548-6435(2012)0000009006

Akbar, M. B., & Barnes, E. (2023) Verification of GPDS planning framework for social marketing: a Delphi method. *International Review on Public and Nonprofit Marketing*. https://doi.org/10.1007/s12208-022-00362-2

Akbar, M. B., French, J., & Lawson, A. (2019). Critical review on social marketing planning approaches. *Social Business*, 9(4), 361–393. https://doi.org/10.1362/204 440819X1563 3617555894

Andreasen, A. R. (2002). Marketing social marketing in the social change marketplace. *Journal of Public Policy & Marketing*, 21(1), 3–13. https://doi.org/10.1509/jppm.21.1.3.17602

Armstrong, B., Reynolds, C., Martins, C.A., Frankowska, A., Levy, R.B., Rauber, F., Osei-Kwasi, H.A., Vega, M., Cediel, G., Schmidt, X., Kluczkovski, A., Akparibo, R., Auma, C.L., Defeyter, M.A.A., Tereza da Silva, J., & Bridge, G. (2021). Food insecurity, food waste, food behaviours and cooking confidence of UK citizens at the start of the COVID-19 lockdown. *British Food Journal*, 123 (9), pp. 2959–2978. https://doi.org/10.1108/BFJ-10-2020-0917

Aya Pastrana, N. and Obregón, R. (2023). Harnessing the power of social marketing for sustainable development. *International Review on Public and Non-profit Marketing*, 20(3), pp.661–692. https://doi.org/10.1007/s12208-023-00382-6.

Barber, R., Beresford, P., Boote, J., Cooper, C. and Faulkner, A. (2011). Evaluating the impact of service user involvement on research: a prospective case study: evaluating the impact of service user involvement on research. *International Journal of Consumer Studies*, 35, pp. 609–615, doi: 10.1111/j.1470-6431.2011.01017.x.

Begho, T., & Zhao, N. (2023). Motivating household food waste reduction: harnessing the power of message context and framing. *Food Frontiers*, 4(1), 432–446.

Bhat, S. A., Darzi, M. A., & Hakim, I. A. (2019). Understanding social marketing and well-being: a review of selective databases. *Vikalpa*, 44(2), 75–87. https://doi.org/10.1177/0256090919861010

Bryant, C. A., Courtney, A. H., McDermott, R. J., Lindenberger, J. H., Swanson, M. A., Mayer, A. B., Panzera, A. D., Khaliq, M., Schneider, T., Wright, A. P., Craig Lefebvre, R., & Biroscak, B. J. (2014). Community – based prevention marketing for policy development: A new planning framework for coalitions. In *Social Marketing Quarterly*, 20(4), pp. 219–246). https://doi.org/10.1177/15245 00414555948

Butler, S. (2022). *Supermarkets Wasting 200,000 Tonnes of Food that Could Go to Needy, Say Charities.* Guardian UK, February 2022.

Dobson, M. (2023). *Christmas Packaging Facts and Waste Statistics (2023 Update)* www.gwp.co.uk/guides/christmas-packaging-facts/ (Accessed October 2023).

Dolan, R., Seo, Y., & Kemper, J. (2019). Complaining practices on social media in tourism: a value co-creation and co-destruction perspective. *Tourism Management*, 73(September 2018), 35–45. https://doi.org/10.1016/j.tour man.2019.01.017

Domecq, J.P., Prutsky, G., Elraiyah, T., Wang, Z., Nabhan, M., Shippee, N., Brito, J.P., Boehmer, K., Hasan, R., Firwana, B. and others (2014). Patient engagement in research: a systematic review. *BMC Health Services Research*, 14, p. 1.

Domegan, C., Collins, K., Stead, M., McHugh, P., & Hughes, T. (2013). Value co-creation in social marketing: functional or fanciful? *Journal of Social Marketing*. https://doi.org/10.1108/JSOCM-03-2013-0020

Evans, D. (2012). Beyond the throwaway society: ordinary domestic practice and a socio- logical approach to household food waste. *Sociology*, 46:41–56

EveryDay Green (2023). *The Environmental Impact of Black Friday in the UK 2023*, Available at: www.everydaygreen.co.uk/blogs/journal/environmental-imp act-black-friday-uk#:~:text=For%20example%2C%20the%20delivery%20 of,every%20year%20in%20the%20UK (Accessed March 2024).

Flaherty, T., Domegan, C., Duane, S., Brychkov, D., & Anand, M. (2020). Systems social marketing and macro-social marketing: a systematic review. *Social Marketing Quarterly*. https://doi.org/10.1177/1524500420925188

Fransman, J. (2018). Charting a course to an emerging field of 'research engagement studies': a conceptual meta-synthesis. *Research for All*, 2, pp. 185–229, doi: 10.18546/RFA.02.2.02.

French, J. (2011). Why nudging is not enough. *Journal of Social Marketing*, 1(2), 154–162. https://doi.org/10.1108/20426761111141896

Gaski, J. F. (2022). Toward social responsibility, not the social responsibility semblance: marketing does not need a conscience. *AMS Review*, 12(1–2), 7–24.

Gbadamosi, A., Bathgate, I., & Nwankwo, S. (2013). *Principles of Marketing: A Value-Based Approach.* London, UK: Macmillan International Higher Education.

Gordon, R., Russell-Bennett, R., & Lefebvre, R. C. (2016). Social marketing: the state of play and brokering the way forward. *Journal of Marketing Management*, 32(11–12), 1059–1082.

Hamid, S. A. R., & Khan, M. K. N. (2020). Value co-creation as a strategic tool of social marketing: analysis of a social service branding process in developing economy. *Turkish Journal of Business Ethics*, 12(2), 155–176. https://doi.org/ 10.12711/tjbe.2019.12.2.0136

Hamidi, F., Gharneh, N. S., & Khajeheian, D. (2020). A conceptual framework for value co-creation in service enterprises (Case of tourism agencies). *Sustainability (Switzerland)*, 12(1), 1–21. https://doi.org/10.3390/su12010213

Hastings, G., & Domegan, C. (2012). *Social Marketing: Why should the Devil have all the best tunes?* (2nd ed.). Abingdon, UK: Routledge.

Ind, N., & Coates, N. (2013). The meanings of co-creation. *European Business Review*, 25(1), 86–95. https://doi.org/10.1108/09555341311287754

ISMA, AASM and ESMA (2017). *Global Consensus on Social Marketing Principles, Concepts and Techniques*. International Social Marketing Association.

Jackman, J. (2023). *Food Waste Facts and Statistics*. www.theecoexperts.co.uk/home-hub/food-waste-facts-and-statistics#:~:text=This%20wasted%20food%20is%20disposed,4.5%20million%20tonnes%20is%20edible. (Accessed November 2023).

Jenkins, E. L., Brennan, L., Molenaar, A., & McCaffrey, T. A. (2022). Exploring the application of social media in food waste campaigns and interventions: A systematic scoping review of the academic and grey literature. *Journal of Cleaner Production*, 360, 132068. https://doi.org/10.1016/j.jclepro.2022.132068

Jeswani, K. H., Figueroa-Torres, G., Azapagic, A. (2021). The extent of food waste generation in the UK and its environmental impacts. *Sustainable Production and Consumption*, 26, 532–547.

Jones-Garcia, E., Bakalis, S.; Flintham, M. (2022). Consumer behaviour and food waste: understanding and mitigating waste with a technology probe. *Foods*, 11, 2048. https:// doi.org/10.3390/foods11142048

Kamin, T., Kubacki, K., & Atanasova, S. (2022). Empowerment in social marketing: systematic review and critical reflection. *Journal of Marketing Management*, 38(11–12), 1104–1136.

Kennard, N. J. (2020). Food waste management. Zero Hunger, 355–370.

Kennedy, A.-M., Kemper, J.A. and Parsons, A.G. (2018), "Upstream social marketing strategy", *Journal of Social Marketing*, Vol. 8 No. 3, pp. 258–279. https://doi.org/10.1108/JSOCM-03-2017-0016

Khajeh, E., Dabestani, R., & Fathi, S. (2015). The role of upstream and downstream social marketing in electricity consumption management. *International Journal of Business Innovation and Research*, 9(3), 311–328. https://doi.org/10.1504/IJBIR.2015.069138

Lee, N. & Kotler, P. (2022). *Success in Social Marketing: 100 Case Studies from Around the Globe*, New York, NY: Routledge.

Lohnes, D. J. (2021). Regulating surplus: charity and the legal geographies of food waste enclosure. *Agric Human Values*. 38(2): 351–363.

London Daily News (2023). *Black Friday 2023: Experts Reveal that 80 Per Cent of Products Wasted*. www.londondaily.news/black-friday-2023-experts-reveal-that-80-per-cent-of-products-wasted/ (Accessed October 2023).

Manikam, S., & Russell-Bennett, R. (2016). The social marketing theory-based (SMT) approach for designing interventions. *Journal of Social Marketing*, 6(1), 18–40.

Meah, A., Watson, M. (2011). Saints and slackers: challenging discourses about the decline of domestic cooking. *Soc Re Online*, 16(2):6

Morgan, E. (2015). Plan A: analysing business model innovation for sustainable consumption in mass-market clothes retailing. *Journal of Corporate Citizenship*. https://doi.org/10.9774/gleaf.4700.2015.ma.00007

NESTA (2013). *By Us, For Us: The Power of Co-Design and Co-Delivery*. Available at: https://media.nesta.org.uk/documents/the_power_of_co-design_and_co-delivery.pdf, (Accessed April 2024).

NRDC (2017). *WASTED: Second Edition of NRDC's Landmark Food Waste Report*. Available at: www.nrdc.org/bio/dana-gunders/wasted-second-edition-nrdcs-landmark-food-waste-report#:~:text=CONSUMERS%3A%20The%20largest%20source%20of,part%20of%20the%20supply%20chain, (Accessed April 2024).

Office for National Statistics (2021). *A Review of Household Behaviour in Relation to Food Waste, Recycling, Energy Use and Air Travel*. Available at: www.ons.gov.uk/economy/environmentalaccounts/articles/areviewofhouseholdbehaviourinrelationtofoodwasterecyclingenergyuseandairtravel/2021-11-01, (Accessed October 2023).

Oliver, K., Kothari, A. and Mays, N. (2019). The dark side of coproduction: do the costs outweigh the benefits for health research? *Health Research Policy and Systems*, 17, doi: 10.1186/s12961-019-0432-3.

Osborne, S.P., Radnor, Z. and Strokosch, K. (2016). Co-Production and the co-creation of value in public services: a suitable case for treatment? *Public Management Review*, 18, pp. 639–653, doi: 10.1080/14719037.2015.1111927

Ramage, E.R., Burke, M., Galloway, M. *et al.* (2022). Fit for purpose. Co-production of complex behavioural interventions. A practical guide and exemplar of co-producing a telehealth-delivered exercise intervention for people with stroke. *Health Research Policy and Systems*, 20(2), https://doi.org/10.1186/s12961-021-00790-2

Rodríguez-Sánchez, C. (2023). The role of social marketing in achieving the planet sustainable development goals (SDGs). *International Review on Public and Non-profit Marketing*. https://doi.org/10.1007/s12208-023-00385-3

Saragih, H.S., Simatupang, T. and Sunitiyoso, Y. (2018). From co-discovery to co-capture: co-innovation in the music business. *International Journal of Innovation Science*, 11(4), pp. 600–617. https://doi.org/10.1108/IJIS-07-2019-0068

Schmidtke, D., Rundle-Thiele, S., Kubacki, K., & Burns, G. L. (2021). Co-designing social marketing programs with "bottom of the pyramid" citizens. *International Journal of Market Research*, 63(1), 86–105.

Stein, M., & Polychronakis, Y. (2023). *Food Waste Issues of Universal Infant Free School Meals in South-East England Schools*. Abingdon, UK: Food Futures in Education and Society.

Stewart, R. and Liabo, K. (2012). Involvement in research without compromising research quality. *Journal of Health Services Research and Policy*, 17, pp. 248–251, doi: 10.1258/jhsrp.2012.011086.

Thaler, R. H., & Sunstein, C. R. (2015). *Nudge: Improving Decisions About Health, Wealth, and Happiness*. UK: Penguin Politics Business.

United Nations (2021). *UNEP Food Waste Index Report 2021*. Available at: www.unep.org/resources/report/unep-food-waste-index-report-2021, (Accessed October 2023).

Vlaholias, E., G., Thompson, K., Every, D. & Dawson, D. (2015). Reducing food waste through charity: exploring the giving and receiving of redistributed food. In: *Envisioning a Future Without Food Waste and Food Poverty*.

Watson, M., Meah, A. (2013). Food, waste and safety: negotiating conflicting social anxieties into the practices of domestic provisioning. *Sociological Review* 60(S2):102–120. doi:10.1111/1467-954X.12040

WRAP (2020). *UK Progress Against Courtauld 2025 Targets and UN Sustainable Development Goal 12.3.* https://wrap.org.uk/resources/report/uk-progress-against-courtauld-2025-targets-and-un-sustainable-development-goal-123 (Accessed January 2024).

WRAP (2023). *Food Waste Reduction Roadmap* https://wrap.org.uk/taking-action/food-drink/initiatives/food-waste-reduction-roadmap (Accessed February 2024).

WRWA (2023). *How to Reduce Waste and Recycle at School.* Available at: https://wrwa.gov.uk/schools-adult-groups/how-to-reduce-waste-and-recycle-at-school/, (Accessed April 2024).

Zainuddin, N., Dent, K. and Tam, L. (2017). Seek or destroy? Examining value creation and destruction in behaviour maintenance in social marketing. *Journal of Marketing Management*, 33(5–6), pp. 348–374.

15

THEORISING PEACE MARKETING FOR NOT-FOR-PROFIT ORGANISATIONS

A Remedy for Community Cohesion

Ahmed Al-Abdin

Introduction

The charity sector revenue in the UK is estimated to total around £51.2 billion (IBIS World, 2023), with industry growth seeing a decline due to reduced funding from the EU, Brexit, high-profile scandals amongst organisations such as Oxfam which has blockaded such organisations under the scandal spotlight from claiming government funding. The impact of COVID-19, falling disposable incomes due to an array of factors such as the current cost of living crisis have resulted in lower voluntary donations with revenue forecasted to decline by around 0.8% in 2023–2024 (IBIS World, 2023). Beyond donations, the social value of charities is significant because it can heavily impact stakeholder engagement, help charities to overcome pressing challenges and contribute to their longevity. Social value is understood to be centred around problematising solutions to measuring and valuing the impact that interventions have on society. A report by the Charity Retail Association (2023) suggests that across predominant stakeholder groups, the topmost important outcome is 'giving back to others' where the estimated social value is in excess of £22 billion.

Indeed, the Charities Aid Foundation (CAF, 2023) estimates that the cost of living crisis has meant that more than two-thirds of charity donors have had to prioritise spending to help manage bills, with 17% indicating that they would be likely to cut their charity donations, with 24% reporting that they had made, or were intending to make changes to their charitable habits, including reducing or cancelling regular and/or one-off charity donations.

Questions remain as to how the not-for-profit sector can leverage the outcome of giving back to others? How can formal (e.g., government, local

DOI: 10.4324/9781003396802-15

authorities, employees, volunteers, board of trustees, donors) and informal stakeholders (e.g., neighbours, families, community, customers) foster greater social cohesion to bring about uplifting changes to important charitable causes and ensure the longevity of the charity sector? Over four decades ago, Galtung (1985) summarised 25 years of peace research by categorising human needs into four essential classes: Survival, Welfare, Freedom, and Identity. He underscored the significance of not prioritising one class over the others, and instead advocated for a holistic approach, satisfying all needs equally to prevent hostilities and promote peace. Since Galtung's (1984) study, an existing problem in the literature is that a plethora of studies have theorised the concept of 'peace' more broadly as relating to war and violence. No studies have theorised peace marketing with respect to not-for-profits or indeed attempted to conceptualise notions of peace outside anthropogenic (i.e., manmade) conflict. Rather, in this chapter, if we recognise that social conflicts arising from macro-environmental factors may prohibit stakeholder engagement amongst not-for-profits, we can better understand how peace marketing can leverage conflict resolutions, which we argue is important to aiding not-for-profit longevity.

Building on peace research, peace marketing as a term has escaped categorisation within the marketing discipline and is aligned to other terms such as 'sustainable peace', 'business and peace', 'charity marketing', 'corporate social responsibility' , 'bottom of the pyramid'. However, peace marketing differs in that it cannot be limited to a single communication campaign (Kotler, 2017) or social responsibility initiative, and it has the capacity to deeply influence formal (e.g., government, charity organisations) and informal institutions (support groups, customers, communities) (Horak & Restel, 2016). Peace marketing would seem to capture the broader sustainability and peace literature and we broadly view it as the desire to expand marketing into a force for peacebuilding efforts and conflict resolution outside of wars and violence and instead, to mend fractured communities and prolong consumer welfare. To this end, and to aid not-for-profits longevity, we offer a peace marketing conceptual framework which we present later in the chapter.

Peace marketing can connote peaceful symbolisms to shape public opinion and alter attitudes through images and communication. Whilst typically within modern day marketing, swaying political attitudes carries its juxtapositions and is closely aligned with political and social marketing, respectively, the problem here is that polarised communication can create fertile grounds for intended and unintended protracted dissent. Consequently, 'pro' this 'belief' or 'pro' that 'belief' can potentially pit communities against each other. To cite some examples, consider the classic contention of whose responsibility is it to support the most vulnerable – not-for-profits or the government? Here, we can appreciate that rising costs and the cost of living crisis has tightened the noose around not-for-profits resources. Local councils are operating with restricted budgets with some going into bankruptcy (e.g., Birmingham) (Wallis, 2024) and shortfalls in funding can be seldom solved by fundraising. The hangover from COVID-19 has meant that not-for-profits and key formal stakeholders such as employees and volunteers are under severe pressure, whilst operating on shoestring budgets, leading to some charities scouring into reserves to fund operating costs (IBIS World, 2023).

First, we discuss the concept of peace more broadly, before reviewing the concept of peace marketing, followed by an application of formal and informal stakeholders to not-for-profits. Conclusions are then drawn with implications for theory and practice.

Peace and Not-for-Profits

As a term, 'peace' is problematic. It is a concept that has gained considerable spotlight across disciplines such as politics, international relations and the wider social sciences, particularly in the context of war and conflict, and because unlike peace, war has a beginning and an end which makes it easier to explore. A collective agreement between scholars is that there can be 'negative peace' where there is a pause in violence (e.g., a ceasefire) between States (Walt, 1987; Waltz, 1988). The flipside of 'positive peace' entails a process through which former adversaries develop mutual compromises to the extent to which war is no longer an option. Peace is what can bind people and communities together via shared common values. We argue that a central problem in the existing literature is that it tends to view peace in the context of war and violence. Rather, we contend that peace can manifest across other anthropogenic crisis and natural disasters. Consider for instance, how the UK population rallied together in support of NHS workers during the COVID-19 pandemic. We might consider the pandemic as fostering greater peace amongst communities in unsettled times. Subsequently, peace would seem to provide hope and a promise for a better future by building trust encounters between stakeholders. We assert that peace can be seldom achieved without having a space for reflection and reconciliation, and there must be a commitment to acknowledging how trauma may have impacted individuals while providing an opportunity to remedy them. For peace to operationalise, there therefore must be a painful past. However, peace experiences are found in the present as it is focussed on what people do part of their daily lives. It would seem to epitomise a mental state and depends on the oscillation between trust and suspicion. For example, consider the resettlement of refugees after fleeing a warzone or hospices where loved ones undergo bereavement support. Key stakeholders such as customers need to be able to trust the not-for-profit and identify with them. Not-for-profits would also seem to serve as peace mediators in terms of their impact locally and nationally. For instance, charities such as Refugee Council, Action Aid and several others support refugees across the country, their resettlement and routes into work and further study. Such not-for-profits are frequently the peace mediator between organisations, the government and the public where views are polarised towards refugees, though over 61% of the population are sympathetic to welcoming immigration (Kantar, 2024).

Peace Marketing and Not-for-Profits

Peace marketing as a nascent term has its roots in broader peace research and in conflict resolution (Melin, 2016) but in 2016, prominent marketing scholar Phillip Kotler coined and equated it to spiritual marketing, stating that "Marketing is love and love is peace" as well as describing 'eras' of marketing including 1.0, 2.0 and 3.0 (Kotler et al., 2019). According to Kotler, most marketers have transitioned from 1.0 (product-oriented) to 2.0 (customer-oriented) marketing. He hopes more companies will consider Marketing 3.0, the 'value era', acknowledging that "consumers today are not only concerned with their own lives but also reflect on bigger issues", especially "today's times of far-ranging conflicts" (Kotler et al., 2019, p. 140). Kotler stopped short of extending further theorisations surrounding peace marketing. The significance of the value era that he speaks of is more important now than ever before, particularly given the decline in donations to not-for-profits following Brexit, COVID-19 and the current cost of living crisis (IBIS World, 2023).

Unlike other terms such as sustainable peace, which argues that peace is required in its various guises to promote sustainable prosperity (Schultz et al., 2007), peace marketing has the capacity to problematise solutions to pressing issues faced by not-for-profits. For instance, COVID-19 was a tale of two halves for not-for-profits operating in the UK. A report by IBIS World (2023) suggests that despite 25% of charities losing at least 40% of their income in 2020, donations reached approximately £5.4 billion over the 6 months through June 2020, up £800 million on the year of 2020, due to an increase in public donations to hospitals and hospices who encountered severe disruption during the pandemic. The impact of COVID-19 significantly impacting individual incomes following an initial surge in donations, coupled with the current cost of living crisis and scandals that have dented charities reputations following allegations against organisations such as Oxfam who were suspected of the sexual exploitation of vulnerable beneficiaries during the Haiti earthquake going back to 2010 (IBIS World, 2023), and the United Nations Relief and Works Agency (UNRWA) who operate in conflict zones to provide vital aid. Most recently, the Israeli–Palestinian conflict has seen more than 34,000 Palestinian civilians killed by Israeli Defence Forces and around 1,200 Israelis following the October 7 attacks in Israel. The UNRWA were accused of housing Hamas terrorists despite submitting staff lists annually with the Palestinian Authority, Israel, Jordan, Lebanon and Syria. At the time of writing the international community is waiting for the Israeli government to provide further evidence and an independent inquiry has been launched into the allegations (Nichols & Perry, 2024).

Peace Marketing as a Tool for Addressing Conflict

Given the continuous sphere of shockwaves encountered by not-for-profit, we argue that peace marketing needs to be viewed as a tool for tackling conflict and to "make the concept of peace more attractive" (Reychler, 2006, p. 13) by influencing social behaviour, changing both attitudes and habits for the good of society and the wider not-for-profit service ecosystem.

Peace would appear to be far more impactful than the selling of tangible products and services to the mass market (Foegen, 1995). Marketing's role is to find solutions to consumer problems, and in the case of not-for-profits for example, "such solutions [do not involve just] products but peace" (Chukwu, Anucha & Nwador, 2018, p. 55), particularly as the core existence of these organisations hinges on filling gaps and providing dedicated resources and support to help the most vulnerable.

Approximately, 170,000 registered charities in the UK provide various forms of direct support to vulnerable individuals and communities with around one million employees in total and an estimated £30 billion derived from generous public donations (Family Action, 2024). Thus, expectations are high and not-for-profits such as Family Action have observed that around 85% of their initiatives stem from commissioned projects by councils, the NHS and the government (Family Action, 2024).

Not-for-profits are supposed to be independent, and they are regarded as formal institutions who have the capacity to build up trust in a quicker fashion because they are unlike government services which are considered 'compulsory' such as social services, hospitals and schools. The danger is that the lines between compulsory and voluntary services is becoming increasingly blurred. For example, record demand for food banks has left them in limbo because they are unable to provide key necessities to everyone. Four in ten food banks are unable to support people due to a lack of resources (Elton, 2023). Further cuts to state and welfare benefits have only compounded the issue. The example of food banks highlights the growing tensions referent to the debate around whose job is it to provide necessities, not-for-profits, or the State?

The dichotomous nature of this debate would seem to impede future directions for not-for-profits. Rather, the way forward is complex, and charities are better served by leaving old adages aside and looking at bridging fractured communities together by maximising stakeholder engagement and using the existing resources at their disposal. In this way, peace marketing can become influential as we can move away from the 'blame game' and viewing peace as integrative propaganda which attempts to unify (in this case), not-for-profits and government by emphasising the importance of a united society with heterogeneous values and beliefs (Bernays, 2005). Instead, and as advocated by Dean and Shabbir (2019), to prevent spillover effects of crises such as poverty and social inequalities, we need to acknowledge that the potency of peace marketing is felt through its intangible presence and impact at the ground level. We hear popular terms when a crisis hits such as 'aggressor', 'oppressor', 'oppressed' and many others, but irrespective of political orientation, the key within a crisis is to preserve and/or provide a better quality of life for individuals and communities. This sentiment is akin to Dean and Shabbir (2019), who suggest marketing should serve as a counter to propaganda and therefore peace marketing plays an integral role in tackling key priorities from the bottom-up or what Baron et al. (2018, p. 145) term "an austerity-driven service ecosystem". It is this unified view of peace which Weiss (2022, p. 621) labels as "peace pluralism" which appears vital to the move from transaction to relational relationships between polarised stakeholders. Peace pluralism would therefore seem to be at the heart of peace marketing strategies because of marketing's ability to bridge communities together and to conjoin in reconciliation efforts via a range of formal and informal stakeholders. But, what role can these stakeholders play in activating peace marketing and supporting not-for-profits? To answer this question, we turn to institutional theory and delve into formal and informal stakeholders in the next section.

Anchoring Not-for-Profit Peace Marketing through Institutional Theory

Institutions are not just the literal sense of 'an organisation'. Rather, they come in many forms, such as government laws, informal social norms and symbolic meanings. Cardinale (2018) suggests that institutional theory relates to the rules that shape and standardised behaviour within a given social structure. These structures provide aides to collaboration, and that of institutional arrangements which are the "interdependent assemblages of institutions" (Vargo & Lusch, 2016, p. 6). Overall, these aides to collaboration can be viewed as the mechanisms that marry multiple stakeholders together and coordinate value co-creation (Baron et al., 2018).

Baron et al. (2018) note that institutional theory can enhance our understanding of service stakeholders and their interactions while Vargo and Lusch (2016) stress that a service ecosystem approach is particularly important and indeed useful, where value co-creation is coordinated through stakeholder engagements in a more complex, dynamic and social system across

TABLE 15.1 A snapshot of formal and informal not-for-profit stakeholders

Formal Stakeholders	Informal Stakeholder
Employees	Donors
Trustees	Customers
Employed volunteers	Casual volunteers
Charity retail stores	Neighbours/community
Government	Families
Local Authorities/councils	Community engagement work
Sustainability groups	Partners of employees/volunteers
Funders	Job centre (e.g. for volunteering work)
Regulators	Media

Source: The author.

three levels: micro (consumer), meso (community) and macro (e.g., not for profit, government). Such a service ecosystems perspective places emphasis on the many-to-many perspective, involving multiple level stakeholders to gain (in this context), a more holistic view of stakeholder engagement. Here, we borrow from institutional theory and adopt Horak and Restel's (2016) extension of Helmke and Levitsky's (2004) typology of informal institutions to aid an understanding of the complex stakeholder engagement for not-for-profits and how peace marketing can support engagement between multiple stakeholders. Table 15.1 presents a snapshot of formal and informal stakeholders surrounding not-for-profits.

In their original typology, Helmke and Levitsky (2004) note two dimensions; 'convergent' and 'divergent'. The convergent dimension is concerned with the level of outcomes produced by formal as well as informal stakeholders while the divergent dimension seeks to assess the extent to which formal norms, rules and practices are observed and obeyed in practice. The convergent dimension also suggests two sub outcomes: 'complimentary' and 'substitutive'. Complimentary outcomes suggest that informal stakeholders collaborate with the existing formal stakeholders they all abide by written rules. In this way, informal stakeholders exist to help solve issues that formal stakeholders either willingly struggle to seldom solve or deliberately neglect. 'Substitutive' – the second sub outcome of the convergent dimension rests on the premise that informal stakeholders take on the role of attaining solutions that are aligned with formal rules and procedures.

Within the divergent dimension, there are also two sub outcomes: 'accommodating' and 'competing'. Accommodating outcomes imply that informal stakeholders are incentivised to modify formal rules but without contradicting them. Efforts are made to stabilise the status quo rather than react against it. Competing stakeholders draw together contested formal rules and produce competing informal stakeholders. When this occurs, competing informal stakeholders are spurned on by the prospects of obeying some rules and reformulating others.

Noting that the typology proposed by Helmke and Levitsky (2004) falls short of describing not-for-profits, Horak and Restel's (2016) extended their typology to include 'transition', which comprises of 'auxiliary' at the convergent dimension and 'suppression' at the divergent dimension. Auxiliary describes the extent to which social cohesion can manifest at the macro-level more explicitly. In most cases, within the auxiliary dimension, opportunity spaces can manifest (Normann, 2001), which help informal stakeholders redefine (via social cohesion at the meso-level) the institutional boundaries by taking actions to alter formal institutional rules, norms and practices. In other words, the more that informal stakeholders coordinate with each other to transform the system, the more likely it is that their actions will influence changes at the macro-level. Conversely, the second suppressing outcome that Horak and Restel (2016) propose suggests that like the competing sub outcome, informal stakeholders can sometimes hamper transitional development and unintentionally infect rather than remedy formal stakeholders. In the conclusion section, presented next, we offer a conceptual peace marketing framework which merges our thinking on formal and informal stakeholders, as well as potential peace marketing outcomes.

Conclusion and Future Proofing Not-for-Profits

Until this point in the chapter, we have theorised how peace marketing can manifest amongst not-for-profits. We have discussed formal and informal stakeholders and can how peace marketing might support stakeholder engagement. Our conceptual framework (see Figure 15.1) illustrates an understanding of the complex stakeholder engagement for not-for-profits and how peace marketing can support engagement between multiple stakeholders. Given the current UK climate, lack of government funding, a fall in donations and the cost of living crisis, stakeholders in 'transition' have never been more apparent. Auxiliary stakeholders here at the convergent dimension such as local communities, volunteers and customers can work together to help support important causes irrespective of macro-environmental factors. Conversely, at the divergent dimension, the suppressing outcome can see stakeholders hamper transitional development. In this regard, the actions of government policies and funding priorities may impact not-for-profit initiatives.

Similarly, informal stakeholders such as donors may limit their donations, which can affect not-for-profit resources. For example, a report by the Charities Aid Foundation (2023) suggests that there has been a decline in people donating, but sustained regular donations have increased, not because of more people donating, but due to donors maintaining their donations and/

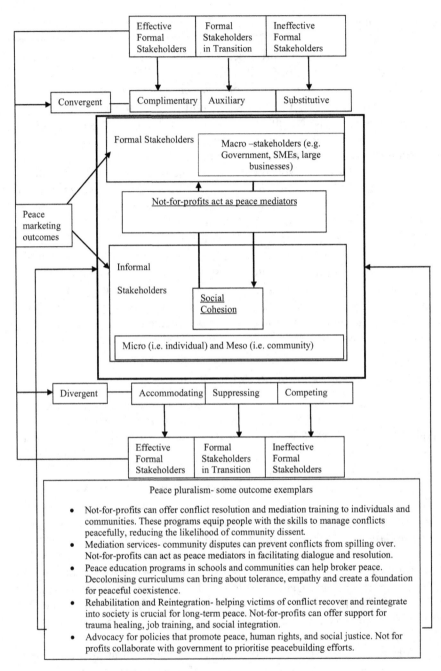

FIGURE 15.1 Peace marketing framework.

Source: The author.

or increasing them. The type of cause donated too remains of high importance, with animal welfare charities the most popular. Donors have a high degree of power in determining what causes they wish to donate too and how much they are willing to give. Trust plays a key role here and those charities with stronger transparency of where donations have been spent stand a better chance of securing donations (IBIS World, 2023).

In a congested industry, overlapping not-for-profit services and/or those operating in the same sector may lead to confusion among donors and the competition for funding, volunteers and customer attention is fierce. For example, of the circa 168,000 charities operating in the UK, there are around 31,115 just in the social services sector (Charity Commission, 2024). More than half of all charities in the UK are worried about their ability to survive due to the increase in cost of living and reduction in customer disposable income, and with demand for targeting funds to those vulnerable persons and communities at a premium, almost one-quarter of all charities have had to reduce services and or use their reserves to help cover core costs (Schweppenstedde, 2023). Facing a conundrum, charities are also reluctant to ask donors to adjust their donations given the cost of living crisis and the fear that some may cancel their donations if asked.

Technology may help propel donations and future proof not-for-profits however, particularly through crowdfunding or apps like JustGiving, in-built online payment systems. Digital funding has transformed the landscape for charitable donations and made donating more readily accessible. While traditional methods such as cold calling has its place, particularly amongst those individuals who may be less digitally savvy, not-for-profits are discovering integrated ways of incorporating online campaigns to raise awareness, sustain and encourage new stakeholder involvement.

From simple videos and stories via social media platforms such as TikTok and Instagram, digital fundraising has the capacity to reach a wider audience and at a fraction of the cost of traditional methods. Donors are also able to champion their preferred charity via online platforms and share with friends and family. Unlike traditional methods, digital fundraising also affords the collection of important data and analytics so that not-for-profits can better understand donor behaviour and improve future campaigns. There is no textbook answer here to future proofing not-for-profits, but we have attempted in this chapter to display how peace marketing can support their longevity, impact, significance and reach amongst target groups.

Practitioners reading this chapter can use our peace marketing framework to engage in stakeholder engagement mapping, particularly considering a variety of formal and informal institutions. Several key initiatives might also take place including public awareness campaigns that highlight the benefits of peace and linking it to respective charity causes. Such campaigns might be used to educate the public about the importance of peacebuilding to garner greater support for peacebuilding initiatives. Moreover, practitioners can engage with a myriad of stakeholders such as civil society groups, business leaders and entrepreneurs, volunteers, government and local councils to deliberate peacebuilding priorities and develop collaborative initiatives. Furthermore, positive peace policies may be designed, developed and implemented, focussing on advocating peace, tolerance and understanding.

Discussion Questions

1 Think of a not-for-profit organisation and use the peace marketing framework to analyse the formal and informal stakeholders, then consider some of the conflicts that they have faced in recent times and how these stakeholders might help overcome them.
2 Develop a marketing plan for a not-for-profit organisation. Conduct a short marketing audit (including a SWOT, PESTLE and 5 forces). Devise some SMART Marketing objectives based on these to advocate peace through marketing initiatives. Consider the target market within your marketing plan and discuss some marketing mix activities and messaging strategies you might use to highlight peace through marketing initiatives.
3 Examine successful examples of collaborations between not-for-profits and for-profit organisations to advance peace through marketing initiatives.

References

Baron, S., Patterson, A., Maull, R., & Warnaby, G. (2018). Feed people first: a service ecosystem perspective on innovative food waste reduction. *Journal of Service Research*, 21(1), 135–150.

Bernays, E. L. (2005). *Propaganda*. New York: Ig Publishing.

Cardinale, I. (2018). Beyond constraining and enabling: toward new microfoundations for institutional theory. *Academy of Management Review*, 43(1), 132–155.

Charities Aid Foundation. (2023). *Charities Aid Foundation UK Giving Report 2023*. Available at: www.cafonline.org/about-us/research/uk-giving-report. Accessed 02/04/24.

Charity Commission. (2024). *About Us*. Available at: https://beingacharitytrustee.campaign.gov.uk/about-us/. Accessed 24 April 2024.

Charity Retail Association. (2023).*The Value of Giving Back-the Social Return of Charity Shops*. Available at: www.charityretail.org.uk/social-value-and-social-return-on-investment-sroi-of-charity-shops/. Accessed 02 April 2024.

Chukwu, G.C., Anucha, V.C., & Nwador, C.A. (2018). Peace marketing in volatile parts of Nigeria: a panacea for national development. *Leadership, Security and National Development*, 582.

Dean, D., & Shabbir, H. (2019). Peace marketing as counter propaganda? Towards a methodology. *Propaganda*, 350.

Elton, C. (2023). *'How Are People Going to Cope?': Almost All Food Banks Helping First-Time Users As Demand Surges*. Available at: www.bigissue.com/news/social-justice/cost-of-living-food-banks-first-time-users-crisis/. Accessed 26 March 24.

Family Action. (2024). *About Us*. Available at: www.family-action.org.uk/. Accessed 02 April 24.

Foegen, J. H. (1995). Promoting peace through marketing. *Business and Society Review*, pp. 29–31.

Galtung, J. (1985). Twenty-five years of peace research: ten challenges and some responses. *Journal of Peace Research*, 22(2), 141–158.

Helmke, G., & Levitsky, S. (2004). Informal institutions and comparative politics: a research agenda. *Perspectives on Politics*, 2(4), 725–740.

Horak, S., & Restel, K. (2016). A dynamic typology of informal institutions: learning from the case of Guanxi. *Management and Organization Review*, 12(3), 525–546.

IBIS World. (2023). *Charities in the UK*. Available at: https://my.ibisworld.com/uk/en/industry/SP0.191/about. Accessed 02/04/24.

Kantar. (2024). *How Does the Public View Immigration in General?* Available at: https://kantar.turtl.co/story/public-attitudes-to-immigration/page/3/1. Accessed 02/04/24.

Kotler, P. (2017). *How Can We Market Peace? [Blog Post]*. Retrieved from www.marketingjournal.org/how-can-we-market-peace-an-excerpt-from-philip-kotlers-autobiography-philip-kotler/.

Kotler, P., Keller, K. L., Brady, M., Goodman, M., & Hansen, T. (2019). *Marketing Management*. Pearson UK.

Melin, M. M. (2016). Business, peace, and world politics: the role of third parties in conflict resolution. *Business Horizons*, 59(5), 493–501.

Nichols, M., & Perry, T. (2024). *Israel Yet to Show Evidence UNRWA Staff Are Members of Terrorist Groups, Review Finds*. Available at: www.reuters.com/world/middle-east/review-says-unrwa-has-robust-neutrality-steps-issues-persist-2024-04-22/. Accessed 23 April 24.

Normann, R. (2001). *Reframing Business: When the Map Changes the Landscape*. London, England: John Wiley.

Reychler, L. (2006). Challenges of peace research. *International Journal of Peace Studies*, 1–16.

Schweppenstedde, D.F. (2023). *Key Challenges and Opportunities Facing the Charity Sector*. Available at: www.cafonline.org/about-us/blog-home/charities-blog/challenges-and-opportunties-facing-charity-sector. Accessed 02 April 24.

Shultz, C. J. (2007). Marketing as constructive engagement. *Journal of Public Policy & Marketing*, 26(2), 293–301.

Vargo, S. L., & Lusch, R. F. (2016). Institutions and axioms: an extension and update of service-dominant logic. *Journal of the Academy of Marketing Science*, 44(1), 5–23.

Wallis, W. (2024). *Bankrupt Birmingham Council Takes Drastic Steps to Balance the Books*. Available at: www.ft.com/content/3ec920d6-d4eb-42fe-8cd4-61ec8a17244a. Accessed 24.04.24.

Walt, S. M. (1987). *The Origins of Alliances*. New York: Cornell University Press.

Waltz, K. N. (1988). The origins of war in neorealist theory. *The Journal of Interdisciplinary History*, 18(4), 615–628.

Weiss, E. (2022). Peace and liberal misrecognition: non-liberal peace initiatives in Israel-Palestine. *The American Sociologist*, 53(4), 604–624.

INDEX

Printed in the United States
by Baker & Taylor Publisher Services